>C1/

D0931073

Date Due

5-1 MAY 1 9 2005			
APR 0 2 2011			

MEN AT MIDLIFE

MEN AT MIDLIFE

MICHAEL P. FARRELL
State University of New York at Buffalo

STANLEY D. ROSENBERG
Dartmouth Medical School

Auburn House Publishing Company
Boston, Massachusetts

To J. Paul, Estelle, Karen, and Eric

Library of Congress Cataloging in Publication Data
Farrell, Michael P., 1942-
  Men at midlife.

  Bibliography: p.
  Includes index.
  1. Middle aged men—United States. 2. Middle aged men—United States—Case studies. 3. Middle age—United States. 4. Life cycle, Human. I. Rosenberg, Stanley D. II. Title
HQ1059.5.U5F37   305.2′4   81-3624
ISBN 0-86569-073-1   AACR2

PREFACE

The concept of life stages is a relatively new one. Historians report that people first began thinking of childhood as a separate stage of life in the eighteenth century. Before that time there was only a dim awareness of the unique needs of children. Adolescence began to be talked about as a separate stage during the nineteenth century. Since then a whole body of theory and an array of institutions have emerged to meet the needs of people in the period between childhood and adulthood. Now, in the last quarter of the twentieth century, we are discovering middle age. Theories and research began to appear during the seventies, and already popular literature is full of advice on how to deal with the needs of the middle aged.

Our study began in 1971, just prior to the explosion of interest in the subject. Although we were not aware of other research in progress at the time, we had both known Daniel Levinson while graduate students at Yale and had worked with some of his colleagues. Some of his emerging interests might well have filtered toward us. In this same period, we both studied with Theodore Mills and were strongly influenced by his in-depth analysis of the interface between personality, group process, and the social system. We felt that his methodological approach, which emphasized qualitative and quantitative data, was most suitable for the range of problems that interested us. This approach guided us in our initial theorizing, our research design, and the analysis of whole families.

In our study we compare men in their late twenties to men in their late thirties and early forties. When we began our research we were close to the age of our younger men, looking at the older men as subjects of study. Over the 1970s, as we gathered and analyzed the data, we have moved closer to the older group, experiencing first-hand many of the events and feelings we had been studying from a distance. This experience of being participant-observers has enriched and deepened our understanding of what the middle-aged men were telling us.

Although the personal meaning is now much clearer, the study began at a more abstract level as an attempt to bring some order to conflicting reports about the experience of men entering middle age. When we first became intrigued by the problem of men entering middle age, we began reviewing the existing literature. A lack of consensus soon became apparent. Some writers argued that a midlife crisis was a universal experience in male development; others suggested that men reached their peak of self-actualization at this point. Looking at the literature more closely, we saw that the research findings seemed to depend upon which methods were used and which segment of the population of middle-aged men was being studied.

On the basis of this review and subsequent sorting and organizing of this data, we developed a model that argued for four different types of experiences of men entering middle age. These were related to both their psychological characteristics and their life circumstances. To test our model we developed a design that incorporated many of the best elements of the previous studies, both quantitative and qualitative.

Our design utilized the most representative sample gathered to date, comparing 300 men entering middle age to 150 men in their late twenties. We used a wide array of scales to measure their attitudes, behavior, defenses, and the current state of their physical and psychological health. In our preliminary analysis of the data we found evidence for our four different types of men, though the model had to be modified somewhat. Guided by this preliminary analysis, we selected 20 men for in-depth interviews. That is, we took pains to ensure that five of each of our types of middle-aged men would be studied. Thus our qualitative findings have a direct bearing on our quantitative findings. In order to get the fullest possible picture of these men, we decided to interview their families as well.

Contrary to our early expectations, we do not find evidence for a universal midlife crisis in men. Although men seem to accumulate the burdens of middle age at roughly the same pace, they show variation in how they respond to these stresses. Some men do appear to reach a state of crisis, but others seem to thrive. More typical than either of these responses is the tendency for men to bury their heads and deny and avoid all the pressures closing in on them.

A second unexpected finding is the discovery of the impact of family relations on the experiences of men entering middle age. Previous studies have emphasized the importance of work in male development. In fact, there seems to be a well-developed myth in our culture that men's emotional lives revolve around their work and are independent of their families. Our contact with the families demonstrated the ways in which a man's experience of midlife is very much dependent on the culture and structure of his family. The changing relationships to wife and children act as precipitants for development in men; at the same time, both wife and children are drawn into a man's defensive strategies, supporting his denial and avoidance of midlife issues. This interlocking of individual and family developmental processes is a critical element in men's experience of midlife.

The results of our study are of potential interest to researchers and clinicians as well as to the general reader interested in the experience of men entering middle age. We have attempted to present the findings in such a way as to be comprehensible to all these potential readers. Although qualitative and quantitative data are mixed throughout the book, the reader more interested in the case studies will probably feel more at home in Chapter 2 and Chapters 5–10. However, we feel that full appreciation of the case studies depends upon an understanding of the more general trends.

As we mentioned above, interest in middle age is a recent phenomenon. There are probably many reasons why the interest occurs now. Both the lengthening of the average life span and the contraction of the child-rearing years to the early stages of the family life cycle probably play a part. The shift away from being a child-centered society also influences the shift of attention to adulthood. Perhaps the women's movement has made men more self-conscious and both sexes more aware of the development that can occur throughout the life cycle.

We might also speculate that the midlife experience is a more accurate symbol of our culture's current concerns. Just as adolescents represented a collective totem in the sixties and early seventies—embodying identity issues, rebelliousness, and fears of loss of control—so do the middle aged now symbolize our concerns about staleness, atrophy, and meaning. Research on adolescence disconfirmed many of our stereotypes and myths, indicating that adolescents aren't so different from the rest of us. So too will midlife research undercut images of the middle aged as stepping out of the continuity of life and development in our culture. We hope that the data presented can contribute to a fuller and more accurate understanding of midlife changes in our society.

MICHAEL P. FARRELL
STANLEY D. ROSENBERG

ACKNOWLEDGMENTS

Much of our understanding of the midlife experiences of men emerged from intensive analyses of twenty subjects in addition to the survey responses of almost five hundred men. We owe these men and their families a great deal, but we cannot identify them here because of our commitment to confidentiality. We have disguised the men thoroughly in regard to location, occupation, and life circumstances, so they may not even recognize themselves. We wish at this point to once again thank them for their help.

John Gorman of Cambridge Survey Research, Inc. played an invaluable part in designing the sample and coordinating the gathering of the survey data. His concern for precision and his enthusiastic support meant much during the early stages of the study. Raymond Volpe of the S.U.N.Y. at Buffalo computing center guided us through the organization and analysis of the data.

Our family interviews were enriched by the participation of Robert Vosburg, M.D., Ann Boedecker, Harriet Rosenberg, M.A., and Madeline Schmitt, R.N., Ph.D.

Our intellectual debt is more difficult to trace. At all stages of the study, discussions with Bernard Bergen have stimulated our thinking and enriched our analysis. Daniel Levinson helped to conceptualize our initial findings and provided us with ideas and encouragement. His generosity and support are greatly appreciated. Harriet Rosenberg and Madeline Schmitt provided support and intellectual input at all stages of this study. As colleagues, they provided ideas during the formal research process and feedback during many phases of the conceptualization and write-up of our data. As our wives, they provided support and insight as we participated in and observed our own entry into middle age. Finally, Farrell would like to thank the participants in his graduate seminars in Marriage and Family Relations, particularly Peter Curtis, Janet Near, Janice Crumrine, and Joan Spade.

Since the authors have been at different universities, preparation of the manuscript has been a tale of two cities. The patience and skill of several secretaries have been necessary to bring about the final product. We wish to thank Maureen Patnode, Peggy Seaver, and Nancy Clark for the work done in New Hampshire, and Lois Oldenbrook, Diane Marlinski, and Patricia Hopkins for the work done in New York.

The initial study was generously supported through grants to Dartmouth Medical School from the Ittleson Family Foundation and the Van Ameringen Foundation, and we would like to express our appreciation to their directors and boards of trustees. During periods of the writing, Rosenberg was supported in part by N.I.M.H. Grant Number 5 T01 MH 15027.

MICHAEL P. FARRELL
STANLEY D. ROSENBERG

CONTENTS

Chaper 1

INTRODUCTION

Though theories of adult male development are now common-
place, empirical validation of those theories remains sketchy. The
theories themselves have generally been built on observations of
narrow segments of the population—primarily middle-class subjects and/or people suffering psychological distress. Of course,
theory-building must begin somewhere, and the clinician's office
or the suburban home may be fertile ground for these initial attempts to conceptualize a complex phenomenon. But if we are to
gain a fuller understanding of male development, we must move
beyond these narrow confines and assess the adequacy of initial
models through studies of the larger population. Our study has
attempted to accomplish this task, generating a fuller picture of
the male midlife transition in our society.

We have chosen to focus attention on one particular period of
adult male development—the transition from young adulthood
into early middle age. It is this period of entry into middle age
that many theorists claim is one of turmoil or "crisis." While our
thinking is dependent on the pioneering work of other writers on
midlife, such as Neugarten,[1] Gutmann,[2] Lowenthal,[3] and Levinson,[4] we have not reviewed their work in any detail in this volume.
This decision was made partly because we have done such reviews
elsewhere.[5,6] In addition, our primary consideration was the continuity of our own presentation. We move from a conceptual
overview to various levels of data presentation and analysis to a
discussion of the theoretical significance of these findings while

1

also considering individual, dyadic, and familial issues. Given this complexity, we thought it best to avoid detailed discussions of other theorists, and have included instead as an appendix an annotated bibliography for the reader interested in more specific analyses of other works on midlife. Perusal of this bibliography should also help to make clear both our intellectual debt to and areas of disagreement with other scholars.

Our initial objective was to gain more specific knowledge of this supposed crisis: Who does it affect? Under what circumstances? How is it manifested and experienced? Beginning with a review of past theory and research, we built a working model that synthesizes past findings, then tested the model using both survey methods and in-depth interviews in a study of a random sample of almost 500 men. We feel that our study provides the widest data base yet on male midlife processes, in terms of both the sample and the breadth and quality of data available for each subject. Lowenthal, Thurnher, and Chiriboga, for example, studied 27 middle-aged men out of a larger sample of 216 men and women spanning the range from adolescence to pre-retirement. Levinson's widely recognized study is based on interviews with 40 men, with a disproportionate representation of college graduates (70 percent) and upper-middle-class professionals (biologists, novelists, and executives), although some hourly workers were also studied.

Our findings have supported some of the propositions of previous theory, notably certain broad aspects of Erikson's theory of identity development. But they have called into question other theories, especially those that propose a universal identity crisis as a part of the transition into middle age. The results of our study have led us to suggest modifications of existing theories, and they raise a number of questions for future research.

The inadequacies of current theories become more understandable if we look carefully at past research. It is readily apparent that different researchers studying different populations present very different pictures of the experience of middle age. While some studies have found middle age to be the apex of satisfaction and effectiveness, others found it to be a period of identity crisis and discontent.

In Chapter 2 we review these diverse findings and present a working model that synthesizes them. The working model serves as a guide to our research.

Research Methodology

Past research has utilized either small samples of intensely studied subjects or large samples of people who answered questionnaires. Both types of studies have their shortcomings.

Studies using small samples may be inadequate, for example, because the population has been too narrowly circumscribed to test and build general theories of development. Clinical studies, based on observations of psychiatric patients, have emphasized the pathogenic aspects of midlife changes, generating predictions of collapse, depression, and confusion. Researchers studying middle-class elites, in contrast, have built theories emphasizing ego-mastery and self-actualization. Popular writers, interviewing friends and chance associates, have often built theories that artificially reduce complexity and reassure readers about the normalcy of their own experiences. An adequate research design should confront these limitations by sampling a larger, more representative segment of the population. However, studies based on large samples also have built-in problems. To be able to study and compare large numbers of people requires standardized questionnaire methods. To reduce expense and time and to insure comparability, each subject responds to the same set of questions. This approach provides information about basic surface characteristics of the subjects and can be a powerful method for testing theories. However, questionnaire responses often do not tell us about the deeper, underlying concerns, feelings, and beliefs of the respondents. To get beneath the surface requires in-depth interview techniques.

In addition to these mechanical issues of sample size and composition, interviewing techniques, and so on, the researcher must articulate the connection between his design and his conceptual positions. Most research on midlife or adult development has portrayed individual experience as the result of impinging economic, social, or physiological forces. A second approach views the life cycle as the unfolding of an epigenetic timetable whereby the man moves through universal stages of development. Assuming the primacy of one or more of these approaches permits a narrowing of focus and the specification of causal relations. We will argue that while such causal relations may exist, they are rather tenuous and account for little of the variation seen in midlife responses. Both our research design and our findings suggest a more complex model, one anchored in the idea that the individual is an active agent in interpreting, shaping, and altering his own reality. He not only experiences internal and external changes, he gives meaning to them. The meaning given shows a wide range of variation. The man, we will attempt to show, responds to the world around him and to his own unique internal needs in a creative and synthesizing fashion. This perspective demands a phenomenological approach to data-gathering. Rather than assuming that we, as researchers, know all the factors that determine the man's experience, we have asked the subject to speak for himself, telling us about the aspects of his world that have meaning for him. While his self-description may display confusion, dissimulation, ambivalence, blind spots, or self-delusion, it nonetheless points to those aspects of self and social reality around which the middle-aged man is attempting to build and maintain a viable existence.

Operationally, this requires us to cast a wide net, inquiring about many facets of the man's day-to-day life, his history, his beliefs about himself, his social world, and those interpersonal connections that are meaningful to him. It also requires a style of inquiry that invites the subject to speak spontaneously, with the freedom to tell the researcher what is significant in his life. This stands in contrast with more structured approaches (for example, multiple-choice questionnaires) in which the researcher must decide on the significant questions prior to contact, yielding comparability and a certain kind of precision at the cost of a rich dialogue with the subject.

In this chapter we present a research design aimed at surmounting some of the problems noted in earlier research. Our design combines both survey questionnaire techniques applied to a large sample and in-depth analysis of case studies of men and their families.

The Cross-Sectional Design

The ideal research design to test theories of midlife experience would be a longitudinal study. A sample of young adult men is located and they are tested on a number of personality and social measures. As they move into middle age, the same group is recontacted and retested. The changes observed are then assumed to be the result of maturation and the impact of midlife stresses. A few such studies have been done, although the populations studied have all been middle-class. However, the expense and time involved set limits on carrying out such studies. Once having contacted the sample, one has to wait twenty years for the data to come in. Moreover, since cultural, historical, or economic change occurs during the span of this study, there is always the possibility that the researcher is measuring these effects rather than aging per se.

An alternative to the longitudinal design is the cross-sectional design that we have chosen. We have taken samples of young adult and middle-aged men and compared them on a variety of scales relevant to aging. This kind of design has its own limitations. One possibility is that the differences we find between the men are due to the impact of middle age; this approach of course assumes that fifteen years ago the average middle-aged man had the same characteristics as the average younger man of today; and fifteen years from now the younger men will resemble the older. However, another possibility is that at least some of the differences between the two groups are due to cultural and historical changes. Most of our middle-aged subjects grew up during the Depression, reaching adolescence during World War II. As they pieced together identities these events must have left their mark. On the other hand, the younger men in our study grew up during a period of unprecedented affluence punctuated by violent protest movements in the cities and on college campuses. These very different environments favored different attitudes, values, and behavior. Thus, it is probable that at least some of the differences between groups are due to these changed circumstances. Since we cannot sort out which differences are due to normal development and which are due to cultural change, we are going to assume that our findings of differences are due primarily to changes associated with aging, recognizing the imperfections of this design.

The Samples

In the spring of 1973 Cambridge Research Associates developed a stratified random sample technique for locating groups of 200 younger men between the ages of 25 and 30, and 300 older men between the ages of 38 and 48. These groups were representative of a major Northeastern urban-suburban complex, as well as of a rural New England county. The age range of the younger group was chosen so as to represent men who had passed through the adolescent identity diffusion stage. Presumably, a majority were engaged in building a stable work and home life. The older men were chosen to represent men moving through the phase of transition from being young adults to being middle-aged.

The sampling technique involved first delineating neighborhoods that were relatively homogenous with regard to social class. Then samples of neighborhoods were drawn. Within each neighborhood we then sampled blocks at random. Finally, a trained interviewer went to the block with pre-assigned instructions to contact people in a randomly chosen house on the block. If the house did not have a male who met the age criteria, the interviewer proceeded to the next house until an appropriate subject was located. If the subject could not be interviewed at that time, the interviewer arranged an appointment for a later time. Demographic data indicated that the areas surveyed were statistically representative of the U.S. population as a whole in terms of age, household composition, income, education, and occupational distribution.

Each interview lasted from 90 minutes to two hours. Part of the interview involved direct questioning and part involved the subject filling out a questionnaire.

Measurement Instruments

In addition to background information and a few direct questions about life satisfaction, a number of scales were administered. First, we administered Keniston's Identity Integration scales. This instrument consists of four subscales developed on a population of college students. We carried out our own factor analysis of the scales and found the items factored into four dimensions almost identical to those located by Keniston. The subscales are as follows:

1. Work role identity—a measure of the extent to which the subject feels at home in his current occupational role.

2. Interpersonal identity—a measure of the extent to which the subject has gained a sense of intimacy with some significant others.
3. Solidarity—a measure of the degree that the person feels a sense of oneness with groups in the larger community.
4. Clinical identity—a measure of the degree that the person has achieved a sense of internal integration (control over impulses, anxiety, conflicts, etc.).

In addition to Keniston's scales we also administered Nettler's Anomie scale[7] and our own Midlife Crisis scale to measure other aspects of alienation. Our Midlife Crisis scale consists of twelve items that have face validity as measures of the degree to which a person is experiencing difficulty in coping with the stresses of middle age (See Appendix 1).

Our model for conceptualizing the responses to midlife stress argues for the importance of authoritarian denial as one component of the response. To measure the degree of denial we administered several preestablished scales. They include a modified version of the F-scale,[8] the Tolerance for Ambiguity scale,[9] the Social Desirability scale,[10] the MMPI Denial scale, the Authoritarian Child-rearing scale,[11] and a measure of attitudes toward war. Finally, the questionnaire included several scales to measure the degree of physical and psychological impairment: Zung's Depression scale,[12] the MMPI Anxiety and Hypochondriasis scales, and a psychosomatic symptom scale, as well as direct questions about current health status.

Follow-Up Family Interviews

Survey data give us self-reported information about people's responses to direct questions. It can tell us about gross differences between younger and older men, and it may even enable us to locate types of middle-aged men. But a two-hour structured interview has many limitations: It gives only a brief snapshot of a man, showing only those portions that we have enough foresight to seek. Also, the interpretations of these snapshots are subject to error, either because of conscious or unconscious distortion on the part of the subject, or because of misunderstanding on the part of the researcher as he analyzes the data. The misunderstanding may even have begun when the researcher formulated the questions. Theory may have led to the wrong questions.

In order to correct some of these problems and provide us with a rich clinical base for interpreting our findings, we arranged for follow-up interviews with 20 men and their families. The follow-up families were chosen after a preliminary analysis of the data. We attempted to find five of each of the emerging types of middle-aged men.

The subjects were contacted by phone and offered $100.00 each to allow us to visit them for dinner on a typical evening and to interview them and their families at our offices. Twenty out of 27 men contacted agreed to the follow-up interview. The interview began with a visit to the person's home. The home visit was loosely structured to allow the conversation and events to flow spontaneously. The objectives were twofold: first, to observe the family interacting in their home environment, and second, to obtain an historical picture of the development of the family with a focus on the father. The interviewers usually had dinner with the family, then conversed about the family's life, toured the house, watched television, or did any of a variety of other activities suggested by the host. After leaving the home, the interviewers then tape-recorded their observations and impressions.

After the home visit a more structured interview was scheduled at our offices. These office interviews were recorded on sound tape in their entirety and a portion of the interviews were recorded on videotape. The interview began with the whole family present, focusing on family history and the current structuring of activity in the home. After approximately one hour the children were separated from the parents and the interview continued with the husband and wife. While they were questioned further about history and their current relationship, the children were interviewed separately. The objective of the interview with the children was to obtain a picture of their current relationships to their parents and their perceptions of their father. Finally, the husband and wife were each interviewed alone. The objective throughout was to obtain as complete a picture as possible of the man's development, his relationship to significant others, his work, his political and social attitudes, and his health. In all, the office interview took from three to four hours.

It is important to note the quality of the relationship that developed between the research team and the subject families, since our analysis depends heavily on the data that emerged during this seven to eight hours of contact. Despite the fact that we often encountered resistance and suspiciousness, upon initial contact these barriers quickly evaporated. All the interviewers* were struck by the rapidity with which a climate of intimacy and rapport developed. Farrell came to the research with an extensive background in running self-analytic groups; Rosenberg and Vosburg have long experience in the practice of intensive psychotherapy. While these skills may have contributed to the almost immediate sharing which occurred, we all felt that the primary impetus came from the subjects' need to share and put into perspective their own lives and histories. Our job was made simple by the fact that these men and their families saw the interview/home visit as a rare opportunity to utilize interested and sympathetic strangers, ones with professional credentials. The rapid intimacy was enhanced by the fact that we were outside their normal life space; they would not need to feel embarrassed or self-conscious when encountering us in other circumstances. Since we were from distant communities and promised anonymity in our data reporting, they did not have to fear our indiscretion.

In this context, it is not hard to imagine the collapse of time that characterized the interviews. Earlier life phases were not simply described, but were often vividly reexperienced. Old victories, pleasures, disappointments, and conflicts, in being anecdotally reported, gave strong emotional coloring to the immediate situation. The families came to regard us, at least temporarily, as old and intimate friends. Many continued to correspond with us over several years, and almost all expressed regret as the interviews terminated. If resources had permitted this, we had the feeling that these families would have liked to talk on for days.

As psychotherapists, we estimated that these interviews probably yielded a data base comparable to 20 or 30 hour-long therapy sessions. That is, they enable the analyst to perceive the major

---

* At various stages of the study, interviews with families were conducted by Robert Vosburg, M.D., Ann Boldecker, Harriet Rosenberg, and Madeline Schmitt. The authors are indebted to them for this direct help and for their subsequent contributions in the discussion and analyses of cases.

configurations of the man's personality, affective state, psychiatric symptomatology, quality of interpersonal relations, coping and defensive styles, and sense of himself as a person. While such data may not be as rich as that uncovered through long-term psychoanalytic treatment (where transference is stimulated and infantile experiences are recalled and reenacted), it does seem to us adequate to the level of description and inference we make in our data analysis.

Research Strategy

Our research strategy is first to compare the men on the various measures of personality and behavior. According to available theories of development, our younger men should be into a second latency phase. They are old enough to have weathered the storms of adolescent identity crisis and the problems of young adult intimacy. At this point (age 25 to 30) they should be working on building skills, putting down roots, and building a stable home for a family. On the other hand, the older men are likely to be going through the transition into middle age. They are at the stage when the stresses of middle age are likely to start hitting them. If the theories of midlife crisis are correct, then we should find them showing more signs of instability and crisis. However, as our working model will illustrate, we expect to find a more complex picture. The second part of our research objective is to describe the range of responses to middle age. Because of this objective we made our middle-age sample larger than the younger sample, and have carried out the two types of follow-up interviews with subsets of this sample only.

In Chapters 3 and 4 we present our test of theories of the male experience of midlife. The results provide some evidence for Erikson's developmental theory, but also suggest important modifications. We do not find support for theories that argue for a single developmental path followed by all men. Rather, we find that the experience of middle age is very different for different men in different environments. Most notably, personality, family situations, social class, and rural or urban residence are all associated with significant differences in patterns of male midlife response.

Having examined the quantitative findings, we then turn to the results of our follow-up interviews with the men and their families, in part to assess the validity of our findings from quantitative data, and in part to deepen our understanding of the midlife experience. In Chapter 5 we present composite descriptions of the variety of male experiences of midlife. In addition to general developmental histories, we focus particularly on the men's experience of work and career.

One of the more important findings of our study may seem obvious when stated blatantly, but it has not been emphasized in previous research. A man's experience of middle age is strongly influenced by and strongly influences the family system in which he participates. Though the family system constitutes an interwoven whole, we have broken the discussion of it into three sections. In Chapter 6 we focus on the husband-wife relationships of different types of men. Here we are particularly interested in the factors that contribute to the sense of distance and marital dissatisfaction characteristic of couples at midlife. In Chapter 7 we focus on the parent-child relationship. We find that the father and mother roles are so interdependent that it makes sense to deal with them together. As the adolescent child goes through the process of building an identity, the parents vicariously participate in the child's struggles and relive some of the concerns and issues of earlier stages in their own lives. In the later part of Chapter 7 we present two cases that illustrate the turmoil that erupts as the adolescent's boundary testing calls into question the identities and values of the parents. In a surprising number of cases (8 out of 20), we find the parents using the adolescent child as a scapegoat for unresolved internal or marital conflicts. In Chapter 8 we present some of our findings on the changes in men's relationships to their parents and in-laws as they approach midlife. Here again we focus on the subjective experience of these relationships—the ways in which the men perceive parental figures and how they feel about them.

A number of theorists have argued that male friendships play an important part in the lives of younger men, but as they move into middle age, male friendships become more superficial and have less of an impact on men's lives. In Chapter 9 we present the findings of our tests of several theories about the reciprocal impact of friendship groups and adult life changes.

Approaches to Understanding Adult Life Transitions

Broadly speaking, we can differentiate at least three alternative approaches to understanding adult life transitions. The empirical approach tends to correlate certain outcomes (such as depression or divorce) with precipitants external to the individual or self system (career progress, maturation of children). The individual is seen as responding to events in the social and physical worlds that impinge on him.

The second approach, the developmental, implies a natural process of psychological growth. The individual does not simply react to events, but changes his capacity to respond by moving to a more differentiated and integrated level of functioning. He develops an increasingly sophisticated and adequate adaptation to his environment, reflected in an increased ability to master internal and external demands and to maintain gratifying relationships with others. At this point few scholars have actually presented a theory that addresses these aspects of development. Erikson's is the best-known developmental theory and has been the most influential in guiding current research in "adult development." His theory implies a predictable and coherent sequence of psychological growth: stages of psychosocial development. This process of development points toward the acquisition and maintenance of an "ego identity," reflected in the person's sense of well-being or "a feeling of being at home in one's body," of "knowing where one is going," and an "inner assuredness of recognition from those who count."[13] Erikson sees each developmental stage as focusing on a given task or problem. In mature adulthood, the two primary identity struggles are seen as "generativity versus stagnation" and "integrity versus despair." The former refers to a parental concern, although not simply directed toward one's own offspring, with helping or guiding the next generation to acquire the skills, perspectives, and values that will permit both their self-fulfillment and their cultural continuity. Integrity seems the more elusive task, involving a developing sense of the meaning and order of one's life, and its inherent dignity. Such a sense of integrity, Erikson argues, permits the maturing self to face death without a sense of despair.

While there are certain points of descriptive agreement with Erikson's framework, our findings do not point to systematic identity development as the basic dynamic of adult life. Rather, we observe halting, sporadic, more and less workable attempts by men to create a self they can value. While the specific expressions of this self may evolve as their roles change through adult life, the basic thematic concerns that guide its construction seem to remain fairly constant. Men entering midlife scramble, as do adolescents and young adults, to find some combination of love, security, respect, power, and autonomy. We focus on the family, the work place, the community, and friendship groups as the primary areas in which these struggles take place. Moreover, they are not limited to any temporal space. Struggles undergone in adolescence or young adulthood can be as emotionally salient as contemporary events. Midlife seems, in fact, often to trigger the reemergence of such emotionally laden memories.

Past research in the area of middle age has not, we would contend, been optimally productive because it has not combined methodological rigor with a holistic and in-depth view of the phenomenon. The biological and role changes that occur around middle age can best be interpreted as experiential rather than literal impingements on the self. That is, their major impact comes about because both the individual and his culture endow these changes with meaning. The processes by which these changes are recognized (or avoided), assessed, and acted upon by the individual thus become crucial areas for examination.

Endnotes

1. Neugarten, Bernice L. (ed.), *Middle Age and Aging* (Chicago: University of Chicago Press, 1968).
2. Gutmann, David L., "The Post Parental Years: Clinical Problems and Developmental Possibilities," in *Mid-life: Developmental and Clinical Issues*, edited by Norman and Scaramella (New York: Brunner/Mazel, 1980).
3. Lowenthal, Marjorie F., Majda Thurnher, and David Chiriboga, *Four Stages of Life* (San Francisco: Jossey-Bass, 1975).
4. Levinson, Daniel J., Charlotte N. Darrow, Edward B. Klein, Maria H. Levinson, and Braxton McKee, *The Seasons of a Man's Life* (New York: Alfred A. Knopf, 1978).
5. Rosenberg, Stanley D., and Michael P. Farrell, "Identity and Crisis in Middle Aged Men," *International Journal of Aging and Human Development*, vol. 7, no. 2, 1976.

6. Farrell, Michael P., Stanley D. Rosenberg, and Madeline H. Schmitt, "Identity, Alienation, and the Life Cycle," presented at the Annual Meeting of the American Sociological Association, Chicago, August 1976.

7. Nettler, Gwynn, "Scales of Alienated Attitude," in *Measures of Social Psychological Attitudes*, edited by J. B. Robinson and P. Shaver (Ann Arbor, Mich.: Institute for Survey Research).

8. Rosenberg, Stanley D., Michael P. Farrell, and John Gorman, "Racism: A 1973 Scale," *Journal of Social Psychology*, vol. 12, no. 4, 1976.

9. Martin, James G. and Frank R. Westie, "The Tolerant Personality," *American Sociological Review*, vol. 24, 1959, pp. 521–528.

10. Ford, LeRoy H. Jr., "A Forced Choice, Acquiescence-Free, Social Desirability (Defensiveness) Scale," *Journal of Consulting Psychology*, vol. 28, 1964, p. 475.

11. Levinson, Daniel J., and Phyllis E. Huffman, "Traditional Family Ideology and Its Relation to Personality," *Journal of Personality*, vol. 23, 1955, pp. 251–273.

12. Zung, W.W.K., "A Self Rating Depression Scale," *Archives of General Psychiatry*, vol. 12, January 1965, p. 63.

13. Erikson, Erik H., "The Problem of Ego Identity," *Journal of the American Psychoanalytic Association*, vol. 4, no. 1, 1956, pp. 58–121.

Chapter 2

CONTRADICTIONS IN CONCEPTIONS OF MIDDLE AGE

Our understanding of adult male development is still at the exploratory stage. A few pioneers have ventured into the territory with crude instruments and methods, but, as is often the case with new explorations, they have come back with contradictory reports. Some of the reports tell a story of men finding fulfillment, of being "in command," or experiencing rebirth. The full flourishing of desirable human qualities is alleged to occur during this period. Others describe a wasteland of marital dissatisfaction, alcoholism, neurotic disorders, and physical breakdown. Still others report an ordeal or "crisis" that must be surmounted if the promise of midlife fulfillment is to be found. Sweeping formulations about the whole adult life-span are also appearing. These seem often to produce general theories of development that are rapidly being assimilated into popular culture. An intriguing aspect of these models, at least to clinicians and those grappling with issues of their own life transitions, is that they outline or imply a developmental timetable. In making such stages appear more or less uniform and predictable, they can provide guidelines for living, or at least a measuring rod for the normalcy or adequacy of one's maturation.

It is our contention that such general theories are useful, but premature. They have been built inductively on very narrow data

15

bases, usually making use of middle-class respondents or people seeking counseling. A careful review of the empirical research reveals many contradictory findings that are ignored by the theorists. At the same time, they are useful in helping us think through and conceptualize the fragmentary and contradictory data at hand. In this sense, these preliminary theories help us to frame new and clarifying questions, suggesting issues on which to focus our attention.

In this chapter we examine some of the contradictions in the emerging portrait of middle-aged men. We first look at the "optimistic reports"—results deriving primarily from survey methodology—that present a relatively positive view of the period. Then we look at the "pessimistic reports" from clinical and demographic studies, ones that link this life phase to various forms of pathology and stress-related symptoms. Our objective is to highlight the contradictions and unanswered questions in the literature. Next, we build a synthesis of past theory and research that will be the basis of a general working model for conceptualizing the male experience of middle age. Finally, we look at the images of middle-aged men that are current in popular literature and movies—images that illustrate the typology of middle-aged men developed in our model.

Definitions of Middle Age

Defining the period of middle age is much like defining a period in history: No one quite agrees when it begins or ends. Neugarten[1] reports that lower-class respondents experience critical life-cycle events at an earlier age than middle-class respondents. Marriage, the birth of the first child, and middle age all occur earlier for the working class. Levinson[2] proposes that middle age begins with a transition period that occurs inevitably between the ages of 40 and 45. During this period men go through changes in their self-concepts and life structures that place them in middle age.

It is probably a mistake to tie the stages of adult development too closely to a timetable, especially the entry into middle age. Unlike adolescents, people in middle age do not have predictable chronological events that define the transition from young adulthood to middle age. Especially for men, there is nothing similar to entry into junior high or pubescence that is closely tied to chronological age marking that transition period. Rather, there is a gradual accumulation of life problems, role transitions, physiological changes, and events that ultimately lead a man to experience himself as having become middle-aged. The order of accumulation may vary, but most men find themselves undergoing transitions and problems that mark the arrival of middle age.

One common problem is that of dealing with aging parents who are becoming increasingly dependent, physically weaker, or dying. Another is that of relating to adolescent children who are dealing with issues of sexuality, disengagement from the parental home, and finding a place for themselves in the adult world. In relation to his children and his parents, the middle-aged man is more or less graciously moving into what Hill[3] has called the "patron" position, giving out more than he receives to both the older and the younger generation. In the area of work, the problems include coming to terms with the contrasts between the youthful dreams of success and the reality of what is possible. For a few fortunate men who succeeded early this problem may never arise, but for most men the disjunction between dreams and reality is something that is faced during this period. Both the successful and unsuccessful find themselves wrestling with the stagnation described by Erikson.[4] Finally, the period is marked by events that drive home to a man his physical vulnerability and force him to come to terms with his own eventual death. Undeniable signs of aging, illness, or the death of a friend may be the events that make one's own death a more salient concern during this period.

It is in the three domains of family, work, and physical self that experiences marking the transition begin to accumulate. The order of accumulation may vary, the chronological age at which the experiences arrive may vary, but once they have occurred, a man has reached the period of midlife.

Once men reach that period, they do not all experience their problems in the same way. Although objectively they may have similar life experiences, their reports indicate a wide range of subjective responses. The range of responses is reflected in the contradictory research reports and the widely divergent pictures of the experience presented in popular culture.

The Optimistic Reports

Many studies of men have presented an image of middle age as a "golden period" of development[2] where men achieve a level of self-actualization not possible in younger adulthood. The period is characterized by security, diminishing external pressures, and the maturity and good judgment to enjoy what life has to offer. Terman[5] reports that men reach a peak of self-confidence and self-esteem during middle age. In a study of 100 successful middle-aged persons, Neugarten[6] describes both men and women as feeling an increased ability to "manipulate their social environments" because of accumulated status and knowledge. These resources permit them to alter or define social rules rather than simply follow them. They also feel more capable of modulating their own feelings and impulses. In regard to both internal and external issues, these middle-aged subjects reported feeling more "in command."

The general thrust of Neugarten's findings are echoed by Deutscher,[7] who examined the "postparental phase of life"; by Estes and Wilensky,[8] who correlated reported life satisfaction with income; and by Lowenthal's research group, who found that male midlife respondents on self-reports, describe themselves rather favorably.[9]

In all these portrayals middle age is depicted as a period of peak development for men. They have mastered their internal and external world, have a highly positive self-concept, and are at the height of their authority. These data might lead one, at first glance, to conclude that the midlife or middle-age crisis is no more than a figment of the overactive literary imagination; but other evidence would indicate that such a conclusion may be too hasty.

The Pessimistic View

Psychoanalysts, psychiatrists, and other writers working with clinical data often see a middle-age crisis as universal—a developmental inevitability.[10-14] Levinson proposes, as did Jaques and others, a developmental sequence, with a period of midlife crisis, that "exists in all societies, throughout the human species, at the present stage of human evolution." Such assertions have sometimes been dismissed on the grounds that the clinician does not see a representative sample of the population, but rather the affluent, verbal, and discontented. These perspectives, that is, seem to originate by contact with a self-selected group: those who are sufficiently distressed to seek professional help for psychological or psychiatric problems. Even if they were only 5 or 10 percent of the middle-aged population, they would appear to the clinician as a virtual tidal wave of distress or pathology. Secondly, problems of anxiety, depression, or self-doubt can occur anywhere in the human life-span. The argument for a midlife crisis, if it is to be valid, must provide evidence of either a special incidence or symptomatology in this life stage, or at the least some evidence of a unique quality to the problems of this as opposed to other phases of maturation. One is then confronted with the issue of subjectivity or latitude of clinical interpretation: Can either the therapist or the patient be trusted in their conclusion about the sources of stress in midlife? The uniqueness of the therapeutic setting makes replication of findings highly problematic, while the goal of the work is obviously curative rather than investigative. These factors combine to evoke skepticism about conclusions drawn from or inspired by treatment-based populations. The large majority of individuals who never seek such help may be totally dissimilar, making "crisis" an atypical rather than a universal response.

Whether or not such conclusions are artifacts of the clinicians' narrow world view, it would seem obvious that the questionnaire approach of simply asking individuals how happy they are cannot adequately tap the phenomenon of middle-age crisis as it has been described. Psychoanalytic writers do not assert that they see overt, conscious confrontation with midlife issues, but rather a myriad of pathological reactions to it. They often note denial of the crisis and subsequent attempts at escape (for instance, frantic activity or sexual adventures which prove burdensome) along with more general forms of decompensation such as anxiety, depression, and diffuse rage. Furthermore, the clinicians are not the only ones reporting that middle age is stressful. A number of surveys and epidemiological studies have supported this view.

Pineo's longitudinal study found that marital satisfaction for both men and women in fact declines in middle age,[15] a conclusion that was subsequently supported by other writers looking at large samples.[16] A large-scale demographic study of Baltimore and the surrounding county indicated a sharp increase in the rate of psychoses in the middle aged as opposed to the young.[17] Leighton similarly found an initial peaking of psychoneurosis for men in their late thirties through their mid-forties in his study of Sterling County.[18] The Midtown study of Srole and his colleagues, one of the most comprehensive studies of psychiatric disturbances ever attempted, also uncovered greater symptom-formation in the middle-aged group than in younger adults.[19] Simple statistical comparisons reveal that first admissions for alcoholism to state hospitals peak for the age group 45–57[20] as do mental hospitalizations for other reasons.[21]

Less severe psychological symptoms appear to follow the same pattern. Middle age is associated in several studies with the "feeling of an impending nervous breakdown,"[22] as well as with general "nervousness" and headaches.

The incidence of a number of psychosomatic ailments shows sharp increase for the middle-aged. Peptic ulcer, in most studies, has its highest incidence in the 40–50 age group, with those in the 30–40 age group showing the next highest rate.[23] Hypertension and heart disease also show an increasing incidence in middle age as compared with young adulthood.[24]

Lowenthal and Chiriboga, writers we cited as being in the optimistic camp, are themselves suspicious of the high satisfaction expressed by their middle-aged male respondents. The authors report that the subjects ". . . seem rather to have a conscious reluctance to report negative circumstances or affect, or to repress them altogether." Yet Lowenthal and Chiriboga seem to be left with the impression that such negative affect persists and finds less direct modes of expression: "The cost of this effort to live up to a strong male image may be great . . . it is the men who have serious difficulties in mid-life. . . ." Men in their study, for example, report greater satisfaction with sex in marriage in middle age, while their wives report a decline in both frequency and satisfaction. While the researchers do not comment on this data, we would suggest that these men reach a kind of equilibrium by lowering their own expectations for themselves while ignoring their mates' dissatisfactions. There is thus a hollow, ostrich-like quality to their sense of having a good sexual relationship with their wives.

Cuber and Harroff[25] studied 37 upper-middle-class Americans between the ages of 35 and 50. Although none of these people had sought psychiatric treatment, they found widespread disillusionment and cynicism among their respondents. Subjects had a strong tendency to rationalize away the disturbing aspects of their existences, in terms of both living with themselves and maintaining a front for others. Many maintained marital arrangements that were either quite empty of meaning or marked by festering hostility. Once again, the men tended to describe such arrangements as workable or convenient, while the wives were more vocal in stating that they represented a disappointing and deadening mode of existence. Cuber and Harroff also cite instances in which respondents imply that they would not have revealed their true feelings about such intimate and significant issues on a questionnaire. This may be one reason why their findings contrast so sharply with those of Neugarten, Deutscher, and Lowenthal. Such contradictory results point to a need for clarification in this area.

Sources of Contradictory Findings

There are at least three possible sources of the contradictions in findings. First, there is a lack of clarity and consensus in defining the period of middle age. Different researchers are studying different periods of the life cycle under the same name. We'll call this the definitional problem. The second source of contradictions may be methodological: Samples studied may not be representative of the whole population, and data-collection techniques may not yield comparable results. The third source actually overlaps the first two sources. It may be that there are several paths of adult male development in our culture. Different researchers may be studying men on different paths and assuming they are observing a universal phenomenon.

Definition Problems

The boundaries of middle age are notoriously vague, both objectively and subjectively. In the research literature they have been defined as ranging from the late thirties to the late sixties, nearly one half the normal life-span. Particular studies have focused on different points in this wide span of time. Some have focused on the "empty nest" phase, when all children have left home. Others have been less precise, focusing on men in a general age period but not specifying what their current life problems are. Some studies may be prematurely precise, focusing on narrow age ranges by the prior assumption of universal developmental patterns that are closely tied to chronological age. It seems likely that different points in middle age may be associated with different experiences in men. Some periods could well be highly gratifying, while others might be devastating. Further research with more precise delineation of the changing life circumstances and response patterns is required for the clarification of these problems.

Methodological Problems

Most of the research on middle age has been based on unclear sampling techniques with subjects most frequently being middle class. Lowenthal's subjects all come from a single suburban neighborhood. One half of Levinson's 40 men work in the same corporation; Block and Haan[26] and Vaillant's[27] subjects are all part of the educated upper-middle or upper class. Neugarten's subjects are middle class. Pineo's subjects seem to be a more diverse group, though they were originally chosen from a college population. To clarify the picture of development during middle age, it is necessary to base studies on larger samples that are representative of the general population.

A second methodological problem that may be contributing to the confusion is the different methods of collecting data. Survey studies tend to produce more positive findings than studies based on in-depth clinical interviews. Epidemiological studies of health data also generate a more negative picture. It may be that the population of middle-aged men is more likely to present a positive picture when interviewed by a stranger who shows up with a questionnaire. But with a more in-depth contact, or with data from sources other than the man himself, the picture becomes less benign.

Assumption of a Single Developmental Path

Theories of adult male development tend to assume a single developmental course followed by all men. In *The Seasons of a Man's Life*, for example, Levinson argues that "the life structure evolves through a relatively orderly sequence during the adult years. The essential character of the sequence is the same for all the men in our study and for the other men whose biographies we examined."[28] Thus "entering the adult world" occurs between ages 28 to 33; "settling down" occupies men between ages 33 to 40, culminating with a phase of becoming one's own man; the midlife transition occurs during the period from 40 to 45; and so on. Gould[29] divides the life cycle into similar stages.

The contradictory research findings indicate potential problems with this kind of model. Perhaps the stages proposed by Levinson apply to a subset of men—most likely a creative and intellectual elite who achieve many of our cultural ideals of success and normalcy. Such data may speak more to our cultural image of "success" and "self-actualization" than to either the reality of most people's lives or to universal psychological processes. The contradictions in the research findings may indicate that there are several paths of adult male development or that the very idea of "development" is a hopeful fiction, simple survival being more the norm. The implications of developmental models for the sequence, timing, and content of midlife changes do not seem to accord with the available data.

The lack of fit between theory and research in this field is reminiscent of the failure to find confirmation for Erikson's theory of identity development. He had proposed a universal identity crisis during adolescence, an idea which soon became the orthodox belief in the field. In its early phases adolescent research was also dominated by clinicians studying those people who sought help during this stage. Later attempts to test their developmental theories on normal populations generated a much more complicated and interesting picture than the original theories proposed.[30-32]

Theory-Building about Middle Age

One way that theory-building begins is with description. The phenomena are observed and described repeatedly, and recurrent patterns are abstracted out of the flow of observations. Eventually the patterns are clustered together into a static typology. A syndrome of variables that regularly co-occur are grouped together. Thus, the medical researcher may group together a syndrome of symptoms—fever, abdominal pain, and nausea. At the second stage of theory-building the scientist begins to build a dynamic model that causally explains the syndrome. A few variables are isolated as key determinants of other variables. Hypotheses are built around the key independent variables, and other properties of the phenomenon relegated to positions of dependent variables —surface indicators or symptoms, but not the causes of the pattern.

In the study of adult development we are still at the early stages of theory-building. Many observers have reported patterns, but the observers do not agree, and the patterns do not yet "make sense." That is, we have not yet reached consensus about the basic patterns let alone agreed upon the key underlying determinants of the patterns. To advance our understanding of middle age we must first organize what we have observed into a working typological model. The model must recognize the divergent findings in the field, yet provide some order to guide future research. Though a lucky guess is possible, it would seem premature to jump ahead to a dynamic theory of the underlying determinants of the observed patterns. First, it is necessary to consolidate what we know. Then, after the patterns have been clarified, it will be time to begin the later stages of theory-building. What is required is a more general conceptualization that suggests relationships between physical, psychological, interpersonal, and cultural variables. In other words, rather than a fully developed theory, we need a model that points the way to appropriate variables and levels of analysis.

Our first step in attempting this study was thus the proposal of a working model of male responses to middle age.[33] The age period being studied, we argued, needed to be more clearly specified, and the sample used more representative of the population as a whole. Finally, the methods of study should be more multifaceted and holistic, allowing for the assessment of psychological distress, symptom formation, alterations of life patterns, values, self-concepts, psychological defenses, and coping styles. The methods should also allow for the possibility of getting beyond immediate defensive covering, perhaps through establishing a more open interviewing relationship.

A Working Model of the Male Midlife Experience

We shall now describe our initial model of the life changes associated with middle age in our society. Our emphasis is on the experiential aspects of these changes and the adaptational patterns they evoke. Since the problems of confronting middle age are more or less ubiquitous (although the midlife crisis may or may not be), there must also be shared mechanisms for dealing with these. All cultures provide psychological supports and controls to guide members through major life transitions, helping them to more comfortably assume new roles and statuses. A common mechanism for accomplishing these ends is the existence of stereotypes that link certain kinds of feelings, attitudes, and behaviors to certain kinds of people. We all know, within limits, how "old people" or "teen-agers" are supposed to act. Similarly, we can find cultural images that can serve to reassure and re-anchor the individual caught in the midlife upheaval. These stereotypes both reflect certain personal realities in our society and also help, by their availability, to encourage and legitimize the enactment of such patterns: They become a conforming response to midlife. Novels, movies, television, and other outlets of popular culture portray alternative images of middle-aged men, images that not only reflect current styles of dealing with middle age, but also provide role models. We draw on these stereotypical patterns to illustrate and elucidate four types of responses to middle age.

Our model assumes a division between the objective press of circumstances that accumulate in middle age and the subjective responses to these circumstances. The objective circumstances are relatively constant for middle-aged men, but the subjective responses vary considerably. We will first examine the objective factors that affect middle-aged men in relation to their work, home life, and bodies.

Work Life: The Shrinkage of Possibilities

Lehman has studied the peak years of productivity of men in different professions.[34] Looking at several professions, he calculates the likelihood of a person making an important contribution to his field at each point in the adult life cycle. He finds, for example, that medical scientists are most likely to make a contribution to progress in medicine during the age span of 35 to 39. Physicists, on the other hand, are most likely to make important contributions during their late twenties. For the most part, Lehman's findings are not very encouraging to the middle-aged man. Most professions peak prior to this period.

However, even if a man is not familiar with Lehman's findings, even if the charts are irrelevant to his chosen vocation, he now has a good idea of what the chances for success are for someone in his position. If he has been climbing a bureaucratic pyramid, he sees the number of possible positions above him getting fewer while the competition is getting more intense. If he has depended on his physical strength, he knows it is already beginning to decline. He's likely to begin measuring his dreams of what he wanted to be against the reality of what he has become and the shrinking possibilities that lie before him. If his life structure has been built around hopes for future fulfillment in achievements or acquisitions, he now begins to assess how well those hopes have been realized. The vague expansive future has shrunk into a very particular present. What's left of "the future" is limited in time and possibilities. For some men, this point is driven home by the death of a friend or associate. For others, the awareness of shrinkage comes gradually. Regardless of when or how it comes, the pressure to redefine one's work goals and one's relationship to work mounts. As Jaques points out, even immensely successful men are likely to begin taking stock at this point, assessing which goals they will pursue within the limited life-span still available.[35] At forty a man has reached full adulthood, and the dreams of youth must confront the hard-edged reality of the present. For many men, new adaptations to work are required that take into account the limits of that reality and the feelings of desperation associated with those limits. The men in Neugarten's study, for example, had well-articulated ideas about the relationship "between life-line and career-line." Middle age was a very relevant marker in this schema, a point at which one was well advised to "take stock." These men expressed the belief that mobility was severely limited after age 45, forcing one to make any major career initiatives prior to this age.[36]

Reaching or approaching the optimal point in one's career does not simply occur; it is also experientially relevant. While men do not necessarily reach peak earnings, the highest rung on the organizational ladder, or maximum recognition until later middle age, indicators of how far they will go in these dimensions tend to appear much earlier. Those slated for top management have been separated from middle managers. There are very few academics or scientists who make major contributions after the onset of middle age who have not made contributions of equal magnitude earlier in their career.[37] These facts appear to be part of the common lore within the organizations and professions and tend to reduce the expectations that one is any longer in the running for dramatic or unexpected career advances. The change-in-life chances associated with age are similar in the working class. They must cope not only with the gradual decline of physical vigor and agility, but also with the fact that younger workers may be better equipped to deal with technological changes that affect the work process.

Home and Family Life: The Husband Role

At home a quite different set of stresses impinges on a man as he moves into his forties. Most men are married and have children by this time. Most have tried to build a home that is a protective environment for their families, one that encourages in their children the behavior and beliefs the parents have come to value. Many men have chosen to build this protective encasement in the suburbs, but some have stayed in the city near their old neighborhood. For the latter, the home is often viewed as an encampment in a hostile environment, requiring constant vigilance to guard it against the encroaching strangers who follow different styles of life.

The emotional center of the family is generally the wife. Her traditional role is to set the routines, mediate disputes, and maintain the physical environment. By the fourth decade most of the wives of these men have begun to emerge from the burdens of constant child care. The husband, who has often built a life structure based on a fixed image of his wife and her role, now must face a developing, changing person less defined by the stereotypical wife-mother role. These changes in his wife's behavior and sense of herself may impinge on the husband, creating pressure to redefine his own self-conception. Certain gratifications and ways in which he has related to his family are no longer supportable.

One study of family relations,[38] for example, suggests that the assertion of authority within the family becomes problematic for the middle-aged male, who experiences guilt about his own aggressiveness. He attempts to deal with this by recourse to either passivity (which is sometimes rationalized as a passive "cerebral" control, particularly by the middle-class males) or by justifying his control on moral grounds, as a force for "good" within the family. The wife, on the other hand, is perceived as exhibiting high emotionality and impulsiveness. In the earlier periods of middle age she is "checked" by the husband, but her hostility and

nurturance are nonetheless crucial to the family's emotional life
and fantasies. The limits of these fantasies may become more
apparent in older age groups, who perceive continuing ascendency
of the mother—eventually to the point where she pushes the
father from the stage and seems to draw strength from his decline.
In general, both middle-age and older males appear to use women
as the focus for much projected material. "The woman is the figure
of 'unchecked' impulse [which] breaks into a scene otherwise peo-
pled by more restrained or affiliative figures. She is a figure of
primal omnipotence and wrath—a 'devil. . . .' "[39]

Home and Family Life: The Father Role

This projective modality seems also to operate in the males' perception of the younger generation and in the social environment
in general. As a group, middle-aged men tend to deny their own
feelings of aggressiveness or impulsivity. They simultaneously
tend to attribute these characteristics increasingly to others, while
also becoming more strident in their demands for conformity and
more punitive and less forgiving toward deviance.[40] The younger
male becomes a particular focus for such projective attribution:
middle-aged men perceive adolescent boys as ridden with those
forbidden desires and traits they totally deny in themselves.

As adolescent children make bids for individuation, they may
experiment with identities that are irrelevant or contradictory to
the dreams that their father has for them. As they try to come to
terms with the social and cultural landscape of their times, they
may take on values and behaviors that are antithetical to the life
structure he has built. At the very least, they begin to move in
wider and wider circles, outside the possibility of his control. His
authority diminishes and he must deal with the loss of control
associated with earlier phases of the fathering role. These strains
create pressures to redefine his basic assumptions about himself,
find new outlets, and alter his approach to the problem of giving
meaning and purpose to his life.

Home and Family Life: The Role of Son to Aging Parents

In dealing with his own parents, a man also experiences strains
that may undermine the adaptations of earlier adulthood. As his
parents age, he finds them becoming dependent on him. As a
young man he was apt to have perceived them as powerful objects

to come to terms with or escape from. He must now come to grips with experiencing them as declining, perhaps needy persons whose demands become insistent, unpredictable, and often burdensome. This may well invoke guilt as well as pressures for him to change his conception of himself in relation to them. He may feel conflicts about loyalty to them as opposed to his own family, and when they die, he loses an emotional tie, whether positive or negative, that is likely to have been a significant part of his universe.

The middle-aged man is called upon to symbolically replace his own father: to assume responsibility for the "family" vis-à-vis the larger culture, to be the rock upon which the interpersonal network rests. The fact that his dominance becomes a point of contention with his wife and children—and perhaps even with his aging parents—does not mitigate the latent expectation that he assume the position successfully. It becomes the ideal against which his potency is measured, by both himself and others. The displacement of his father evokes stress and internal conflict in the middle-aged son. While supplanting or out-achieving the father may have been a central project for the maturing adult, his ascendency is over a now-weakened and sympathetic figure. Guilt and depression would intermingle with any potential elation. To the degree that the middle-aged male's identification with his father is strengthened by the role shift, it functions to emphasize the sense of deterioration and mortality associated with his own physiological changes. Finally, looking to the father or cultural "elders" as a source of strength, control, and wisdom becomes a mechanism no longer available to the middle-aged. As the source of control, he becomes less free to express vulnerability or find external agents to lean on, in either fantasy or reality.

Bodily Changes

Finally, the middle-aged male is more likely to experience physical problems that undermine his image of himself and his mode of relating to the world. Heart attacks, ulcers, back problems, and other maladies affect him or his friends. Pressures mount to restructure his own routines to take into account the possibility of serious illness. Even if these tangible signs of aging do not affect a man, the sheer fact of advancing age is likely to become more salient to him. Age 40 is a momentous hurdle that many men interpret as the halfway mark in life. A poem by Longfellow illustrates the concerns this hurdle may precipitate:[41]

Mezzo Cammin

Half of my life is gone, and I have let
The years slip from me and have not fulfilled
The aspirations of my youth, to build
Some tower of song with lofty parapet . . .
Though, half-way up the hill, I see the Past
Lying beneath me with its sounds and sights,
A city in the twilight dim and vast,
With smoking roofs, soft hills, and gleaming lights,
And hear above me on the autumnal blast
The cataract of Death far thundering from the heights.

All of these factors impinge on a man at this point, creating pressure to redefine his life structure. The pressures may come crashing in on him or they may accumulate gradually. But inevitably they build, creating strain on his earlier modes of relating to the world and on his long-standing assumptions about himself.

Limited Maneuverability

These potentially crisis-inducing elements in the life space of middle-aged males are made even more difficult to manage by the matrix of social demands in which he is generally embedded. He is often in the position of having to be a role model and socializing force for his maturing children. Witnessing their adolescent struggles may reawaken or threaten his own identity conflicts, yet he is not nearly so free as the adolescent to work through or express his problems. While his physical strengths may be declining, he is just approaching the height of his symbolic and social power. In work, community, and family social structure he is expected to provide strength and commitment commensurate with his status. Thus, expression of the doubts and conflicts inherent in reaching middle age would be mitigated by both the need for internal integration and by cultural expectations.

Like the adolescent, the middle-aged male is confronted by biological, status, and role changes that precipitate efforts to redefine who he is; but, unlike the adolescent, he is not granted an institutionalized moratorium for exploring identities. Instead, he is more constrained than ever by the expectations of others, his obligations to them, and his concern for his already established identity, which is a known if not entirely satisfactory commodity.

However, there are some culturally legitimate identities open to him that allow for stabilization (if not resolution) of the crisis.

By providing intra- and extra-familial roles as well as modes of self-perception and self-system organization, these cultural stereotypes can be seen as providing congruent "solutions" to the myriad problems of transition to middle age. These solutions may themselves be more or less problematic and are subsumed in our typology.

Responses to Stress: The Masks of Middle-Aged Men

Though the objective circumstances may be similar for most men at middle age, the discrepant findings from past research indicate that the responses to the circumstances vary considerably. Some researchers find men with very positive experiences during this period, while others report very negative experiences. We call the men's reports of their experience "masks" to emphasize our suspicion that the subjective experience of men and their presentations of self are not necessarily congruent with each other or with the realities of their observed responses. What is remarkable about the masks described in the literature is that they are all derived from the interplay of a limited number of themes and concerns and portray personal responses as being built around relatively few devices. Since the stereotypical masks represent the extreme points along these dimensions, they help to highlight the significant variables for investigation and to generate firmer expectations about the relations between variables.

While we recognize the pitfalls inherent in attempting to extrapolate personal modes of response from group data, some general characteristics of the middle-aged male and a tentative typology of response types of syndromes might be hypothesized. We advance this set of assumptions and typology as a potential structuring device for research. They have the properties of being: (1) a logical way to integrate the findings bearing on the topic; (2) consistent with many of the persuasive portrayals that abound in popular culture; (3) the basis for specifying the major dimensions or variables associated with the midlife crisis and reactions to it. In presenting each of the types we will make use of examples portrayed in popular culture. The examples not only elucidate theoretical categories; we feel they also provide models that influence the behavior and self-presentations of men.

For purposes of illustration, the typology of responses to midlife stress might be arranged on the following two dimensions:

Denial of Stress	*Open Confrontation with Stress*
IV Punitive-Disenchanted	**I Anti-Hero**
1. Highest in authoritarianism	1. High alienation
2. Dissatisfaction associated with environmental factors	2. Active identity struggle
	3. Ego-oriented
3. Conflict with children	4. Uninvolved interpersonally
	5. Low authoritarianism
III Pseudo-Developed	**II Transcendent-Generative**
1. Overtly satisfied	1. Assesses past and present with conscious sense of satisfaction
2. Attitudinally rigid	
3. Denies feelings	
4. High authoritarianism	2. Few symptoms of distress
5. High on covert depression and anxiety	3. Open to feelings
	4. Accepts out-groups
6. High in symptom formation	5. Feels in control of fate

Dissatisfied applies to rows IV and I; *Satisfied* applies to rows III and II.

Figure 2-1   Typology of Responses to Middle Age Stresses

One working assumption underlying the typology is that the personal disorientation, distress, and fears associated with entering middle age are often denied under direct questioning. Nonetheless, these emotional responses have a greater degree of emotional saliency than is overtly admitted. Many men entering midlife work to deny any weakness or distress they may be experiencing.

Direct confrontation with the issues of middle age appears to be a privilege of the affluent. Those who have consciously confronted the stresses as outlined would fall into two categories: the "transcendent-generative" (II) and the "anti-hero" (I).

The Anti-Hero or Dissenter (I)

Those who are self-reflective and overtly dissatisfied with life and work would tend toward the image of the struggling anti-hero (I). We expect them to be somewhat more symptomatic than the first group, but to be distinguished primarily by a strong sense of alienation and an active identity struggle. The anti-hero, highly ego-oriented in his concerns, would be basically uninvolved interpersonally and hence show relatively little concern about controlling his children. He would be neither ethnocentric nor authoritarian attitudinally. This would be the true or active middle-aged identity crisis and would be overrepresented in the middle or upper class, especially in individuals who have undergone extreme status mobility. Hypothetically such a response is precipitated in this group by a sudden "crisis." The stresses of middle age accumulate to the point that a more satisfactory adaptation, more like that seen in Group II, suddenly deteriorates. Another possibility is that men in this group have suffered more long-standing difficulties, never having achieved the same sense of being at home with themselves or their culture.

The Transcendent-Generative (II)

The transcendent-generative (II) can be described as able to assess his past and present and match them to inner feelings with a positive sense of satisfaction. This type would tend to exhibit few symptoms of psychological and psychosomatic distress. He would exhibit genuine and positive feelings toward work and marriage and have a definite and satisfactory sense of self. This positive sense of himself would be based on and reflected in an openness to feelings, good relations with his children, and a nonpunitive and accepting orientation toward out-groups. He feels in control of his own fate and exhibits a high tolerance for ambiguity.

The Pseudo-Developed Man (III)

The pseudo-developed men (III) would represent themselves, in response to overt questioning, as similar to the transcendent-generative. They present a facade of masculine potency, of having mastered all the basic problems of life. In fact, they would embody many of the characteristics attributed to the faceless American in existential writing,[42] black humor literature,[43,44] and similar critiques of mass culture. The pseudo-developed man deals with the stresses of middle age with denial and avoidance. He presents a facade of cheery self-confidence. However, there is a large gap between his presentation on self-reports and the way he appears on indicators less amenable to conscious manipulation. His facade is maintained through rigid control buttressed by a highly structured life and avoidance of new situations, people, or ideas. His basic discontent or sense of entrapment may find expression in religion, alcoholism, hypochondriasis, or psychosomatic ailment; and he may exhibit unrecognized signs of depression and anxiety.

Some evidence also suggests that, in the paternal role, this group's ambivalence may lead not only to repressive rigidity but also to covert reinforcement of the son's tendency to rebel and "act out." Such reinforcement would obviously serve the function of permitting the father, in the name of innocence, to enjoy vicariously expressive release and aggression against a system that he overtly supports but that he too may experience as oppressive. That is, the father may indirectly communicate to the son a sense of his own dissatisfaction and impotence, making the son's emulation of him highly improbable.

Keniston's study of alienated youth seems strongly to indicate that these young men perceive their fathers—who tend to be successful by external criteria—as in reality acquiescent to an alien external system. They describe their fathers as having "sold out" something within themselves, thereby killing off a most important part of themselves.[45]

And in the implicit descriptions of their parents' relationship with each other, we have noted how alienated subjects described their mothers as the more vigorous, decisive and strong. But the most specific instance of Father's defeat by life comes in these subjects' account of their fathers' vocations. Here they emphasize the abandonment of early hopes and youthful dreams, and the attendant breaking of their fathers' spirits.

The subjects imply a certain sympathy for the abandoned dreams of their fathers, and perhaps for their image of the youthful father themselves; but toward their fathers as they are now, they feel (or communicate) a lack of basic respect. Their sympathy for their fathers is more attached to their fantasy of what their fathers were like twenty-five years ago.

Such perceptions of the father are thus reflective of a profound ambivalence. Rebellion seems to be linked to love of the father, at least to some part of him now lost. A crucial question is to what extent the father indicated to the son that this is the only lovable part of himself. The father can espouse any number of ideologies while encouraging his son to act out his rebellion indirectly.

The Punitive-Disenchanted or Authoritarian Type (IV)

The fourth type combines denial of inner feelings with projection, turning anger and self-hatred toward people considered "outsiders." This stereotype is, of course, congruent with Adorno's characterization of the "authoritarian personality" whose need for controls is expressed in a paranoid world view, a denial of aggressive impulses within the self, and the adoption of a rigid and punitive socio-moral code.[46] While Adorno's work had obvious methodological shortcomings,[47] his conceptualization may nonetheless be useful in ordering the particular phenomenon of reaction to middle age. Those approaching the authoritarian stereotype may openly express discontent, but they do so in terms of the necessity of controlling the environment ("This country is falling apart," "Kids don't have enough respect for their parents") or of altering one's circumstances in terms of income and status. This stereotype is associated with the working or lower middle class. This kind of discontent is thus vocalized and experienced in highly conservative terms, supporting the status quo or an idealized past.

We would expect the two types of response based on denial to be preponderant among those for whom middle age is, in fact, problematic. The individual's tendency to deny this issue and its associated affect is socially reinforced. By reaffirming those values by which he has lived, the middle-aged male can both justify himself and support those values he has grown up with. In so doing he is enabled to retain symbolic potency as recompense for his declining physical and emotional vigor. To denounce the meaningfulness of the culture in which he has gained (or at least sought after) some measure of power, prestige, and respectability would be to admit the meaninglessness of his own existence. The middle-aged have, by and large, established a behavioral commitment to the value system of self-denial, striving, and conformity to social norms which may be most difficult to undo. In fact, as an existence based on these organizing principles becomes more problematic, the need to reaffirm them becomes more urgent.[48]

Literary Images of Middle Age

Though the stresses of middle age have been a subject of literature throughout this century[49,50] they have become an increasingly
common theme in recent times. The characters portrayed in this
literature reflect and influence current styles of dealing with middle age. In this section we will highlight some of these images
with the objective of elucidating our typology of responses to
midlife stresses.

The Anti-Hero or Dissenter: Open Confrontation with Crisis (Type I)

The most consistent and explicit view of middle age in contemporary literature reflects our Type I responses. In these portrayals
the transition into middle age is viewed as inextricably bound up
with a sense of frenzy, if not a total crisis in identity. Time and
again, the aging protagonist emerges as anti-hero, trying to recapture some lost sense of wholeness or integrity by denouncing the
existent value schema. The previous adult period of his life is seen
not only as mismanaged, but also as a kind of malignant fantasy,
a fog of self-deception in which the individual has given up the
potential vividness of experience and life. Saul Bellow's Herzog,
one of contemporary fiction's most notable characterizations, provides a case in point.

> *Late in spring, Herzog has been overcome by the need to explain,
> to have it out, to justify, to put in perspective, to clarify, to make
> amends . . . he sometimes imagined he was an industry that manu-
> factured personal history, and saw himself from birth to death. . . .*
>
> *Considering his entire life, he realized that he had mismanaged
> everything—everything. His life was, as the phrase goes, ruined.
> But since it has not been much to begin with, there was not much
> to grieve about. . . .*[51]

Vonnegut's Billy Pilgrim leaves the reader with little doubt that
his life experience has only left him with a sense of futility, absurd-
ity, and staleness.[52] He continually ruminates over the fire bomb-
ing of Dresden in World War II, a formative event in his life.
Billy recalls children's street rhymes that convey both the fascina-
tion and pointlessness of this memory. The first is:

There was a young man from Stamboul,
Who soliloquized thus to his tool:
"You took all my wealth
And you ruined my health,
And now you won't pee, you old fool."

The second epitomizes the endless circle of his obsession with memory:[53]

My name is Yon Yonson,
I work in Wisconsin,
I work in a lumbermill there.
The people I meet, when I walk down the street,
They say, "What's your name?"
And I say,
"My name is Yon Yonson,
And I work in Wisconsin . . ."
And so on to infinity. . . .

Billy's entire existence is portrayed as such a "nightmare of meaninglessness."

> *And we were flown to a rest camp in France, where we were*
> *fed chocolate malted milkshakes and other rich foods until we*
> *were all covered with baby fat. Then we were sent home, and I*
> *married a pretty girl who was covered with baby fat too.*
> *And we had babies.*
> *And they're all grown up now, and I'm an old fart with mem-*
> *ories and his Pall Malls, My name is Yon Yonson, I work in Wis-*
> *consin, I work in a lumbermill there.*[54]

Nor is the situation seen as rectifiable; there is really no one other than one's self to blame. Ultimately, Vonnegut's hero, like Bellow's, penetrates his being to sense that his own rationalizations and fears are the basis of his dilemma. While the heroes totally renounce the values of society, they come to recognize that they have not been misled by the flawed wisdom of the culture so much as they have eagerly embraced and even helped to generate it, finding it a convenient device for temporarily escaping the basic issues of their existence. Formulations vary here: The protagonist may be escaping from freedom, from fear, from desire, or some combination of these.

While details and conclusions may differ, an extensive and popular literature portrays the midlife crisis in substantially similar terms: Kazan's *The Arrangement*, several of Miller's plays, Friedman's *Stern* and *The Dick*, the ubiquitous *Portnoy,* and Updike's

Rabbit Redux are representative. In all of them the middlescent must experience a new identity crisis and, in so doing, realize that his "maturity" was not based on the successful resolution of the issues of childhood, but rather on their denial. The "rational" goal-seeking adulthood comes to be reinterpreted as largely compulsive and meaningless.

In a very few cases the middle-aged man is portrayed as transcending the dilemmas into which he has descended. In Fowles's *Daniel Martin* the death of a college friend triggers an excursion home for the middle-aged anti-hero. He leaves his current mistress and reestablishes contact with people, places, and parts of himself that he left behind in order to "make it" in movie writing. In attempting to rekindle authenticity in his friend's widow, he abandons the false aspects of his own life and recommits himself to the dreams of his youth. Cheever portrays a similar though more muted version of rebirth during middle age in his highly successful book *Falconer*. Such positive outcomes to the open confrontation with crisis are rare in literary portrayals. More often the anti-hero is depicted as lost in a meaningless world.

The dissenter anti-hero may thus engage in a variety of behaviors, but tends to experience a limited range of emotions and to perceive himself in fairly regular terms. As he arrives at "successful" middle age, he seems to evince a sense of shock and disbelief, as if to ask, "Is this all there is?" Finally released from the drive for achievement in the quest for status and material comfort, he finds that "having it made" is in no sense the gratifying state of affairs he foresaw when he gave up the freedom of youth to enter the "system." In one way or another, he strives to look into himself and find a way out of the box of his intolerable, self-chosen existence.

The Pseudo-Developed and Punitive-Disenchanted Types (III and IV)

Less commonly, the middle-aged male is portrayed as depressed, suffering with a sense of declining potency and preoccupied with themes of death. Instead of attempting to reverse his life course, he turns his despair outward, directing his rage at those who would repudiate the very mode of life that constitutes his misery. The protagonist in this reactive modality needs confirmation that he has chosen an inevitable path, that his basic assumptions remain correct. He must thus struggle to repress and deny many of his feelings and consequently project them onto out-groups, particularly deviants and dissenters who would overthrow the system that is the object of his own ambivalent rage and need; this is a portrayal of our Type IV punitive-disenchanted reactive pattern.

For example, in the movie *Joe* a strange alliance develops between an affluent advertising executive and a factory worker—both fathers of adolescent children—who review their existences and confide to one another: "Didn't you ever get the feeling that it's all a crock of shit?" This revelation is portrayed as intimately tied to attitudes toward youth, who are seen as representing erotic expression. After participating in an orgy with several hippies, and subsequently being rebuffed by them, the two men go on a rampage and kill the residents of a commune. Their erotic release—although an emotional high point—makes them hate the hippies even more for having the youthful potential and tolerance for nonstructure that the men themselves have wasted. Joe, the blue-collar father, epitomizes the macho repressiveness, racial and ethnic prejudice, and belligerent jingoism we associate with the authoritarian posture.

This type of treatment, like Vonnegut's, is clearly not in the genre of realism, but rather attempts to highlight latent anxieties and fantasies and their relation to overt behavior and beliefs. More commonly, the reactive modality is dealt with in terms of recognizable intra-familial conflict. The father becomes more rigid, authoritarian, and punitive as he senses his son's maturation and potential for choice while experiencing himself as becoming impotent and trapped. The television character Archie Bunker is a highly successful version of this image.

The difference between the authoritarian and pseudo-developed deniers is that the authoritarian type admits to dissatisfactions, but perceives them as located in the tensions around him or in the flaws of others. The pseudo-developed man, on the other hand, lives in a world of pretense. In literature he is portrayed as the male figure in the background who is out of touch with the tensions building around him. He is oblivious to the ridicule, anger, or pain that he generates in his environment. The husband in the movie *Diary of a Mad Housewife* captures many elements of this type. He presents a confident, cheerful facade to his family and associates, pretending to have mastered his life situation and achieved a sense of integration at home and in his social world. Meanwhile, his wife and marriage are on the verge of collapse; she is carrying on an affair, while his "friends" treat him with contempt. The recent movie *Ordinary People* also portrays some aspects of the father attempting to maintain such a facade.

The pseudo-developed man mimics the behavior and self-presentation of the secure, content, mature male. Resisting any challenge to this persona, he insists that his wife and children adopt the facade of "the happy family" while rigidly denying any signs of unhappiness or desperation.

The Transcendent-Generative (Type II)

Positive images of middle age are less often portrayed in serious literature. Rather, such images of successful middle age tend to be encountered in the genre of the television series. The wise, kind, and clever detective is portrayed in characters such as Barnaby Jones and Ironsides. Matt Dillon of "Gunsmoke" and Lorne Green's portrayal of the father in "Bonanza" are probably the most classic representations of the wise, mature, strong father. This type is shown as a representative of law and order who is able to attain real intimacy with other characters and maintain deep commitment toward noble goals. He is at once kind and nurturing, but also strong and aggressive when provoked. Interestingly enough, this type is most often a stable background character rather than the major protagonist. He is the voice of the wisdom of the culture who often clears up the disruptions caused by other characters and restores the situations to equilibrium.

As we have attempted to show, these four primary stereotypes are not only common in the culture, they are also congruent with both the direct and tangential findings of middle age. Each can be seen as representing a strategy of being in the world, an integrated mode of response to a common set of role and psychological issues associated with a major status shift. Individuals may tend to move out of one mode of response on a transitory basis, as when the pseudo-developed (Type III) go on a "binge" and move closer to the perceptions and behavior of the anti-hero (Type I). Men may, on a transitory basis, show a combination of responses. The pseudo-developed, for example, are sometimes portrayed as being amenable to adopting the authoritarian response when under sufficient stress. In general, however, we hypothesize that individuals move toward one mode or another as an overall means of ego-defense and as an accepted way of dealing with the social environment. Culture provides well-delineated role models for each type of response, increasing the probability of such movement. That is, the existence and popularity of the stereotypes themselves represent a concretization of these choices which the self may choose to adopt.

Summary and Discussion

We can summarize our working assumption as follows: Men entering middle age, as a group, confront a common set of life space alterations which predispose them to undergo a crisis. That is, their relation to self and social environment tends to become problematic in a way that represents a qualitative shift from earlier adulthood. For some, these changes are minimally disturbing or even viewed positively, and new modes of integration are easily forged or old ones perpetuated.

More commonly, we would hypothesize, the problem is not so easily resolved. Relatively few men openly recognize and confront the disturbing issues associated with middle age in our culture. For those who do, a total reopening of assumptions and a reexamination of self and its relation to the world may ensue. Such a reaction tends to be associated—at least initially—with a dissatisfaction with one's life, one's commitments, and socially approved values. For many more, it would seem, the distress experienced in relation to midlife changes is misidentified, attributed to other sources, or is totally repressed and denied. Whether articulated or not, these midlife reactions represent a psychological reality, predisposing certain men toward symptom formation, reactive behavior patterns and attitudes. The strength and consistency of the denial operate to make the reaction to the crisis even more extreme and personally damaging, and may have important implications for those who share the interpersonal matrix of the middle-aged male. The combination of depression, agitation, and refusal to acknowledge distress serves to undercut the possibility of real connectedness or interchange while enhancing the likelihood of interpersonal conflict.

Endnotes

1. Neugarten, Bernice L., "The Awareness of Middle Age," in *Middle Age and Aging*, edited by B. Neugarten (Chicago: University of Chicago Press, 1968).
2. Levinson, Daniel J., Charlotte N. Darrow, Edward B. Klein, Maria H. Levinson, and Braxton McKee, *The Seasons of a Man's Life* (New York: Alfred A. Knopf, 1978).
3. Hill, Reuben, Nelson Foote, Joan Aldous, Robert Carlson, and Robert MacDonald, *Family Development in Three Generations* (Cambridge, Mass.: Schenkman Publishing Co., 1970).
4. Erikson, Erik H., "The Problem of Ego Identity," *Journal of the American Psychoanalytic Association*, vol. 4, no. 1, 1956, pp. 58–121.
5. Terman, Lewis M., *Psychological Factors in Marital Happiness* (New York: McGraw-Hill, 1938).
6. Neugarten, Bernice L., "The Awareness of Middle Age," *op. cit.*, p. 98.
7. Deutscher, Irwin, "The Quality of Post Parental Life: Definitions of the Situation," *Journal of Marriage and the Family*, vol. 26, February 1964, pp. 52–59.
8. Estes, Richard C., and Harold L. Wilensky, "Life Cycle Squeeze and the Morale Curve," *Social Problems*, vol. 25, no. 3, February 1978.
9. Lowenthal, Marjorie F., Majda Thurnher, and David Chiriboga, *Four Stages of Life* (San Francisco: Jossey-Bass, 1975).
10. Erikson, Erik H., *Childhood and Society* (New York: W.W. Norton, 1950).
11. Jaques, Elliott, "Death and the Mid-Life Crisis," *International Journal of Psychoanalysis*, vol. 46, October 1965, pp. 502–514.
12. Pearce, Jane E., and Saul Newton, *The Conditions of Human Growth* (New York: Citadel Press, 1963).
13. Bergler, Edmund, *The Revolt of the Middle Aged Man* (New York: A.A. Wyn, 1954).
14. Gould, Roger L., "The Phases of Adult Life: A Study in Developmental Psychology," *American Journal of Psychiatry*, vol. 129, 1972, pp. 521–531.
15. Pineo, Peter C., "Disenchantment in the Later Years of Marriage," *Marriage and Family Living*, vol. 23, 1961, pp. 3–11.
16. Rollins, Boyd C., and Harold Feldman, "Marital Satisfaction over the Family Life Cycle," *Journal of Marriage and the Family*, vol. 32, February 1970, pp. 20–28.
17. Pasamanick, Benjamin, "A Survey of Mental Disease in an Urban Population, VI: An Approach to Total Prevalence by Age," *Mental Hygiene*, vol. 46, pp. 567–572.
18. Leighton, A.H., *My Name is Legion* (New York: Basic Books, 1959).
19. Srole, Leo, Thomas Langner, Stanley Michael, Marvin Opler, and Thomas Rennie, *Mental Health in the Metropolis* (New York: McGraw-Hill, 1962).
20. Moon, Louis E., and Robert E. Patton, "The Alcoholic Psychotic in New

York State Mental Hospitals, 1951–1960," *Quarterly Journal of Studies in Alcohol*, vol. 24, December 1963, pp. 664–681.

21. Jaffee, Abraham, and J.B. Gordon, *Demography of the Middle Years: An Interim Report of the Highlights* (New York: Bureau of Applied Social Research, 1968), pp. 1–8.

22. U.S. Department of HEW, *Vital and Health Statistics*, Series 11.

23. Blumenthal, Irwin S., *Research and the Ulcer Problem*, RAND Corporation Report, June 1959.

24. U.S. Department of HEW, *Vital and Health Statistics*, Series 11, no. 37, p. 8.

25. Cuber, John F., and Peggy Harroff, *The Significant Americans* (New York: Appleton-Century-Crofts, 1965).

26. Block, Jack, and Norma Haan, *Lives Through Time* (Berkeley: Bancroft Books, 1971).

27. Vaillant, George E., *Adaptation to Life* (Boston: Little Brown, 1977).

28. Levinson et al., *op. cit.*

29. Gould, Roger L., "The Phases of Adult Life: A Study in Developmental Psychology," *American Journal of Psychiatry*, vol. 129, 1972, pp. 521–531.

30. Douvan, Elizabeth, and Joseph Adelson, *The Adolescent Experience* (New York: John Wiley, 1966).

31. Marshall, James, "Development and Validation of Ego-Identity Status Scale," *Journal of Personality and Social Psychology*, vol. 5, 1966, pp. 551–558.

32. Weiner, Irving, *Psychological Disturbance in Adolescence* (New York: Wiley-Interscience, 1970).

33. Rosenberg, Stanley, and Michael Farrell, "Identity and Crisis in Middle Aged Men," *International Journal of Aging and Human Development*, vol. 7, no. 2, 1976, pp. 153–170.

34. Lehman, Harvey C., "The Creative Production Rates of Present Versus Past Generations of Scientists," *Journal of Gerontology*, vol. 17, no. 4, October 1962.

35. Jaques, *op. cit.*

36. Neugarten, in *Middle Age and Aging, op. cit.*

37. Fried, Barbara R., *The Middle Aged Crisis* (New York: Harper & Row, 1967).

38. Neugarten, Bernice, and David L. Gutmann, "Age-Sex Roles and Personality in Middle Age: A Thematic Apperception Study," *Psychological Monographs*, vol. 72, no. 17, 1958.

39. *Ibid.*, p. 70.

40. Riley, Matilda White, and Anne Foner, *Aging and Society*, vol. 1 (New York: Russell Sage Foundation, 1968), Chapter 4.

41. Longfellow, Henry Wadsworth, in *The American Tradition in Literature*, edited by Bradley, Beatty, Long, and Perkins (New York: W.W. Norton, 1957).

42. Laing, R.D., *The Divided Self* (London: Tavistock, 1960).

43. Excerpted from the book *Slaughterhouse Five* or *The Children's Crusade*

by Kurt Vonnegut Jr. Copyright © 1969 by Kurt Vonnegut Jr. Reprinted by permission of Delacorte Press/Seymour Lawrence.

44. Friedman, Bruce J., *Stern* (New York: Simon and Schuster, 1962).
45. Keniston, Kenneth, *The Uncommitted: Alienated Youth in American Society* (New York: Harcourt Brace Jovanovich, 1965).
46. Adorno, Theodore W., Else Frenkel-Brunswik, Daniel J. Levinson, and R.N. Sanford, *The Authoritarian Personality* (New York: Harper & Row, 1950).
47. Hyman, Herbert, and P.B. Sheatsley, "The Authoritarian Personality— A Methodological Critique," in *Continuities in Social Research*, edited by Jahoda and Christie (Glencoe, Ill.: Free Press, 1964).
48. Festinger, Leon, *A Theory of Cognitive Dissonance* (Evanston, Ill.: Row Peterson, 1957).
49. Dreiser, Theodore, "Free," *The Saturday Evening Post*, March 16, 1918.
50. Cather, Willa S., *The Professor's House* (New York: Alfred A. Knopf, 1925).
51. Bellow, Saul, *Herzog* (New York: Viking, 1964).
52. Vonnegut, *op. cit.*
53. Vonnegut, *op. cit.*, pp. 2–3.
54. Vonnegut, *op. cit.*, p. 6.

Chapter 3

ASSESSING MIDLIFE CRISIS THEORIES

In Chapter 2 we argued that as a man approaches middle age a number of factors converge that tend to disrupt his previous modes of experiencing himself. For some men, this stress may culminate or be expressed in a "midlife crisis." This crisis has been variously described as a pervasive sense of alienation from one's own being in the world, unidentified or misunderstood feelings of anxiety or depression, and/or physical symptoms expressive of psychic distress. The crisis may or may not trigger a search for a more meaningful sense of self; it is essentially an experiential state rather than a defined set of behaviors. One aspect of our research design was to operationalize and test these various "midlife crisis" hypotheses. Are alienation, depression, and psychosomatic illness in middle-aged men part of an interrelated syndrome, functional equivalents for each other, or merely coincidental symptoms appearing differentially in certain age groups? With regard to the attitudinal dimension of the midlife crisis, the sense of alienation per se, it was clear that adequate data did not exist for us to estimate the relative amount, type, or distribution we would find in the population of middle-aged males. Yet it seemed important to measure alienation, since this particular variable has been the direct focus of theoretical interest by many of the major schools interested in adult life change and personality processes.

In this chapter we assess several of the more prominent theories that associate midlife with a sense of alienation or crisis. The theories range from economic-historical analyses, like that of Marx, which conceptualize the position of men in modern industrialized societies, to more individual, psychologically oriented attempts to outline the development of persons through the life cycle. In weighing these theories against our findings, we conclude that a more adequate theory of human development must take into account both the socio-historical environment, on the one hand, and internal psychological and biological processes on the other. In attempting to specify the nature and relative contribution of and interaction among these variables, we find it useful to estimate the relative predictive power of each type of theory. Can economic or social structural variables, for example, be shown to account for differential midlife responses? We argue that such factors become more salient in a context of psychological vulnerability.

The experience of the social world is characteristically a psychological mixture. Sometimes the world is seen as providing necessary elements for exploration, self-discovery, and interpersonal connection. At other times, it may be experienced as alienating —constricting, negating, and disconfirming the self. For most people, these processes probably go on constantly and simultaneously, representing only vaguely differentiated aspects of the flow of experience. There may exist, however, certain key moments of sensitivity in which these external assaults and pressures come acutely into awareness. Adolescence is sometimes portrayed as one such developmental juncture, where issues of self-definition may become a preoccupation, and the person develops a heightened sensitivity to the identity inputs in his social environment. Other psychologically and culturally meaningful life transitions, such as the initial phase of becoming a parent,[1] seem to have this same effect of stimulating consciousness of one's being in the world. In this sense, adult development can be seen as an episodic heightening and diminishing of self-consciousness. The person enters periods of struggle to define, understand, or alter his self in terms of his roles, institutions, relationships, and values. Such moments give way to longer phases of stability where there is no compelling force to these issues. The struggle phase is characterized by active alienation, the stable phase by either positive adjustment or a more profound alienation, depending on one's theoretical orientation. That is, "stability" may be an alienation that is not even aware of itself. Adult roles can thus be seen as institutionalized means of adapting to both cultural, interpersonal stresses on the one hand and internal distress on the other. In an ideal situation the role complex of the middle-aged man is a creative resolution that enhances his sense of himself and his own capacities. Alternatively, the role behavior of the midlife male may represent a disguise whereby his own disquietude, misgivings, and disappointments are hidden. These hidden aspects of alienation will be explored in the next chapter. In this chapter we examine the men's responses to direct questions. If something resembling a midlife crisis is characteristic of men in our culture, one of its prime manifestations would be a heightened sense of alienation.

Alienation, The Life Cycle, and Society

Although their explanations may differ, many theorists claim that alienation is one of the fundamental characteristics of men in modern, industrialized societies. Marx[2] views alienation as a consequence of the deprivation imposed on the lower classes by the economic structure of capitalist societies; Weber[3] sees the dehumanizing properties of huge bureaucracies as responsible; Simmel[4] and others see urbanization as the principal cause. More recently, theorists like Slater,[5] Laing,[6] and Henry[7] have focused on the alienating effects of socialization into a culture based on denial, distortion, and repression. Culture, that is, works to deny and distort what is most human in us. Regardless of whether we see alienation as a consequence of social structure or culture, many theorists tell us that alienation from work, community, and self are widespread phenomena. These theorists are self-consciously social critics, focusing on the individual as he confronts the fragmented, changing social and economic structure around him.

Another body of theory—based on ego psychology—deals with alienation as a complex interaction between personality, early life experience, and the demands and opportunities the maturing self encounters in a particular cultural and historical context. These writers analyze the individual as a developing personality system, isolating stages in the life cycle when a person is most likely to be vulnerable both to his own internal conflicts and to the alienating effects of modern society. Erikson[8] is the most well known of this group. Rather than arguing that alienation from self, interpersonal relations, the community, and work occurs as an undifferentiated

reaction to a stressful environment, Erikson proposes that alienation—or its converse, integration—unfolds in stages as the individual matures.

Through interaction in the family and among peers, the developing child gains some balance of a sense of trust/mistrust,
autonomy/self-doubt, initiative/guilt, and industry/inferiority.
These are not "problems" to be solved in some ultimate sense, but
rather ongoing issues which reemerge around stress and new life
stages. If a person emerges from childhood with relatively constructive resolutions to these issues, he is better able to cope with
later developmental tasks. In adolescence he confronts the problem of severing childhood ties, expanding adolescent identifications, and finding a place in the adult work world, a place
congruent with the self he has become through earlier experiences.
His task is to forge a workable sense of identity in the economic
structure of his society (identity versus identity diffusion). If
these problems are adequately dealt with, his next developmental
challenge is to establish close human relationships expressive of
the person he feels himself to be (intimacy versus isolation). Only
if these earlier developmental hurdles are negotiated is he free to
confront the issues of middle age—finding a sense of relatedness
to his interpersonal environment as a whole in a role that gives
him a sense of being meaningfully and productively connected to
his children, the community, and posterity (generativity versus
stagnation). Erikson suggests that resolution of these issues proceeds in regular phases, with satisfactory resolution of preceding
issues being a precondition for resolution of later issues.

Either of these theories, or some more general position incor-
porating aspects of each, may help us to explain the incidence and
quality of alienation at midlife. Empirically, we would ask, what
form of alienation is likely to occur at what points in the life cycle
of persons in modern societies? That is, do midlife men experience
the self-doubts, malaise, and concern over issues of meaning and
continuity implied by Erikson's developmental schema? Can
adaptation to midlife changes be predicted by relative success in
dealing with earlier developmental issues (work and intimacy)?
Conversely, do midlife males manifest an explicit, angry form of
alienation where the more psychologically integrated person self-
consciously repudiates his social world? This latter response would
support the Marxist and existential approaches, which represent

alienation as a consciousness of an oppressive reality rather than as a failure of adaptation.

Hypotheses

In this chapter we attempt to assess the adequacy of these two broad approaches by testing four hypotheses derived from the literature on alienation and development. We feel that understanding the nature of alienation and its link to life stages is crucial in the study of the midlife experience in our culture.

Hypothesis One: Hierarchical Development

The resolution of alienation-integration issues unfolds in a regular developmental sequence. More specifically, the resolution of the childhood issues (trust/mistrust; autonomy/self-doubt; guilt/initiative; and industry/inferiority) gives one the necessary internal integration to proceed with later developmental issues. The resulting sense of self-esteem and mastery are preconditions for achieving a sense of identity in one's work role; achieving a sense of occupational identity is a precondition for achieving a sense of intimacy; and finally, a sense of intimacy is a precondition for achieving a sense of generativity or connectedness to the community as a whole. Regardless of age, men will not confront later developmental issues until they have achieved constructive resolutions to earlier issues.

Hypothesis Two: Maturation

The older a man, the more likely he is to have constructively resolved early life-cycle developmental issues. Erikson's developmental hypothesis argues that an individual does not fully confront and resolve all dimensions of alienation–integration at once. Men do not confront the intimacy and generativity issues until later in the life cycle, after having achieved constructive resolutions to childhood and adolescent issues. This developmental theory implies that on the average older men will have achieved integrative solutions to more issues than younger men since the latter have not yet reached a life stage where they can be expected to grapple fully with issues of intimacy and generativity.

Hypothesis Three: Midlife Crisis

Men in the early middle-age, "midlife transition" phase will show more signs of alienation than young adult men. Recent theories of midlife crisis suggest a hypothesis that contradicts Erikson's sequential developmental and maturation hypotheses. Unlike Erikson, these theorists propose that the entry into middle age is likely to be associated with an "authenticity crisis" during which a man's whole "life structure" comes apart. These theories would lead us to expect to find men in early middle age showing more signs of alienation on our dimensions than young men.

If we follow their reasoning, we find that, like Erikson, they propose that adolescence is likely to be a troubling time in a person's life. Particularly for males, the problems of defining an adult identity that fits into the economic structure of the society may become acute. A "temporary neurosis" may even emerge at this time, receding after the individual finds himself and is accepted in a supportive work role. After this plateau, he establishes a sense of intimacy—most likely through marriage—and he moves into a second latency phase. Thus young men in their middle and late twenties (the age range of our younger group) are portrayed as relatively stable individuals working hard at developing skills and establishing some status and security in the positions they have chosen. This struggle to establish themselves and, if married, provide a secure home, continues on through their thirties, at which point new stresses and role demands require new adaptations to be forged, often a difficult and painful process.

According to this "midlife crisis" theory, by comparing men in their middle to late twenties with those in their forties, we should find the middle-aged group showing more signs of identity diffusion and alienation than the younger group.

Hypothesis Four: Social Class Effects

The lower the socio-economic status (SES), the greater will be the alienation. In general, an examination of the literature relating social structural variables to alienation shows that men in lower-status occupations are less likely to achieve a positive resolution to integration issues than men in higher-status positions. The former are likely to have less autonomy on the job and fewer educational and economic resources. They are exposed to experiences that can diminish their sense of self and of positive connection to the community. Their problem becomes one of self-protection—attempting to build life routines or psychological defenses which shield them from experiencing the alienating aspects of industrial society. They are more exposed to various forms of mortification and have fewer resources with which to defend themselves.

In order to operationalize Erikson's life-cycle schema, we sought measures of the separate dimensions of mastery to which he refers. Keniston's Identity Scales appeared to be the best available indicators of these dimensions, representing an explicit attempt to translate Erikson's concepts into a reliable and valid research tool. Keniston has collapsed the primary identity issues of childhood (trust, autonomy, initiative, and industry) into a single scale, which he calls Personal Identity. The high scorer describes himself as "self-confident, sure of his inner capacities, and positive in his self-image. His avowed self-concept is one of being on extremely friendly terms with himself, as if he were certain of his adequacy to cope with whatever life brought, and trusted his own personality." According to Erikson, this sense of internal integration is a precondition for moving on to the issues of adulthood.

The following examples are illustrative of items on the Personal Identity Scale (Internal Integration): *

1. I am concerned that my standards are unrealistic or inadequate. (reversed item)
2. I wish I were different in a great many ways. (reversed)
3. I am usually confident that the choices I make are the best ones for me.
4. I have a quite strong sense of my own worth.

Identity versus role diffusion, which is intended to tap the sense of work identity, is operationalized with Keniston's Prospective Identity Scale. The items have a "sense of forward motion, especially in work and career." The low scorer "corresponds most closely with Erikson's description of role diffusion" —that is, he sees himself going nowhere in a work role that is meaningless.

---

* These examples are derived from Kenneth Keniston, "Scales for the Measurement of Identity," unpublished manuscript, Yale University School of Medicine, 1963.

Examples of items from the Prospective Identity Scale (Work Role Identity) follow:

1. If circumstances permit me to do the things I hope to do, my own personal future seems pretty clear-cut.
2. I sometimes feel as if I were riding on a merry-go-round, going around and around but really getting nowhere. (reversed item)
3. I have had great trouble finding a career or profession. (reversed)

Intimacy versus isolation is operationalized with the Social Identity Scale. Scores on this scale indicate the degree to which a person is able to gain a sense of identity in his interpersonal relations. The low scorer is uncertain about whether others understand him, feels unable to communicate his deepest feelings and most important concerns, and feels isolated from others around him.

Examples of items from the Social Identity Scale (Intimacy) follow:

1. I find it hard to express many of the things I feel most deeply. (reversed)
2. The way I present myself to the world does not coincide with my deeper feelings about myself. (reversed)
3. Knowing that I can usually express my deepest feelings is a great source of pleasure to me.

Finally, the extent to which a person has achieved a constructive resolution to generativity issues is measured by the Solidarity Scale. This scale taps the extent to which a person has gained a sense of oneness with some elements of the community that share his values and goals. Gandhi and Martin Luther King represent extreme cases of a constructive resolution to these issues. Each identifies with a wide segment of his community, and each uses his skills to confront what he sees as the community's most pressing needs. A person who scores low on this dimension finds no groups in the community whose values he identifies with or whose opinions and needs matter to him, and he feels no sense of continuity with his past.

Examples of items from the Solidarity Scale (Generativity) follow:

1. I have rarely if ever found a group enough like myself that I would want to be identified with it. (reversed)
2. My own way of life is, in the last analysis, very different from that of most people. (reversed)
3. Despite the passage of years, I feel that in some ways I still belong in the place where I grew up.

Findings

In this section we discuss the test of each hypothesis in turn. Since the findings compose an interlocking whole, we conclude with an overall interpretation.

The Hierarchical Development Hypothesis

According to Erikson, if a person has not satisfactorily resolved earlier developmental issues, he will experience great difficulty in his attempts to resolve later ones. If this is true, by placing the scales in the appropriate order we should find that they approach a Guttman scale.* People who have not successfully resolved an earlier, more basic issue, should not have resolved later issues. The extent to which the scales approach a Guttman ordering is presented in Table 3-1. Since the Keniston items are answered with a six-point Likert scale, an average score of three or less on an alienation scale is considered successful resolution of an issue.

Examining Table 3-1, we see that the developmental hypothesis receives a modest degree of support. There is a 21 percent improvement in our ability to predict scores, assuming the scales fit a Guttman scale. However, there are clearly points where the order does not fit the Guttman criteria.

The first row of the table shows all zero percentages because it includes the 71 men who have not yet achieved integration on any of the developmental issues. The last row shows men who present themselves as having achieved integration on all four

---

* The authors wish to thank Madeline H. Schmitt for suggesting this line of analysis.

Table 3-1   Percentage of Respondents Following Erikson's Developmental Timetable

	Dimensions of Development in Sequential Order (left to right)			
	Internal Integration	Identity in Work Role	Intimacy	Generativity
Positive Integration on no dimension (N = 71)	0	0	0	0
Positive Integration on 1 dimension (N = 78)	36	51	4	9
Positive Integration on 2 dimensions (N = 97)	61	69	34	36
Positive Integration on 3 dimensions (N = 88)	87	89	60	64
Positive Integration on 4 dimensions (N = 99)	100	100	100	100
Overall Percent with Positive Integration on Each Dimension (N = 433)	61	66	43	45

Coefficient of Reproducibility = 0.80
Minimum Marginal Reproducibility = 0.59
Percent Improvement = 0.21

Note: If Erikson's theory were correct, for each row all cases would fall on the left hand side of the stepped break in the grid.

dimensions. Rows two through four contain the information necessary to test the hypothesis.

The second row contains the results for the 78 men who achieved a positive score on only one dimension ("one-milestone men"). If Erikson's theory is correct, that one dimension should be the first, Internal Integration; it should not be one of the dimensions that are confronted later in the sequence. Contrary to Erikson's theory, we find only 36 percent of these one-milestone men achieved their single aspect of identity resolution in the domain of Internal Integration. Row two shows that these men are most likely to gain a reported sense of identity in their work role. However, in support of Erikson, we find that one-milestone men are not at all likely to skip far ahead to later life-cycle issues. Only four percent report a positive sense of intimacy, and only nine percent experience a sense of generativity. Thus, although we do not find total confirmation of Erikson's predicted sequence of development, we do find some support for the thrust of his argument.

Among those men who have achieved two developmental milestones, the bulk of the findings support Erikson. The majority of these two-milestone men report satisfactory resolutions on the first two issues.

Finally, looking at the three-milestone men, we find that the sequential development theory is strongly supported for the first two dimensions. Over 85 percent of these three-milestone men report positive integration in the first two columns. However, as shown in the last two columns, these men are slightly more likely to achieve a sense of generativity than a sense of intimacy. Although the theory predicts that intimacy issues are more easily resolved than generativity, it appears that a sense of intimacy is at least as hard to achieve as a sense of generativity. In fact, looking at the bottom marginals, we find that only 43 percent of all the men see themselves as having successfully resolved the intimacy issue, less than for any other issue.

In general, our findings show support for Erikson's perspective, but there are two interesting deviations. First, we find that men are most likely to report themselves as having successfully resolved the identity-in-work-role issue. Even many men who have not successfully resolved childhood issues may report a positive resolution to this issue. Thus, it is possible that mitigating circumstances may permit one, vis-à-vis work identity, to step out of Erikson's proposed sequence. Second, we find that men are least likely to successfully achieve a sense of intimacy. This finding supports theorists like Slater,[9] who argues that males in our culture are systematically socialized into a pattern of denying feelings, avoiding exposing themselves in interpersonal relationships, and placing career success above other concerns. These findings will shortly be discussed at greater length.

Midlife Crisis versus Maturation

Although we have examined the unfolding of integration according to Erikson's developmental timetable, we have not yet looked
at the direct relationship between age and integration. Many recent theorists have suggested that younger men achieve some
positive resolution of developmental issues, only to proceed to
the ordeal of a midlife crisis, with subsequent undoing of earlier
ego integration.

Gould[10] and Levinson et al.[11] propose that the entry into middle
age is likely to be a crisis period in one's life. The age range
where they expect a crisis (38 to 45) includes the bulk of the
middle-aged men in our study. They argue that status changes
and chronological aging impinge on men at this point, leading
to a massive upheaval of identity, intimacy, and generativity
issues. By this "crisis" theory we would expect our middle-aged
men to score higher than our young adults on all the alienation
scales.

However, Erikson's developmental hypothesis implies just the
opposite conclusion. Having had more time to confront issues of
the later life cycle, middle-aged men should be at least potentially more "mature" and show more signs of integration than
younger men. Thus, this maturation theory would lead us to expect younger men to score higher on alienation than older men,
especially on those dimensions of alienation that are not fully
resolved until later in the life cycle.

The crisis and maturation hypotheses were tested by means
of analysis of variance* (see Table 3-2). Looking at the means
for young and old on each dimension of alienation, we see that
in every case the older men score lower on alienation than the
younger. Though neither the intimacy nor generativity dimensions show differences with $P<.05$, the differences are in the same
direction as the other three tests. Furthermore, if we compare
the means for issues earlier in the life cycle (Internal Integration
and Identity) with those of the later life cycle (Intimacy and
Generativity), we see that alienation is more likely on the later
life-cycle issues, especially for the younger men. However, the
failure to reject the null hypothesis of no difference between age

---

* To test both this hypothesis and the social-class hypothesis, we used a two-
way analysis of variance test on each of our alienation-integration dimensions.

Table 3-2 Results of t-Test: Comparing Younger Men (25–30) to Older Men (38–48) on the Alienation Dimensions (A high score indicates high alienation)

	Dimensions of Alienation-Integration										
	Internal Integration		Identity in Work Role		Intimacy		Generativity		Alienation Factor*		N
	$\overline{X}$	s.d.	$\overline{X}$	s.d.	$\overline{X}$	s.d.	$\overline{X}$	s.d.	$\overline{X}$	s.d.	
Young	3.14	.77	2.82	.84	3.20	.88	3.20	.87	7.43	3.27	(111)
Middle	2.74	.62	2.66	.78	3.13	.91	3.08	.87	6.36	3.36	(322)
Total	2.84	.73	2.70	.80	3.15	.90	3.11	.87	6.64	3.37	(433)
t	5.19		1.99		.54		1.24		2.99		
P	.001		.05		N.S.		N.S.		.01		
Eta	.239		.089		—		—		.138		

* In a factor analysis of twenty scales, all four of the alienation scales loaded on the first factor with loadings above 0.50.

groups on these dimensions suggests that they are still as much a problematic issue for middle-aged men as for younger. These findings are consistent with the maturation hypothesis.

It is interesting to note that alienation on the intimacy dimension showed the least difference between groups and the highest means of all the dimensions, suggesting that both younger and older men are reporting the most difficulty in experiencing gratifying, close interpersonal relations. Only 43 percent of all the men tell us they have someone with whom they can share their "deepest feelings" and most personal problems, lending credence to Slater's hypothesis that our culture socializes men into loneliness and emotional isolation. Emphasis on competition, repression of feelings, and denial of problems produces individuals who are unable to trust in or make themselves vulnerable to others. To the extent that men cannot achieve a constructive resolution to the intimacy issue, Erikson would predict that they would be handicapped in dealing with the subsequent life-cycle issues of generativity and integrity.

Instead of this building block phenomenon—where difficulty in regard to the earlier issue produces an insubstantial base for dealing with later isues—we find a less systematic pattern. A sense of generativity, it appears, can be gained through more impersonal means. As our case studies will illustrate, the roles and enterprises men utilize to enhance their sense of generativity do not necessarily require any pronounced capacity for emotional openness, warmth, or self-exposure. We might regard this stance as a type of pseudo-generativity whereby general concern for doing good is substituted for more immediate forms of caring for others. On the other hand, it is rather arbitrary to dismiss these men's reported sense of accomplishment in a given sphere because a theoretical schema implies that such an achievement is unlikely.

Status and Alienation

Marxian theory suggests that lower-class men are not only alienated from their own labor in modern industrial societies, but also suffer the consequences of this alienation in other aspects of their life. Their position in the socioeconomic structure leads to alienation from work, self, and others. On the other hand, Freudian and existential theorists have argued that alienation is not related to

Table 3-3 Results of Analysis of Variance: The Effects of Socio-Economic Status on Alienation Dimensions

	Internal Integration		Identity in Work Role		Intimacy		Generativity		Alienation Factor		N
	$\overline{X}$	s.d.	$\overline{X}$	s.d.	$\overline{X}$	s.d.	$\overline{X}$	s.d.	$\overline{X}$	s.d.	
SES Level: 1	2.74	.67	2.37	.67	2.83	.92	2.94	.84	5.47	3.20	(48)
2	2.68	.82	2.56	.78	2.96	.88	2.77	.67	5.42	3.17	(50)
3	2.91	.67	2.60	.74	3.11	.84	3.20	.86	6.83	3.21	(96)
4	2.75	.66	2.80	.78	3.22	.89	3.07	.84	6.57	3.17	(188)
5	3.29	.85	2.99	.93	3.42	.96	3.58	.98	8.82	3.59	(51)
Total	2.84	.73	2.70	.80	3.15	.90	3.11	.87	6.64	3.37	(433)
F Ratio	7.05		5.35		3.57		6.72		9.21		
P	<.001		<.001		<.05		<.001		<.001		
Eta	.244		.217		.179		.243		.280		

class, but results rather from socialization into a culture that denies expression of emotion, blocks instinctual urges, or otherwise hinders the development of an authentic self. Alienation would thus be seen as the result of any role in such a culture, varying only in specific form. The results of our tests of these hypotheses are presented in Table 3-3.

Looking down the columns, we see that as status decreases alienation increases on all dimensions. Differences due to status are significant at least at the 0.05 level, but the etas are never higher than 0.280. The structuralist or Marxian hypothesis receives some support from this data, but class certainly does not explain all, or even most, of the variance in expressed alienation. It is obviously necessary to examine the effects of variables other than social class if we are to understand the reported sense of alienation as it appears differentially in middle-aged men.

Age, Status, and Alienation

As mentioned above, all the alienation scales are correlated and load on the first factor in a factor analysis of twenty scales. For the sake of brevity, we will make use of this single alienation factor when discussing the relationship between age, SES, and alienation.

Looking at the first order and partial correlation coefficients, we found that controlling for one of the independent variables (age or SES) has little effect on the relationship between the other and alienation. However, if we look within age groups at the correlation between SES and alienation, we find a stronger association in the middle-age group ($r = 0.23$ versus $r = 0.14$). Furthermore, if we look at mean alienation factor scores for each age group (Table 3-4), we find that the least-alienated group are the highest status middle-age men, but *the most alienated group are the lower status middle-age men*. This finding is the reverse of the general trend, which shows the younger group is more alienated than the older group on all dimensions. It implies that, while increasing age leads to less alienation in middle and upper classes, aging in the lowest social class simply leads to more alienation. Low social status has an increasingly detrimental impact on men as they get older. In fact, this impact is felt most severely as the men deal with the issues of the later life

Table 3-4   Means and Standard Deviations of Alienation Factor Scores for Age Groups and Socio-Economic Status

		Young Men			Middle-Aged Men		
		$\overline{X}$	s.d.	N	$\overline{X}$	s.d.	N
SES Level:	1	8.13	4.20	7	5.02	2.75	41
	2	5.43	3.31	12	5.42	3.12	38
	3	7.66	2.62	21	6.60	3.32	75
	4	7.12	3.01	43	6.40	3.20	145
	5	8.43	3.34	28	9.30	3.81	23
Total		7.43	3.27	111	6.36	3.36	322

	F Ratios	Eta	P
Column	8.95	.138	<.001
Row	9.21	.280	<.001
Interaction	—	N.S.	N.S.

cycle: the intimacy and generativity issues. Class five older men have the highest mean alienation scores on these dimensions—higher than an other group on any other dimension (3.74 on Interpersonal or Intimacy Alienation; 3.78 on Generativity).

A concrete explanation for the higher generativity scores for middle-age and upper-class men is that these men have more access to ready-made roles in organizations that seem specifically designed to meet generativity needs. When they begin searching for ways to gain a sense of connectedness to the community as a whole and to the needs of the next generation, they find many organizations such as the Rotary Club, the Kiwanis Club, the Knights of Columbus, or a college alumni group that welcome their participation and offer them institutionalized means to direct their resources toward community needs. Even if such organizations do not provide the concrete realization of generativity concerns, they at least supply a set of myths that give a man a sense of connectedness to noble purposes in the future and to heroic figures of the past and present. Lower-class males are less likely to find these roles and myths available to them.

We find, then, strong association between SES and alienation among older men. This implies that social class influences how men deal with the developmental issues of later adult life; whether they experience an increasing sense of adequacy, self-acceptance, and connectedness, or an exacerbated sense of estrangement from self and community. As status increases among older men, the likelihood of achieving a sense of integration increases, and as status decreases, the likelihood of being alienated increases—particularly on the intimacy and generativity dimensions.

Summary and Conclusions

In this chapter we have tested four hypotheses derived from the theories of alienation and personality development. First, we tested Erikson's hypothesis that confrontation with alienation-integration issues unfolds in a developmental fashion such that internal integration must precede a sense of identity in work role; both of these must precede the achievement of a capacity for intimacy; and finally, all three of the former must precede the attainment of a sense of generativity. This hypothesis was not fully supported, the results suggesting a more variable and complex set of possibilities.

We find that if a person has resolved only one developmental issue, it may be *either* internal integration *or* work role identity. In other words, many men achieve a sense of identity in their work role without having successfully resolved "earlier" developmental issues regarding basic trust, self-esteem, etc. These men appear to define themselves, and relate to the interpersonal world, through the mechanism of their occupation and its associated social identity. Outside of their work roles, they may feel alienated, purposeless, and display signs of a highly tenuous sense of self. While this pattern does not fit Erikson's theory, it is congruent with critiques of the "one-dimensional" quality of personality development in industrial society.

In support of Erikson's theory, however, we find very few of these "one-milestone" men who have achieved a sense of integration on the later life-cycle issues. Further support for this pattern is found when we look at men who have resolved two issues. Bearing in mind that the two issues could be any two of the four, we find that the two issues most likely to be resolved are those Erikson predicts: internal integration and identity.

When we look at the pattern of resolution among those reporting positive adaptation on these issues, the results are less congruent with Erikson's theory. We find that the capacity for intimacy is slightly more difficult to achieve than the capacity for generativity. In fact, many men report a sense of generativity without having first achieved a sense of intimacy. Fifty-seven percent of the men score in the alienated direction on the intimacy dimension, making it the most problematic issue of the four.

We also tested hypotheses about midlife crisis and maturation. The concept of a universal midlife crisis would lead us to predict that middle-aged men would be more likely to experience a sense of alienation than men in their middle and late twenties. On the other hand, Erikson's maturation perspective does not imply any such increase in alienation through the life cycle—especially since there are dimensions of identity resolution that one would not even confront fully until later in life. The findings support a maturational perspective. There seems to be no systematic movement toward alienation associated with the entrance to middle age.

Finally, we tested the structuralist hypothesis that lower-status men are more likely to be alienated than higher-status men. This hypothesis received strong support, particularly when we look at the association between SES and alienation among the older men.

In general, our findings call for an integration of the developmental, cultural, and structural theories of alienation. While older men are more likely to have confronted and resolved the later life-cycle issues, younger men are likely to be still struggling to attain a sense of identity, intimacy, and generativity.

Our findings indicate that the intimacy issue is the most difficult to resolve, suggesting the necessity of altering Erikson's hypothesis about the order of resolution of the alienation-integration issues. We found no significant difference between younger and older men on the intimacy dimension. Both are equally likely to experience loneliness and frustration in their attempts to relate to others. If it is interpersonal alienation that is most common to men in our culture, then we must give great credence to Slater's critique. Socialization into American culture, with its emphasis on individualism, denial of emotionality, and stress on competition blocks men from achieving a sense of intimacy. Alienation is not necessarily unidimensional: To be well integrated into cultural clues vis-à-vis work and institutional role-making may appear highly functional—may in fact imply or demand an alienation from intimate relationships. If Slater's critique, like those of Marcuse,[9] Brown,[10] Laing,[6] and Henry,[7] are accurate, such a pattern constitutes a hollow or inherently alienated "success." The individual is left with outward achievement in the absence of any enhanced experience of himself or capacity to trust, love, or be loved: He has dehumanized himself.

Finally, our findings show that the lower a man's socioeconomic status, the less likely is he to achieve a constructive resolution to the alienation-integration issues. This association is strongest for the older men. In conjunction with the other findings, this suggests that the Marxian conception of the alienating effects of one's relation to the means of production might be enriched by consideration of the developmental dimension. While lower status may lead to alienation for young men as well as older men, it does not have its full alienating impact until later in the life cycle. While for higher-status men integration unfolds with age, for lower-status men age increases the sense of alienation and may lead to qualitative alterations of the experience.

We must once again look to our case studies to understand this shift. In younger men, the sense of being an "outsider" and a victim of the socioeconomic order is partially allayed by the idea of possibility. As young men, most of our subjects had at least vague dreams or expectations of transcending their situations. As they progress into middle age, this hope evaporates, until they feel trapped in an unfolding future over which they have no control. Instead of being a temporary situation, their poverty and lack of power and status becomes experienced as the defining reality of their lives—a characteristic of their very selves. It is this realization that is linked to the bitter alienation we see in lower-class, older men.

Finally, our questionnaire suggests that the literary image of a widespread midlife crisis in middle-class, middle-aged men is not supported. If we are to believe our respondents' portrayal of themselves, we must conclude that Portnoy and Herzog are relatively rare phenomena, while their counterparts in the lower class are relatively frequent.

However, it should be emphasized that we have been looking at questionnaire responses—self-reports on scales designed to measure a conscious sense of integration or alienation. It may be that middle-aged men in our culture deny or repress any doubts or feelings of alienation they may be experiencing. As discussed in Chapter 2, role demands in the family and at work as well as cultural ideals of "manliness" encourage such an exaggerated or fraudulent self-presentation. The suppression of doubts or signs of disintegration are necessary to the maintenance of such a persona. Our findings of the lack of intimacy in the lives of the majority of men may be a consequence of the denial pattern. Distance is necessary to maintain the facade.

This pattern of development of a false persona in response to the private experience may even unfold with the same timetable as Erikson's developmental model. In other words, the deniers may attempt to simulate the responses and attitudes defined by the culture as indicating successful resolution of life-cycle issues. We will thus have to put these findings in the context of other indicators to better estimate this pattern of pseudo-development. To the extent that this pattern exists, it is clearly a manifestation of the more profound level of alienation referred to earlier in the chapter. Herzog comes to know and articulate his own misery, creating the potential to extricate himself from it. The pseudo-developed man, absorbed in his own distortions, becomes increasingly unable to find alternatives. As we suggested in Chapter 2, the self-deception, denial, and dissimulation associated with pseudo-development will inevitably have consequences in other spheres of the middle-aged man's existence. In the next chapter we explore this issue.

Endnotes

1. Rosenberg, Stanley, and Harriet Rosenberg, "Identity Concerns in Early Motherhood," in *Understanding the Family: Stress and Change in American Family Life*, edited by C. Getty and W. Humphreys (New York: Appleton-Century-Crofts, 1981).
2. Marx, Karl, *Economic and Philosophical Manuscripts of 1844*, edited by D. Struik (New York: International Publishers, 1964).
3. Weber, Max, *Max Weber on Law in Economy and Society* (Cambridge, Mass.: Harvard University Press, 1954).
4. Simmel, Georg, "The Metropolis and Mental Life" in *The Sociology of Georg Simmel*, translated by K. Wolff (Glencoe, Ill.: Free Press, 1950).
5. Slater, Phillip, *The Pursuit of Loneliness* (Boston: Beacon, 1970).
6. Laing, R.D., *The Politics of Experience* (New York: Ballantine, 1967).

7. Henry, Jules, *Culture Against Man* (New York: Random House, 1963).
8. Erikson, Erik H., *Childhood and Society*, 2nd ed. (New York: W.W. Norton, 1963).
9. Slater, *op. cit.*
10. Gould, Roger L., "The Phases of Adult Life: A Study in Developmental Psychology," *American Journal of Psychiatry*, vol. 129, 1972, pp. 521–531.
11. Levinson, Daniel J., Charlotte N. Darrow, Edward B. Klein, Maria H. Levinson, and Braxton McKee, *The Seasons of a Man's Life* (New York: Alfred A. Knopf, 1978).

Chapter 4

DEVELOPMENTAL PATTERNS IN MIDDLE-AGED MEN

Contrary to popular theorizing, we did not find the men moving into midlife showing, as a group, signs of increased alienation or social disconnection. In comparison to young adults, middle-aged men describe themselves as both coping adequately and feeling well integrated with the institutions around them. Those in the lowest socioeconomic class are the exception to this general trend. These findings are in accordance with some of the earlier social-psychological studies of development, which see the movement from early to middle adulthood as a gradual acquisition of coping skills and self-esteem.

While these data argue against the notion of a more or less universal identity crisis occurring in middle-aged men, it leaves us with a number of unanswered questions. Is it possible, for example, that the psychological upheavals of midlife are expressed indirectly; and if so, what are their typical manifestations? In order to address this issue, we attempted to incorporate other measures of symptom formation (for example, depression, hypochondriasis, and anxiety) that could potentially reveal alternative modes of midlife response. As we suggested earlier, the current array of bewildering, contradictory findings can begin to make sense if we look at responses to middle age as varying along two basic dimensions. We characterized the first as a crisis or alienation dimension, ranging from those who are finding a progressive sense of satisfaction with their lives to those who are experiencing intense unhappiness, alienation, or crisis. We hypothesized a second "denial" dimension, whereby responses to midlife stresses could also vary from open confrontation, through attempts to deceive others, to exclusion from conscious awareness. Such a construct leads us to a more complex set of possibilities.

The initial question attacked by researchers was essentially that of whether or not the entrance into midlife precipitated a crisis for the individual. We saw this question as too limited, hypothesizing the possibility of different kinds of midlife response such as disguised or denied crises. Our working model thus implies that not all our middle-aged respondents are as well off as they present themselves. At least some of these men may be reacting to midlife stresses by increasing defensiveness through such mechanisms as repression, projection, and denial. Rather than showing an orderly pattern of development through Erikson's psycho-social stages, some of these men may be showing an orderly pattern of denial of life stresses, a pattern of pseudo-development.

We also recognized a possible distinction between alienation per se and forms of personal disorganization and psychopathology. Alienation is an experience of disconnection from one's group or culture, a disconnection which does not necessarily imply psychopathology. While the ego-psychological (as well as other) models of adjustment argue for a fit between self and society as an optimal situation for personal well-being, the lack of such a fit can be engendered by a variety of circumstances. Rapid social change, for example, or extreme forms of group reaction (for example, as in Nazi Germany or contemporary South Africa) may work against the experience of group identity for the better-integrated individual. Alienation itself is thus neither a necessary or a sufficient basis for judging the presence or absence of a midlife crisis.

Rather than limit our exploration of "crisis" to the dimension of alienation, we also administered several standard scales aimed at measuring aspects of physical and mental health pertinent to possible aspects of reaction to midlife stresses: Zung's Depression scale,[1] the MMPI Anxiety and Hypochondriasis scales,[2] Gurin's Psychological Symptom scale,[3] and several direct questions about ulcers, asthma, and other diseases likely to be psychosomatic. In order to assess whether or not the pseudo-development or pseudo-integration pattern exists, we administered several scales aimed at measuring aspects of denial. These scales include the MMPI Denial scale,[4] the Tolerance of Ambiguity scale,[5] an updated measure of ethnocentrism,[6] a measure of authoritarian child-rearing attitudes,[7] and a Social Desirability scale.[8] In the next section we compare the scores for the younger and older men on these scales, as well as on our own Midlife Crisis scale. This scale was formulated to tap those aspects of the altered self-experience most often referred to as constitutive of the midlife upheaval. The primary qualities that emerged in the clinical and literary descriptions were those of introspection, staleness, disappointment, and desperation to recapture lost opportunities. After considerable pretesting, we narrowed this scale to a set of 12 questions (see Appendix 1) inquiring about these experiences in relation to work, marriage, family life, and general sense of self.

What we find, in fact, is a pattern closely resembling the model presented in Chapter 2. While those reporting an openly acknowledged crisis of identity at midlife are a clear minority, significantly more than half of our middle-aged respondents are showing evidence of denied or displaced feelings of personal disorganization. Fewer than one third of these men seem to manifest a true sense of positive development or self-acceptance, even though a far greater number claim this status on overt self-report questions.

Self-Reports of Overt Crisis

If we look first at our measures of overt "crisis" or a sense of increased social disconnection, we find significant differences between the men on four out of seven scales (see Table 4-1).

Table 4-1 Comparisons of Young and Middle-Aged Men on All Crisis Scales

	Mean for Younger Men	Mean for Older Men	t	P
Nettler's Anomie	1.44	1.36	4.28	<.001
Midlife Crisis*	3.41	3.45	.63	N.S.
Work Dissatisfaction	1.81	1.73	1.98	<.05
Internal Integration	3.14	2.74	5.19	<.001
Work-Role Identity	2.82	2.66	1.99	<.05
Interpersonal Identity (or Intimacy)	3.20	3.13	.54	N.S.
Generativity	3.20	3.08	1.24	N.S.
N	(111)	(322)		

* Reversed scale: The lower the score on this scale, the more a person shows signs of midlife crisis.

Specifically, the middle-aged men portray themselves as less anomic and more satisfied with their work than the younger men. As discussed in the last chapter, we also find the older men show fewer signs of internal disintegration and work-role identity diffusion than the younger men. However, we find no difference between the groups on the generativity and intimacy scales. Surprisingly, we also find no differences on our Midlife Crisis scale. The general trend reinforces our earlier analysis that shows the middle-aged men reporting fewer signs or at least no more signs of crisis, identity diffusion, or alienation than the young adult men.

This trend toward presenting themselves as being relatively "together" at middle age is repeated in the comparisons of the two groups on measures of physical and psychological health (Table 4-2). On these comparisons we find either no difference between the men (depression, hypochondriasis, and psychosomatic diseases) or a trend toward younger men being worse off than older men (anxiety and psychological symptoms).

The theories of midlife crisis, even when cast in their most general terms, would lead us to predict that men entering middle age will show signs of distress: anxiety, depression, anomie, identity diffusion, or at least some doubts and questions about their life structure. If the transition to middle age generates these phenomena, we would expect to find the men in this stage showing more problems than men in the comparatively tranquil young-adult stage. Our initial findings do not support this line of reasoning. If anything, we find the young adult men showing more signs of psychological stress than the older men.

Table 4-2 Comparisons of Young and Middle-Aged Men on Measures of Health

	Mean for Younger Men	Mean for Older Men	t	P
Zung's Depression	1.70	1.71	.07	N.S.
Psychological Symptoms	1.71	1.62	1.98	<.05
Psychosomatic Disease*	1.90	1.89		N.S.
MMPI Anxiety*	1.53	1.55	1.14	N.S.
MMPI Hypochondriasis	1.34	1.35	1.20	N.S.
N	(111)	(322)		

* Reversed scale.

Pseudo-Development versus Integration

Having not found support for the overt crisis theories, we proceeded to examine our indicators in the hypothesized pseudo-
development model. If middle-aged men are in fact presenting a
facade of integration, we would expect to find them showing more
signs of authoritarian denial and other related defensive patterns.

Looking at our measures of denial and projection, we find significant differences between the groups on all six scales (Table
4-3). The middle-aged men show more signs of denial, rigidity
in their thinking, authoritarian attitudes toward child-rearing,
bigotry, favorable attitudes toward war, and a tendency to present to the world a conventionally desirable facade. These findings
support the idea that many of the middle-aged men are dealing
with the stresses of midlife by increasing utilization of repression,
projection, and denial, becoming increasingly estranged from their
own feelings, and becoming fearful and hostile toward the world
around them. The denial pattern is associated with the presentation of a facade of integration, thereby confounding our direct
test of the crisis theories. These pseudo-developed men do not
exhibit signs of overt crisis because they are out of touch with
their own affect and chronically enmeshed in denying troubling
perceptions.

This obviously does not imply that all middle-aged men defensively deny stress and falsely present themselves as better integrated than they are. The problem is one of empirically differ-

Table 4-3   Comparison of Young and Middle-Aged Men on All Authoritarian Denial Scales

	Mean for Younger Men	Mean for Older Men	t	P
F-Scale	3.95	3.75	2.28	<.05
MMPI Denial	1.53	1.60	3.19	<.01
Intolerance of Ambiguity	3.81	3.72	1.58	<.10
Authoritarian Child-Rearing Attitudes*	2.33	2.21	2.52	<.01
Social Desirability	1.46	1.54	2.91	<.01
Attitudes toward War	1.64	1.80	3.68	<.001
N	(111)	(322)		

* Reversed scale: The lower the score on these scales, the more a person manifests
the trait being measured.

entiating these patterns of response to middle age. We thus moved to a factor-analytic approach to separate out our four hypothesized responses: men who are openly confronting a midlife crisis; men who are open to their feelings yet well integrated; men who are denying problems and presenting themselves as integrated; and men who acknowledge distress but still use denial and projection to locate the sources of their distress elsewhere. This step in the data analysis was thus our first attempt to validate our working model as a way of ordering statistical or survey data on midlife. This examination is not, in and of itself, conclusive but rather part of a process that also includes more intense, phenomenological scrutiny.

The Typological Model: An Examination

We have hypothesized that men's responses to life stresses vary along two basic dimensions: crisis or disintegration versus integration, and denial versus open confrontation. If this hypothesis is correct, then a factor analysis of our scales should generate two orthogonal factors corresponding to our two dimensions.

We carried out a principal components factor analysis and found four factors with eigenvalues greater than one (Table 4-4). Together they account for 53.3 percent of the variance in the scale scores. After performing a varimax rotation on the four factors, we find that the results are very much as our typological theory would predict.

Eight scales load on factor I with loadings greater than 0.50. On the positive end of the factor are seven scales that measure some aspects of disintegration, crisis, or alienation. This finding suggests that disintegration constitutes a pervasive syndrome; men showing disintegration in one area of their life are likely to show problems in other areas. However, on the negative end of this factor we find the MMPI Denial scale with a moderate loading ($-.56$). This finding suggests that many men scoring low on the disintegration factor are in fact manifesting the denial pattern.

On factor II we find our five direct measures of the authoritarian denial syndrome, including, once again, the MMPI Denial scale with a loading of 0.40. Those who score high on this factor tend to have low tolerance for ambiguity, deny problems, reject

Table 4-4 Factor Analysis of Scale Scores: Orthogonal Rotation

Factor I Disintegration vs. Integration		Factor II Egalitarianism vs. Authoritarian Denial	
Scale	Factor Loading	Scale	Factor Loading
Internal Integration	.79	Authoritarian Child-Rearing	−.82
Work Role Identity	.72	Intolerance of Ambiguity	−.75
Midlife Crisis	.64	F-Scale	−.68
Anxiety	.60	Social Desirability	−.56
Generativity	.57	MMPI Denial	−.40
Interpersonal Identity	.55	Depression	−.30
Nettler's Anomie	.52		
MMPI Denial	−.56		
Eigenvalue: 5.71		Eigenvalue: 2.55	
% of variance: 28.6		% of variance: 12.8	

Factor III Psychological Health		Factor IV Orientation toward Community	
Scale	Factor Loading	Scale	Factor Loading
Psychosomatic Diseases	.73	Attitudes toward War	.67
MMPI Hypochondriasis	.68	Generativity	.40
Psychological Symptoms	.67	Nettler's Anomie	−.39
Anxiety	.40	Dissatisfaction with Work	−.59
Eigenvalue: 1.36		Eigenvalue: 1.03	
% of variance: 6.8		% of variance: 5.2	

minority groups, use authoritarian child-rearing practices, and present a conventionally acceptable facade.

Factor III includes our various measures of psychological and physical health. Factor IV contains scales measuring aspects of a man's relationship to the community.

The finding that our strongest factors are those predicted by our typological model provides support for our hypothesis. The two principal dimensions of variation in men's responses to life stresses are psychological distress or crisis versus integration, and denial versus open confrontation. The fact that the MMPI Denial scale loads moderately on the "integration" end of factor I as well as the "denial" end of factor II lends support to our suspicion that many, but not all, of the apparently integrated men are simply presenting a facade of psychological well-being.

Having established these relationships among the scales, we proceeded to examine the developmental patterns for rural and urban, middle- and lower-class men.

Average Developmental Trends: Rural-Urban, Middle and Lower Class

Since factors I and II are orthogonal to each other, they can be represented as a two-dimensional space with four quadrants. Quadrant 1 men are characterized as high on distress and low on authoritarian denial—corresponding to our anti-hero type who openly wrestles with a midlife crisis. Quadrant 2 men are high on integration and low on authoritarian-denial—corresponding to our transcendent-generative type. Quadrant 3 men are high on integration but also high on denial—corresponding to our pseudo-developed type. Finally, quadrant 4 men are high on both disintegration and authoritarian denial. This type corresponds to our punitive-disenchanted type.

One way to obtain an overview of how men move through the space as they age is to plot the factor scores for young and older men. In Figure 4-2 we report mean scores for younger and older men, subdividing them into groups based on social class. Using Hollingshead's measure of social class, we grouped together classes 1 and 2 and classes 3 and 4. Because of their unique developmental pattern, class 5 is presented separately.

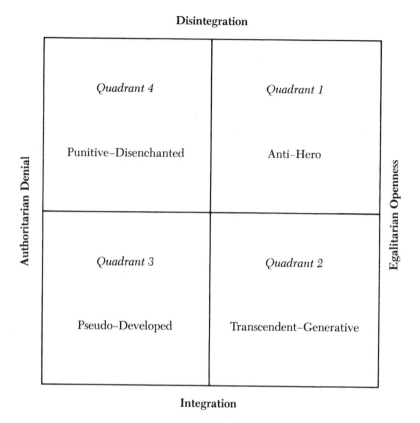

Disintegration

Quadrant 4 Punitive–Disenchanted	*Quadrant 1* Anti–Hero
Quadrant 3 Pseudo–Developed	*Quadrant 2* Transcendent–Generative

Authoritarian Denial | Egalitarian Openness

Integration

Figure 4-1 Factors I and II Represented as a Two-Dimensional Space

Assuming, once again, that the differences between younger and older age groups is due largely to the effects of development rather than cohort, we see that almost all men begin adult development in quadrant 1. That is, they present themselves as alienated but open to their feelings and not relying on projection and denial as means of coping with disturbing affect. In other words, on the average, they have not yet resolved adult developmental problems and they have not developed rigid defenses that protect them from life stress at the cost of inner impoverishment. Class 1 and 2 men move from this position toward greater openness and less alienation, the social and psychological resources of the upper class seeming to facilitate more optimal development. Class 3 and 4 men move into the pseudo-development quadrant. They present

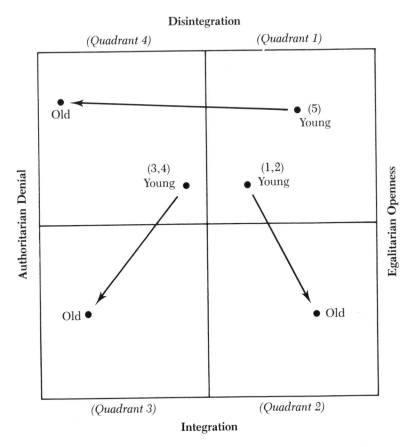

Figure 4-2 Hollingshead's Social Classes (1 and 2, 3 and 4, and 5) Plotted in the Factor Space

themselves as integrated and at home with the self they have created, but this persona is confounded by their pattern of defensive denial. The majority of this group appear to be presenting a facade of integration that disguises their awareness of depression, agitation, and unresolved conflict in their lives. They are our most probable candidates for the pseudo-development pattern. Finally, as we saw in the last chapter, class 5 men become increasingly alienated with age. However, as they move toward middle age, they, like their class 3 and 4 counterparts, attempt to defend themselves against the stresses confronting them by repression and denial. Of course, since they are the most likely group to express a sense of identity diffusion, lack of intimacy and generativity, high anxiety, etc., these defenses are no longer working to ward off all negative perceptions. Instead, they represent tenuous attempts to control inner rage and to locate the source of chronic depressive affect outside the self or to concretize them through somaticization.

Rural-Urban Comparisons

Theories about the relative merits of rural life over urban existence have abounded for at least the past century. Sociologists from LePlay[9] through Wirth[10] to Slater[11] have presented a picture of life in urban areas as fragmented and alienating. In contrast, life in the more communal rural villages and the countryside is described as psychologically healthier and more fulfilling. Our findings are not in accord with this view.

Comparing developmental changes in rural and urban areas, we find, first of all, that reported alienation tends to be slightly greater in our rural sample and denial tends to be much greater. In other words, the pseudo-development pattern seems more likely to emerge in rural areas. If we look at the developmental trends for middle- and lower-class subjects in rural and urban areas, these findings become clearer (Figure 4-3).

First, we find less difference between young and older men of both classes in rural areas. Lower-class rural men show some change, but never get out of quadrant 4. Rural middle-class men move slightly toward less alienation and more denial. It would appear that "midlife" as a developmental phase is less clearly demarcated for rural men, their attitudes, personality characteristics, and coping styles remaining relatively unchanged from early to middle adulthood. There is also less diversity, these styles being more similar despite social class.

In urban areas we find greater differences between young and middle-aged men. The urban lower-class men start as the most alienated and least-denying group, but they move into a position on the border of quadrants 3 and 4. They present themselves as less alienated but seem to retreat heavily into the denial pattern.

Middle-class men in urban areas appear to show more positive adaptations. As young men they are likely to be alienated yet in touch with their feelings and surroundings. As they move toward middle age they experience life as much more gratifying. Our data suggest that this self-description is less likely to be based on repression or denial for these men.

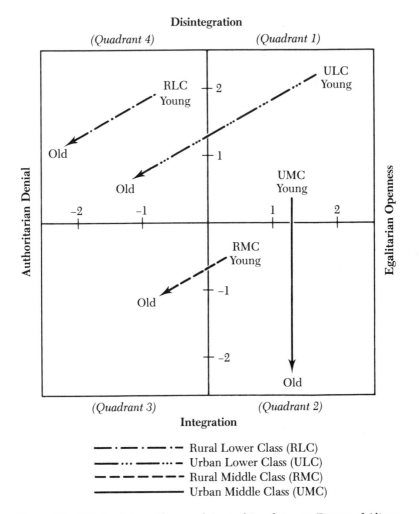

Figure 4-3   Effects of Age, Class, and Area of Residence on Degree of Alienation and Authoritarianism: Mean Factor Scores Plotted on Factors
I and II. (*Note:* See Appendix 2 for comparison of young and old
men from middle and lower classes and rural and urban areas,
using analysis of variance.)

In general, these findings reveal a number of common developmental paths linked to both social class and area of residence.
The men most likely to be in a state of alienation or crisis are the
middle-aged class 5 men. As young men they are dissatisfied with
the life circumstances, and as they age they become even more
unhappy, bitter, and symptomatic. The relentless stress associated
with their marginal economic and social position, along with their

lack of resources or options in dealing with these pressures, leads them to retreat into a defensive pattern that includes rigidity, denial, and a readiness to find fault with and attack easy victims: their children and minority groups. They are hard pressed to find others more powerless and socially marginal than themselves, and tend to turn their bitterness and self-loathing toward such targets.

At the other end of the spectrum are the class 1 and 2 men, especially those living in urban areas. These men fit the pattern of positive development first described by Neugarten in the Kansas City study. By the time they reach their forties, they present themselves as satisfied and in control of most areas in their lives, and there is little evidence to make one suspect that this presentation is a distortion of their self-experience. The educational, social, and psychological resources of these men, coupled with the opportunities in urban areas, seem to lead to a more positive sense of one's self and one's existence. We do however, reserve some questions about this apparently optimal mode of development. These men are fulfilling cultural ideals about what they should be, about what makes a human being worthwhile. Education, career success, wealth, and family, even though they are largely determined by social processes outside the self, are taken as indicators of personal value. There may well be a certain shallowness or smugness to self-esteem based on one's ability to adopt these forms, and a concomitant lack of self-awareness or depth of relationships. In our intensive case studies we shall be particularly aware of these issues and attempt to get a clearer picture of them.

In between these extremes are the class 3 and 4 men and the rural middle class. They do not begin adulthood as alienated as the class 5 men, but, like them, they move into the denial quadrants. They present themselves as well integrated, but their high scores on various indicators of defensiveness lead us to suspect they have built a shell around themselves, avoiding and denying life stresses rather than confronting and resolving them.

For the rural men, the retreat into an exurban community may be part of this pattern of withdrawal and psychological impoverishment. Rather than confront and cope with the complexities and demands of urban life, they attempt to retreat into the imagined tranquillity of life in the country. To better understand the implications of these adaptational modes, we need to look more closely at the reports of the middle-aged men. In the next section we examine the characteristic profiles of middle-aged men in each of our four quadrants.

Types of Middle-Aged Men

We have seen the variety of developmental paths men follow as they move toward middle age. In general, they move away from an experience of alienation and identity diffusion toward either a greater sense of fulfillment and self-acceptance or defensive denial. Once again we have not found evidence of a midlife crisis —if such a crisis means an upsurge of anomie, identity problems, and alienation. Most men either surmount life stresses or they retreat into a superficially compliant and conservative stance of pseudo-development. However, there are some middle-aged men in our crisis quadrant who do report openly experiencing a crisis in middle age. They are a minority who, without feigning a sense of contentment or seeing their problems as caused by others, report intense feelings of dissatisfaction. In this section we examine these men more closely. We also look more closely at the other types, comparing them to each other in order to flesh out our understanding of the types of men in each quadrant. (All comparisons are reported in Appendix 2.)

Looking at the middle-aged men only, we will report the mean scores on our scales, as well as differences in the percentage of respondents agreeing with specific items when appropriate. Of course, since the factors that were used to define the types are made up of the scales, the scales will be strongly related to the types. However, to provide a more detailed description, we will look at which types score highest and lowest on each of the scales.

The Anti-Hero Type

The 12 percent of the middle-aged men who are openly wrestling with feelings of alienation, the ones who come closest to experiencing a midlife crisis, show a number of characteristics that differentiate them from the other types. First, they score highest in anomie on Nettler's Anomie scale. In other words, they are the least likely to be involved in the mass popular culture and local community. They do not enjoy television, spectator sports, or *Readers Digest*. They are least likely to vote in local elections or participate in church activities.

These men score lowest on work satisfaction, portraying themselves as not feeling fulfilled in their work. They also feel dead-ended, seeing little chance of a promotion or a raise in the future.

Eighty-four percent of these men report "thinking about the kind of person I am and what I really want out of life," and 86 percent report wishing to "start afresh and do things over, knowing what I do now."

Although over 50 percent report having had difficulties with their wives in the past, they do not seem especially dissatisfied with their marriage now. Only 9 percent report dissatisfaction with their sexual relations. It is interesting that close to 50 percent of the wives of these men are working, compared to only 30 percent of the wives of other men. This suggests a more egalitarian, less stereotypical set of roles in the home.

These men are the most likely to perceive their children as rebellious, with 25 percent reporting such behavior. However, they are no more likely than some of the other groups to express disappointment with their children or wish they were young again. Of all our respondents, they are least likely to present a socially desirable facade. They admit to everyday faults such as sometimes keeping extra change when they receive it at a store or feeling jealous of others. In a related area they are the most tolerant of ambiguity and are able to see the "gray" side of issues.

Men who experience themselves as being in a state of crisis are our most overtly anxious, scoring highest on the MMPI Anxiety scale. They also score high on certain related psychological symptoms, being more likely to report feeling agitated and restless, having trembling hands and sweaty palms, and other signs of anxiety. They have difficulty getting up in the morning and sometimes feel weak. In response to more overt questions about health, 39 percent claim to have some health problems, 19 percent complaining of ulcers, 31 percent complaining of hay fever, and 64 percent complaining of headaches. Thirty-nine percent report drinking too much either "often" or "sometimes."

The composite picture that emerges of this group is that they are openly grappling with feelings of anomie and are especially dissatisfied with what they have become in their work life. They are least likely to defend themselves with repression and denial or resort to use of projection, scoring lowest on prejudice and bigotry. However, of the four types they are most likely to describe themselves as drinking more than they should.

The open awareness of their plight generates symptoms of anxiety and depression and, in some cases, is associated with psychosomatic or stress-related health problems such as ulcers or hay fever. Whether their physical disorders are the cause or consequence of the feelings cannot be decided from these data, but it is plausible to assume that their emotional distress is being manifested partially in physical symptoms.

The Transcendent-Generative Type

This group, consisting of 32 percent of the middle-aged men, is most likely to report that "in general, life has measured up to expectations," and we are inclined to believe them. They score lowest on our Midlife Crisis scale, with over 90 percent reporting they still find new challenges in work, find their marriages rewarding and their children gratifying. In addition to being satisfied with their work and family, they also are most likely to report good physical and psychological health. Less than 10 percent complain of problems with sleeping, eating, feeling nervous, or showing signs of anxiety. They score lowest on our measure of depression with over 90 percent reporting their lives are full. They still enjoy the things they used to, they feel needed, and are hopeful about their future.

These men have little need for destructive attitudes or self-inhibiting psychological defenses. They are our least prejudiced group and least authoritarian in their child-rearing practices. They appear to be open to their own feelings and to the needs of people around them. The composite picture indicates a group of men who have successfully coped with the developmental problems of life and are not about to have a "midlife crisis." As we will show in the next chapter, rather than having experienced a crisis in the process of reaching this point, they seem to have moved through each phase of life with relative ease and a growing sense of self-assurance. There may have been many serious sources of stress, but active coping behavior has enabled these men to deal with them in ways that have reinforced their emergent sense of themselves.

The Pseudo-Developed Type

Twenty-six percent of the middle-aged men fit this type. Superficially, this group resembles the integrated type, reporting satisfaction with their wives, children, and jobs. In general, they score low on measures of physical and psychological symptoms, acknowledging few overt signs of anxiety or serious physical problems.

However, attention to the test variables specified earlier (denial, distorted self-presentation, and authoritarianism) do permit us to differentiate them from the truly integrated. First, they score by far the highest on our scale measuring the tendency to present a conventionally desirable facade to the world. Second, they are least likely to tolerate ambiguity, believing that work assignments should be clear, preferring an "even regular life" with few surprises, and preferring to be with familiar people in familiar surroundings. Third, they are most likely to be authoritarian in their child-rearing practices, supporting rigid values such as cracking down on children's morality, demanding complete obedience to parents, and bringing up orderly, disciplined, and compliant children. Fourth, they are among the most ethnocentric men we found. Finally, they score highest on our measure of favorable attitudes toward war.

In general, these men report being in good health, only 15 percent having some health problem; and they score lowest on our measures of typical psychosomatic symptoms. However, a number of items indicate that these men are more likely to be suffering a masked depression than our truly integrated types. Compared to the integrated men, twice as many of the deniers report that a "good part of the time" or "most all the time" they do not feel their minds are as clear as they used to be (35 percent), they don't eat as much as they used to (41 percent), they do not find it as easy to do the things they used to do (39 percent), they are not hopeful about the future (21 percent), they wish their children were young (51 percent), and they have difficulty making decisions (29 percent). Though the percentages are smaller, they are also more likely than the integrated men to have trouble sleeping (12 percent vs. 2 percent), to not feel needed (12 percent vs. 4 percent), to feel their lives are not full (16 percent vs. 2 percent), to feel they just can't get going (13 percent vs. 5 percent), and to have ill health affect their work (15 percent vs. 7 percent).

Although these men are least likely to report drinking too much at times (only 22 percent vs. 35 percent of the integrated), they are the most likely to have unsatisfying sexual relations. Over one quarter of these men report not enjoying sex as much as they used to, compared to only 9 percent of the previous two groups discussed. Yet they are least likely to report ever having trouble with their wives (only 28 percent vs. 44 percent of the integrated men and 65 percent of the open-crisis type).

Brief reference to in-depth interviews data may be helpful in clarifying the picture of these men and their mode of functioning. Mr. Brodsky, a middle-class professional, and Mr. Fielding, a blue-collar worker, both score in this quadrant. They reported few health problems and satisfaction with all aspects of their lives. Yet in the home interviews we found that Mr. Fielding's wife was fed up with him and would consider leaving him if it were not for the children. Her prodding led Mr. Fielding to admit that because of work pressures he had "stomach problems" which he treated with valium. Mr. Brodsky turned out to have been unemployed for most of the preceding eighteen months, only recently having taken a job that does not match his qualifications. Though he reports not drinking too much, his wife revealed in the private interview that he had been drinking heavily over the years and still does, even though he has kidney problems and his doctor advises him that he may suffer from kidney failure if he continues. (More will be said about these two cases in the next chapter.)

The composite picture of these men indicates that they are making use of a variety of living strategies, attitudinal configurations, and psychological defenses to avoid confronting the stresses of midlife. In general, they attempt to cope by playing ostrich, refusing to acknowledge their own failings, distress, or the unhappiness of those around them. They present to the world, and perhaps to themselves, a facade of integration. For the most part, it is their facade that is reflected on the questionnaire responses, though some of the cracks appear even in that brief contact. They prefer an orderly, unambiguous environment, hoping that such a setting will permit them to keep this fragile facade intact.

The denial of negative traits in themselves stands in contrast to their perception of their children as needing severe controls in order to keep their impulses under control. Similarly, they perceive blacks, Jews, and other minorities as possessing devious and dangerous traits. Though these men admit to few strains in their own life structures, they perceive these minority groups and their own children as a source of problems to them. In other words, they manifest the classical authoritarian pattern of denial and projection: All badness is taken out of the self and placed "out there" on what comes to be perceived as a hostile and alien universe.

Our in-depth interviews reveal the shallowness of this facade in the men we visited, but even in the questionnaire data we find signs that the defenses are not fully effective. The items that differentiate them from the truly integrated indicate that this defensive style is associated with various symptoms of lethargy and depression. Many have difficulty making decisions and find their minds are not as clear as they used to be. They report not eating as much or enjoying sex as much as they used to. Some show even more direct signs of depression, reporting that they don't feel needed, their lives are not full, they have trouble getting going. For this group, the effort to avoid experiencing their own feelings and changing selves seems to be taking its toll in immobilization, loss of appetites, and depression.

The Punitive-Disenchanted Type

This group, constituting 30 percent of the middle-aged men, is the most symptomatic and unhappy group of our typology. They score highest on our Midlife Crisis scale as well as on other measures of alienation and identity diffusion. Fifty-three percent report directly that "in general" they are "not very happy" with their lives. Eighty percent report thinking a lot about their lives and wishing to start over. Sixty percent report that their friends are having a middle-age crisis.

These men are our most depressed group. Approximately one half of them report that they are hopeful about the future, find it difficult to do the things they used to do, have difficulty making decisions, are not eating as usual, and drink too much. Compared to the other groups, twice as many of these men report feeling restless (27 percent), irritable (17 percent), and fidgety (33 percent); having trouble sleeping (21 percent); losing weight (16 percent); and having many aches and pains (13 percent). Like the open-crisis men, they also report finding middle age difficult (57 percent), having stomach problems (22 percent), ulcers (15 percent), and trouble waking (34 percent), and being too ill to work (18 percent).

A third of these men feel that children are bound to disappoint parents and nearly two thirds report having had difficulty in their relationship with their wives. Twenty-six percent report that marriage is not rewarding after 20 years.

Like the deniers, these men also score high on our measures of authoritarianism. They are likely to present a socially desirable facade and have a low tolerance for ambiguity in their lives. They are our most bigoted group, scoring highest on our revised F-scale. They also tend to utilize repression, projection, and denial to a high degree, but the anxiety, depression, and dissatisfaction with their life structure nonetheless break through. Not surprisingly, more of these men than any other group see themselves as middle-aged or old (31 percent).

The composite picture that emerges is that these men are experiencing severe strain and dysphoria. They feel unable to cope with these pressures, and efforts to employ their usual defensive strategies (similar to those of the deniers) are ineffective in the situation of increasing loss of esteem and diminishing hope.

One example of this type is a man who works in a foundry at a grueling job sandblasting cast metal parts. He hates his "dead-end" job and is ashamed of how "filthy" he is when he comes home. Feelings of resentment about his dilemma are linked to a long history of conflictual relations with his mother; he sees her as responsible for his never going to college. He also resents the success of black youths in the local community college and feels his small town is being overwhelmed by the influx of too many diverse groups. He travels during his vacations but doesn't enjoy it. Aware that his nieces and nephews call him "the grouch," he makes no attempt to enhance his relations with them. His wife, who works as a secretary, can sometimes pull him out of his chronic depression, but his envy of her working conditions and her middle-class co-workers adds an element of tension to their relationship.

Instead of a midlife crisis, these men seem to have experienced a chronic sense of alienation, identity diffusion, and depression. The chronic suffering may be reaching new depths because of the new stresses of middle age, but the midlife transition can hardly be said to represent the basis of their current difficulties. However, there are indications—in descriptions of both self and family—that these men at an earlier point resembled our deniers. The stresses of midlife appear to have precipitated a more overtly symptomatic picture. Unlike the open-crisis men, this type shows little predilection toward introspection. Rather than questioning themselves or their own life choices, they attribute their unhappiness to external circumstances and other people in the environment.

Summary and Conclusions

Past writers have presented conflicting models of midlife changes in our culture. One group argues that men reach their most stable and satisfying adaptation at this life stage, while others argue for a more or less universal crisis period somewhere within the age range of the late thirties to the early forties. Our findings imply that neither model is complete. We do not see evidence of a uniform crisis that cuts across social class and ethnic and personality variables. Instead we find a variety of paths of development with few signs that sudden, discrete midlife crisis is common.

The particular developmental path men follow is related to their position in the class structure and their area of residence. Professionals and middle-class executives in urban areas have the greatest opportunity, as a group, to find comfortable, asymptomatic modes of development. Like the subjects Neugarten describes, as these men approach middle age they move toward a peak in their adaptation to life demands. They report satisfaction with work, family, and their positions in the community. They show neither signs of the identity problems that characterize men in their late twenties nor signs of the authoritarian denial pattern that characterizes other members of their age cohort.

On the other hand, men who are still unskilled laborers give much evidence of personal disorganization and psychopathology as they approach middle age. They begin adulthood in a state of alienation and experience increasing stress as they move toward middle age. They have chronically relied on a limited set of defense mechanisms (denying faults in themselves, projecting negative feelings onto minority groups and their children, maintaining rigid ways of thinking and behaving), but these devices do not seem to totally block out awareness of their pain. They suffer from anxiety, depression, and physical illness, and they are very much aware of not having found gratification in the spheres of work, family, or community.

Perhaps our most interesting finding is the developmental path followed by the bulk of lower-middle-class men—skilled workers, clerical workers, small businessmen, and so on. On the surface these men report resolution of life stresses. But a closer look shows they are living out a more or less fragile personal myth. Rather than having come to terms with life stress, developing the skills and resources to deal with internal and external conflict, these men have followed a path of pseudo-development. They deny any problems with themselves, live in a narrow circumscribed world, and project a variety of faults onto minority groups. They report feelings of depression and lethargy, but these feelings are not well understood or articulated. The sources of their distress, to the extent they can be identified, are seen as remote and outside of their control, for example, "social change." Rather than developing more effective coping patterns with age, these men have retreated into a shell fortified by avoidance and denial. For some men this shell may be fragile, and they may be candidates for a midlife crisis given some precipitating events that undermine their limited adaptations. But on the basis of our follow-up interviews with many of these men, such a crisis seems unlikely. They show a remarkable ability to ignore or distort and then assimilate any information that challenges their personal myth system and world views. While only 12 percent of our respondents manifest what we can describe as an overt "midlife crisis," another 56 percent either externalize their frustration and despair or seek to hide it. These data help to explain the discrepancies in findings to date: The researcher's level of measurement and conceptualization of crisis can permit him to place this majority of middle-aged men into either descriptive category. We would argue that along with diversity of response, the escalation of denial emerges as one fundamental characteristic of midlife for men in our society. Understanding midlife as a developmental stage requires us to look at the origins and implications of this stance as a manifestation of both cultural or familial and individual dynamics.

In the next section we look in more detail at each of these types of men, reporting a series of brief psychobiographies. Using our home interview data, we examine their relationships to their wives, children, friends, and community.

Endnotes

1. Zung, W.W.K., "A Self Report Depression Scale," *Archives of General Psychiatry*, vol. 12, January 1965, p. 63.
2. Dahlstrom, W. Grant, and George S. Welsh, *An MMPI Handbook* (Minneapolis: University of Minnesota Press, 1960), pp. 53–55.
3. Gurin, Gerald, Joseph Veroff, and Sheila Feld, *Americans View Their Mental Health* (New York: Basic Books, 1960), p. 420.
4. Dahlstrom and Welsh, *op. cit.*, pp. 50–53.

5. Martin, James G., and Frank R. Westie, "The Tolerant Personality," *American Sociological Review*, vol. 24, 1959.
6. Rosenberg, Stanley D., Michael Farrell, and John Gorman, "Racism: A 1973 Scale," *Journal of Social Psychology*, vol. 12, no. 4, 1976.
7. Levinson, Daniel J., and Phyllis E. Huffman, "Traditional Family Ideology and Its Relation to Personality," *Journal of Personality*, vol. 23, 1955, pp. 251–272.
8. Ford, LeRoy H., Jr., "A Forced Choice, Acquiescence-Free, Social Desirability (Defensiveness) Scale," *Journal of Consulting Psychology*, vol. 28, 1964, p. 475.
9. Zimmerman, Carle C., and Merle Grampton, "Theories of Frederick LePlay," in *Kinship and Family Organization*, edited by B. Farber (New York: Wiley & Sons, 1966), pp. 14–23.
10. Wirth, Lewis, "Urbanism as a Way of Life," *American Journal of Sociology*, vol. 44, 1938, pp. 1–24.
11. Slater, Phillip, *The Pursuit of Loneliness* (Boston: Beacon, 1970).

Chapter 5

MEN AT MIDLIFE: CASE STUDIES

When we began this study we were highly sensitive to the idea of the "midlife crisis." The results of our questionnaire data thus represented a surprise: Being in a clearly demarcated state of "crisis" was unusual for men entering middle age. Where we had expected to find men reaching a peak of discontent, we discovered a relatively high level of reported tranquillity and satisfaction. As we have shown in the previous chapter, many of these apparently satisfied men are chronically unwilling to be honest with themselves or others about their feeling states. While they present a facade of identity achievement and satisfaction with their lives, they also manifest a rigid set of ego-defenses. They apparently work to avoid acknowledging the concerns and stresses that threaten to undermine their surface equanimity. However, other men who also report satisfaction seem to have achieved a more solid mastery over new life stresses. Overtly and covertly they show signs of having actively wrestled with life stresses and reached, at midlife, a maximal peak of satisfaction. Finally, we did find a minority of middle-aged men in a state of crisis—unhappy with themselves and in a state of conflict with others in their world.

A Closer Look

Having used the quantitative data to locate these types of overt responses to middle age, we felt a need to look more closely at the men. We wished to know whether a more intensive study of men from each quadrant would validate our quantitative findings. We also wished to look at examples of the statistical types, to discover the fuller human reality behind the scale scores. Thus, as was described in Chapter 1, we carried out in-depth interviews with 20 men. We deliberately selected five men from each quadrant and obtained permission to visit each in his home and interview members of his family. After each home visit the man, his wife, and as many of his children as possible came to our offices for a more systematic follow-up interview. After the interviews were complete, the two authors separately analyzed each man and his family, then met together to resolve differences and build a complete analysis. The analyses were then shared at graduate seminars and were further revised on the basis of feedback.

Results of Follow-Up Interviews

The results of the follow-up interviews corroborate and enrich the quantitative data. The men from the transcendent-generative quadrant (2) did indeed appear to be manifesting a high sense of self-acceptance, greater awareness, and more satisfying interpersonal relations. Though they all have seen their share of stress —even tragic losses and repeated adversity in some cases—they have faced up to the stresses and created workable solutions. By the time we contact them in their early forties, they have based their sense of themselves on hard–earned occupational identities and developed a capacity to respond with a greater depth of compassion to people and events around them. They act on their world rather than evade or suffer from it. They feel positive about themselves and hopeful about resolution of their current problems.

On the other hand, the pseudo-developed men show many signs of living out a myth of adult masculinity. Chronic problems go unresolved or unconfronted, while new problems appearing in their lives are avoided or denied in their accustomed style.

Finally, the follow-up cases selected from our two "alienated" quadrants manifest multiple difficulties and symptoms of stress. They show signs of being overwhelmed by accumulated life problems. Many seem to have given up hope of achieving mastery. Their problems range from relationships with their families to work, neighbors, and health. In every case the distress these men are in does not appear to have descended on them precipitously. Instead, the strains and conflicts seem to have been building over their whole adult life. Rather than suddenly experiencing a crisis, these men seem to be in the midst of a never-ending onslaught, with middle age simply adding to their baggage of unresolved problems.

As with the quantitative data, we find in the follow-up cases that social class influences how men experience middle age. The range of resources and styles of response are quite different in the different social strata.

Typical Styles of Coping with Stress

Because of this difference we have decided to present descriptions of men who exhibit the "typical" style of each class in dealing with the stresses of midlife. However, to present a middle- and lower-class version of each type would be cumbersome and lead to redundancies. Therefore, we have decided to present six portraits—three from the middle class and three from the working class. Each portrait consists of a composite of the patterns observed in the group, highlighting the basic trends. Of course, all names are fictitious although all quotes and life situations are actual representations of data reported to us. While a number of the men studied were divorced or involved in second or third marriages, we treat each composite case as if the husband were still involved in his first marriage. This expedient was chosen for a number of reasons: Single marriage is still the modal pattern in this generation, and it was logistically awkward to interview first spouse or children not living with their parents. We thus could not really obtain comparable data on earlier marriages. While this serves to make our data appear somewhat skewed, the divorced men in each quadrant are represented in the case prototype. Although literal case reports might have been more satisfactory in a number of ways, the need to maintain our subjects' anonymity requires us to use amalgamated portraits.

We will also, in the succeeding chapters, use these same six composites to illustrate midlife changes in marital and family dynamics. Let us begin by briefly introducing each of the men.

Six Portraits

Bob Wilson, a man in his early forties, is a social service worker with a wife and two adolescent sons. He is at once under- and overeducated for his job, having studied for but not completed a doctorate in another field. Bob is representative of the subjects whose survey responses place them in Quadrant 1: those experiencing an overt midlife crisis.

Anthony Williams, a forty-year-old manual laborer with three children, illustrates the midlife reaction of Quadrant 4—a mixture of acknowledgment of symptomatology, escalating authoritarianism, and externalization of his problems. In contrast to Wilson, who feels that he has himself to blame for his failures and disappointments, Tony sees himself as a victim of circumstance and others' perfidy.

As we move to our denial quadrants, we find John Brodsky, a chemist with children ages 17 and 21. John illustrates the middle-class pseudo-development pattern of Quadrant 3. He provides the self-descriptions we associate with positive integration, while also giving much evidence of reliance on denial and the presentation of an idealized persona.

Ed Fielding is John's blue-collar counterpart. Although several years younger than John, Ed's two eldest children have already left home for the express purpose of "going it on their own." The Fieldings live in rural New England, in the residential section of a former mill town and commercial center for the surrounding counties.

Finally, our Quadrant 2 cases combine positive self-reports with evidence of less rigid patterns of ego-defense and a greater willingness to acknowledge faults or difficulties. Tom Conley is the successful eldest son of an affluent and ambitious family. These advantages appear to have been important to him, both in terms of his image of himself as someone with great possibilities, and in terms of the doors that these origins opened to him. Bill Mayne's accomplishments, although externally more modest—he is a construction foreman—are perhaps even more impressive because he began with none of these advantages.

The Middle-Class Midlife Crisis

The man we shall call Bob Wilson lived in a well-maintained suburban home. Its meticulous landscaping stood out even in a neighborhood where the residents seemed to work compulsively to maintain a park-like atmosphere on a gently winding street in a suburban development near Boston. Mrs. Wilson, attractive, gracious, and carefully dressed, greeted the interviewer at the door, holding the aluminum screen door open as he walked up the walkway. Though not as outgoing, Mr. Wilson was equally friendly, showing good humor and a readiness to laugh even at himself. The total impression is one of normalcy. To the middle-class interviewers, the Wilsons seem like people we have known all our lives: outgoing and verbal with a sense of what is socially appropriate. The middle class are adept at maintaining good form.

As an adolescent Bob had not been close to his father, a moderately successful entrepreneur who ran his own printing company. He describes his father as stoic and distant. This distance from father seemed to heighten his sense of insecurity and desire for guidance. Even in his twenties Bob consulted his mother in making decisions about his college major and which graduate school to attend. Out of a sense of compliance, he worked for the family business during summer vacations. His father wanted him to take over the firm when he retired. He felt, however, that his father kept from him the inner secrets of the business which, once learned, would enable him to fully grasp how to be a successful entrepreneur.

Besides, Bob developed other aspirations. After high school he wasn't certain he would go to college. But he ran into a respected English teacher while working for his father that summer, and the teacher urged him to apply at a small local college. The teacher tapped Bob's vague interest in doing intellectual work; he applied and was accepted.

He originally planned to major in history or psychology, but the influence of the English teacher and the advice of his mother led him to choose English. After telling of this decision, Bob points to his head and say, "Dumb." In retrospect he feels that with better guidance he would have chosen a more practical subject with more possibility for employment, or he would have gone to work for his father. The theme of fortuitous circumstances leading to unwise choices pervades Bob's description of his early adulthood. Lack of preparation and guidance leads him, in his own perception, to making decisions that later become handicaps, forcing him to make compromises with life.

While Bob was in college his father died, leaving less inheritance than was expected. Bob and his mother decided to sell the business, using the money to complete his education and support her. During this period Bob developed an interest in philosophy and hoped to become a college teacher.

Though Bob lived in the dormitory at college, he spent a lot of time at home. One of his activities included driving his sister and her friends to local high school events. During these trips he met Sarah and gradually began to date her. He says they did not experience a dramatic romance, but rather they gradually came to feel at home with each other. When he graduated from college and joined the Air Force, he wrote to her and they dated during his leaves. After two years of courtship at a distance they decided to marry, and Sarah followed Bob to Alabama, where he was stationed.

Though they disliked Alabama in general, they look back on the period fondly. Bob taught new recruits about radar and Sarah was happily involved with other wives in the Air Force community. In this period, their first child, Robert, Jr., was born. Many couples on the base were at a similar stage of life, and the Wilsons still enjoy occasional reunions with these friends. After being discharged from the Air Force, Bob decided to act on his ambition to be a college professor in philosophy. He applied to Catholic University in Washington, D.C., and was accepted. However, after arriving and beginning his first term, he discovered that he would have to know both Latin and Greek to complete his degree. He found himself ill prepared and decided he could not reach his goal. Since his wife was pregnant again, he decided he had to make some practical decisions and chose to enter the social welfare department and train to be a social worker. It was a compromise, but one he perceived as necessary. When telling about his late discovery of the language requirements, he again points to his head and says, "Dumb."

After graduation he took a job near New York City, but found the cost of living too high and felt too far away from his family. He moved back to Massachusetts and took a job in an employment office in a town outside of Boston. Though he never really enjoyed the work, he made accommodations, and at home there were some compensations.

The Wilsons lived with Bob's mother for two years; then when their oldest son was seven, they bought their present home. They described their early years in this pleasant suburb as busy and exciting. Sarah tells us she was involved "up to her ears" in Cub Scouts and PTA. The Wilson home became a hub of neighborhood activity. Several women visited each other every day. Mrs. Wilson baked brownies when the women came to her place. In

the afternoons she enjoyed having the children in the neighborhood play in their yard where she could keep an eye on and enjoy
her sons. The only discordant notes in her account recalling these
days are hints of envy at some of the more successful neighbors
—a TV weatherman, a self-made appliance store manager, and an
engineer.

Bob, Jr., delighted his parents by being very successful at school
and actively involved in sports. He sang well, and several times
in grade school he had a prominent part in the school play. In his
final year of junior high he got involved in local politics, cam-
paigning for a congressional candidate.

The Wilsons look back on this period as the "golden years."
Although some of their dreams were unfulfilled, they were happy
then; they had friends, a house they were proud of, and it was
clear that Bob, Jr., had a bright future.

It was during this period that Mr. Wilson decided to leave his
bureaucratic job to work as counselor in a rehabilitation program
for handicapped children and adolescents. Although this job was
still far from his earlier aspirations, it did use the skills he had
developed in both social service and personnel work. Counseling
seemed to him to be more than a way of earning a living; it had
inherent value. He hoped to be able to provide young people
with the kind of advice and guidance that he wished he had had
as a young man. He attacked the job with exuberance, taking
courses to expand and freshen his skills as a social worker. He
had not felt at home in the employment office, but with this new
job he could at least help people avoid the mistakes he had made.

At this point Bob Wilson saw himself as a man who had built
a workable life structure. The disappointments of his early adulthood had made him sensitive, he believed, to the needs of the
next generation. His efforts to work through his own identity
struggles and dependency problems were being focused in a way
that promised to be of value for his young clients. He appeared
to be laying the groundwork for a stage of generativity, devoting
his resources to fit the needs of the wider community and the
next generation. At home he had an attractive wife. She envied
the greater success of some of their neighbors, but nevertheless
maintained warm relationships with both them and Bob. Both
husband and wife had reason to hope to compensate for the failures in their own lives through the successes of their sons.

However, by the time we interview Mr. Wilson (seven years

later, when he is 42) we find that most of these positive or hopeful features of Bob's life have gone awry. At work, a new team approach has been introduced, and younger people with more advanced training in counseling the handicapped have been hired. Though Bob spent some time orienting them to the program, he soon began taking a back seat as they began redefining the job. Conflicts were recurrent, finally culminating in Bob's being fired. When we talked with him during the summer, he had no idea where he would be working the following year. Although he knew he would be without a job in September, he had not begun to look actively for work. Bob sounded both defeated and indifferent when describing this situation, as if he were talking about someone else's problems.

At about the time the conflicts began at work, the Wilsons started to have problems with Bob, Jr. He began to break out of their world, looking for new friends and getting into activities they felt were going nowhere—such as acting and drugs. In February of the past year young Bob was arrested for a drug offense. Two weeks later Mr. Wilson suffered a heart attack. Although neither severe nor physically debilitating (Bob is allowed a full range of activities), this illness has been treated by the family as a sign. Bob, Jr., alternates between extreme guilt and remorse, on the one hand, and even more angry defiance of his parents on the other. He feels both responsible for his father's heart attack and angry at his father for staging such an event to punish and constrict him. The boy's response has been stimulated by his parents, who clearly represent the arrest and his father's heart attack as cause and effect. Although they are not explicit, they also hint at a belief or expectation that Mr. Wilson has "suffered enough." This places an obligation on young Bob to stop making his father unhappy, an obligation he is unwilling to accept.

Not surprisingly, when we interviewed Mr. Wilson in the summer of that year, he was in a state of crisis, overtly talking of his despair, lack of direction, and sense of his own life being a failure. Even if he could, he felt no desire to go back to his counseling job. He had had enough of "the unrealistic dreams and emotional demands" of the handicapped youngsters he had previously been so eager to counsel. He no longer had confidence in his ability to provide them with the right information to build a meaningful life in this system. If he could get into a secure administrative job until retirement he'd be satisfied. He felt estranged from his son with no hope of reconciliation in sight.

The old neighbors had either moved away or withdrawn their interest. The contrast between the Wilsons' current isolation and past sense of the neighborhood as a sort of extended family had been recently dramatized for them. New people had bought the house next door during the spring, and a running feud has ensued over children coming into the Wilsons' yard and damaging their garden. The neighbors seem callous about the matter, and Bob feels unable to assert his rights.

Bob Wilson manifests the basic characteristics of the midlife crisis. External precipitants have exacerbated long-standing problems, upsetting compromise solutions that had served in earlier adulthood. Changing conceptions of his work role have made Bob's skills obsolete, a situation worsened by his intransigence about continuing his training or accepting a different place in the organizational hierarchy. As this situation became apparent to him, it seemed to paralyze his serious search for a new position where his skills would be desired. This inertia can be understood in the light of his mixed motivation toward work. His career was never seen as something he had chosen and felt committed to. It was, rather, an expedient; something he had drifted into and stayed with because that was "easier" than trying to do a job that was personally meaningful.

At home his son's advance into adolescence is experienced as a disaster. The son's sexual explorations, experimentations with drugs, and attempts to become an actor are seen as attacks on Bob, meant somehow to hurt him. He is in a state of despair over the whole situation, feeling unable to control his son or adapt to occupational experiences. Even if he does begin to confront these problems, it seems unlikely that their resolution can be in the terms he envisioned five years earlier.

It is important to note that this crisis did not suddenly appear as a result of an internal maturational process. Rather, it seems to be the result of a lifetime of compromises and drifting toward second-choice decisions. The accumulation of unsatisfactorily resolved life problems, coupled with new problems unique to middle age, have overwhelmed Wilson. This leaves him expressing only the hope that he can find some "secure niche to hide in" while waiting for retirement. He has, at this point, surrendered to his situation and envisions the rest of his existence as a waiting for death. His recent heart problems have further stimulated his sense of the fragility of his existence, concretizing his feeling that he is living on borrowed time.

The Working-Class Midlife Crisis

Anthony Williams is a maintenance man at a nearby college who lives on a dead-end street just two blocks from the main corner of a village outside of Boston. He lives with his wife, two daughters, and son in a large square home covered with brown asbestos siding. As one approaches the house, a small two-room section added on the back becomes visible. His parents had lived there until recently. The neighborhood consists of broken sidewalks and houses in various stages of deterioration and patchwork repair. Next door the front porch is propped up by two-by-fours. Williams' garage door is new, but it still hasn't been painted. From the sidewalk it is possible to see a tall stockade fence, surrounding the backyard.

Williams welcomed the two interviewers. He shook hands with a hard squeeze and stared into their eyes with a stony unsmiling expression until they turned away. It seemed crucial to Tony to establish some form of dominance, as if he were anticipating an attempted put-down. The living room was furnished with old, inexpensive furniture upholstered in dark colors. On the wall above the piano were large school photographs of the children taken at an earlier age. Williams' 19-year-old son, Ron, was standing with his coat on, obviously impatient to go out. He shook hands weakly, grunted a few times as his father joked about his busy social life, then left in his car—a new American Rebel. The two daughters, Mary, age 20, and Debby, age 15, stayed in the living room throughout the interview. As everyone was being seated, Anna Williams came in from the kitchen and sat down quietly. Without looking at her, Tony pointed to her with his thumb and said, "This is my wife, Anna."

The interview began in a choppy fashion; direct questions were answered with a few words. Anna and the girls watched Williams for cues as to when to speak. Sometimes they looked amused at his swaggering, cocky style; at other times they seemed worried and puzzled. Eventually Williams loosened up and told his story.

Both his career and his married life got off to a rough start. After graduating from a training school, where he learned to be a machinist, Tony joined the Army in 1946. He returned home and decided to start a trucking business. His grandfather lent him $2,000 and a friend became his partner by putting up a small amount of capital to cover the rest of the initial expenses. While

Tony worked long hours at the business, his partner wasn't as devoted. Tony blames his partner for the eventual failure of the business after a two-year struggle. Tony then went to work at a large factory as a machinist. He also worked evenings with an undertaker to make enough money to repay his business debts. In the private interview we found that during this period Tony had been occasionally dating a girl whom he hoped to marry. However, after his business folded, she lost interest in him.

The double defeat seems to have been devastating to him, precipitating a prolonged if undramatic depression. He would go to work, come home, go to work again. Occasionally under pressure from his mother to "get out of the house" he would take long drives alone, returning home late at night. Throughout this period he lived at his parents' home, trying to save money.

One Saturday afternoon, coming out of church after confession, he met Anna. They knew each other through mutual friends, and he asked her out. After a year of courtship they married, amid great fanfare from the two large extended families.

Unable to afford their own apartment and anxious to remain in the old neighborhood, the Williamses moved in with his parents. As the children began arriving, a small apartment was built on the back of the house and his parents moved into it. Relations with his mother were strained, but with two incomes they were all able to survive. Tony's mother seemed to have as much difficulty in letting go of the parental role as Tony did in seeing himself as an adult and head of a household. Anna tells how her mother-in-law always criticized her housekeeping, and when Tony came home she always had something for him to do. At night when everyone had gone to bed, Tony's mother would frequently get up and come into their side of the house to check the gas stove and the doors.

Tony seems to have borne these strains with resignation, perhaps even being gratified by the continued nurturance, support, and direction from his parents. His part in the exchange was never acknowledged: Tony presented himself to Anna as a man who had to forebear his elderly parent's quirks. Although his mother may have been difficult to live with, he developed a warm relationship with his father. Together they worked on the house, and every Sunday they played cards with friends. Even now Tony idolizes his father, a contractor skilled at many building trades. He speaks with an air of pride and wonder of his father's abilities to build and repair things around the house and his strength and resilience in old age.

Tony's relationship to his own wife and children is somewhat patriarchal. When asked who makes the major decisions about spending money, he raised his index finger in the air, then pointed to himself. When asked who disciplined the children, he raised a finger again and pointed to Anna. His older daughter, Mary, described dinner table scenes when Tony was in a rage over something. Anna would rush around saying, "Shhh! Shhh!" to the children's questions about what was wrong or their requests for permission to go out. "Everyone had to walk on eggs."

Over the years Anna developed a close relationship to Mary and Ron. When they needed something, they came to her first. A sort of underground resistance to Tony's tyranny developed among them. Debby developed a close relationship with her grandmother and was an outsider to the underground. However, she appeared oblivious to the forces around her. Tony describes her as "living in a daze."

A number of midlife stresses have hit Tony in the past five years. They began with the death of his mother when Tony was 40. Tony tells of the death with the same apparent stoicism he showed throughout the evening. "When your time is up, you gotta go," he says. But he says that his father went into a prolonged depression, moping around watching television, having no energy for family activities.

Then two friends from childhood died within a year. Tony says, "Better them than me." He doesn't seem to overtly mourn their loss, but he does appear to exaggerate his fatalistic willingness to accept fate as he reports on this period, insisting that he does not fear death.

Over the years Tony had become active in the Knights of Columbus. He helped organize an annual Christmas party for retarded children, and told of how good it felt to stand by as the kids came up to sit on Santa's knee and receive their gifts. But during the past few years he has pulled away from this activity, claiming that younger men coming in are "messing up" what he helped to build. His final break with them came last year, when he ruptured a disc in his back while lifting a heavy barrel at work. He had to spend three weeks in the hospital and none of his friends came to visit him.

This back injury marked a sharp turning point, evoking all the bitterness and depressive symptomatology kept in check after earlier life reversals and his mother's death. His medical treatment required that he stay home a month after returning from the hospital, but that was seven months ago. Tony's doctor tells him he is fine, but Tony has not returned to work because he ostensibly is trying to obtain workman's compensation for the injury and lost work time. His lawyer is still working on the case, and Tony fears that if he goes back to work he'll lose his case. So he stays at home, takes occasional walks, listens to police calls on a police radio, and watches television. His children have grown increasingly annoyed with him. "All he does is pick," says Mary. "He won't let Mom sit down to do a crossword puzzle. He won't let me sew because it interferes with his radio. And if you stay around the house, he starts reading stories out of the newspaper to you. So me and my brother, we leave the house."

She goes on to tell of his unpredictable sarcastic attacks on her friends. Recently, Mary had been entertaining one of the neighbors. The friend's mother, though on welfare, had just purchased a new chair. Soon afterwards the Williamses purchased a couch and chair. The visiting girl told Tony that her mother admired his new furniture. Tony replied, "Oh yeah! Tell her I paid for mine." Tony's feelings of alienation from neighbors finally led him to build the new stockade fence "for privacy." This fence is, moreover, a symbol of his isolation from a world in which he is not accepted and which he cannot accept.

As we spoke to him alone, his facade of tough indifference was occasionally dropped. There was genuine warmth when he spoke of the retarded children at Christmas time. And once, when he was speaking about the lost girl friend, he almost cried. He said he found himself thinking about her often lately, wondering what his life might have been like if things had worked out with the trucking business and her. But he is firmly committed to his present marriage and would never consider leaving.

With Williams, we see the mixture of unresolved stress and dissatisfaction coupled with stoic denial that characterizes the lower-class crisis type in Quadrant 4. Having failed to achieve his desired occupational identity and mate, he retreated into his parent's home and an old-world life style unreflective of his own generation and community. Although he is proud of his record of hard work—working two jobs over most of his adult life—the output has not paid off in income. He claims to accept this situation in the same stoic way he claims to accept the losses of his mother and friends. His health problems have made him doubly resistant to returning to a job he dislikes and considers demeaning, although secure.

In the face of these mounting problems, he presents a facade of being in control of the situation. Rather than confront his job dissatisfaction, he poses as a crafty legal tactician who is going to beat the insurance company and win a hefty compensation suit. Although maintaining a boyish dependent relationship with his father, he plays tyrannical lord over his own family. His wife and children reluctantly support his myth of masculine patriarchy, while covertly resisting his tyranny and finding means to meet their needs. They seem to recognize his need for support as he alternates between chronically complaining about uncontrollable irritants in his life, denying anything is wrong, and lashing out at them, their neighbors, or friends.

Once again we see that, rather than having a sudden crisis, this man is experiencing the consequences of many unresolved developmental problems. The accumulated problems generated by a failure to break free from dependency on his parents, establish a work identity with any positive meaning for him, or to achieve intimacy with friends, spouse, or his own children, all contribute to his withdrawal. The adaptation of earlier adulthood, although supportable, looks very fragile in retrospect. Although he makes use of denial and displaces his anger onto others, he is not capable of totally escaping the real sources of pain in his life, nor is he able to deny the sense of running out of time.

The Middle-Class Denial Type: Pseudo-Development at Midlife

John Brodsky portrays himself as being in perfect health and harmony with his life circumstances. Like most middle- and upper-middle-class respondents, he generally does a good job of maintaining this facade. As one enters his gracious custom-built home to be entertained with small talk, good liquor, and a sophisticated family dinner, it is easy to assume that John is what he has declared himself to be: a successful man who epitomizes the rewards of hard work and achievement. The entire family is circumspect about betraying any chinks in this armor; they cooperate in trying to appear "successful" for the visitor.

Only after several hours of talk does Mrs. Brodsky reveal that her husband has been an alcoholic and recently suffered a complete kidney shutdown that nearly killed him. Characteristically, John explains that he "never really had a drinking problem" but rather "an unusual sensitivity to alcohol." "Social drinking" alone led to his condition. Despite medical warnings that continued drinking will probably kill him, he still has an occasional cocktail before dinner. In his own perception John is in perfect health because he has "recovered" from his kidney problems. This vignette illustrates well his ability to minimize and deny any input that contradicts the persona he attempts to foist on the world and on himself.

Other areas of concealed discontent became apparent as the evening progressed. First, Mr. Brodsky has become emotionally estranged from his family. We hear once again about a marriage that began in the traditional mode. Mr. Brodsky worked while Loraine was essentially anchored to the home. One difference here is that Mrs. Brodsky had begun a teaching career before her marriage at age 24. She had the opportunity for some taste of an independent existence and some sense of her ability to perform in the larger world. She is two years her husband's senior. After the arrival of their first child, she agreed to stop full-time employment. Apparently, however, there was a long period of struggle when she agitated to work part-time or have more freedom from marital chores—moves which John always resisted. His wishes prevailed, and Loraine eventually stopped protesting against his patriarchal conception of an ideal marriage. These conflicts were apparently most overt in the first six or seven years of the marriage.

This one issue represented a sort of axis around which many elements of family life were crystallized. Mr. Brodsky, a man from a lower socioeconomic background than his wife, but with great ambition, became the family achiever. He demanded much support (and even direct help) from her in regard to his work, and their joint effort was the major interactional modality of the early years of their marriage. This dedication and joint effort fed his career achievements and he established a reputation as a young "comer." To maximize advancement, he switched from company to company in his field, rarely staying in one location for more than a year or two.

This period of his twenties and early thirties was very good for John in comparison both to the present and to his youth. He came from a hard-working, emotionally distant family and never felt much affection or caring from them. He responded, as he reconstructs it, with attempting to "prove his worth" to them through school achievement and later through a lucrative mail–order business he founded while still in high school. He was a competitive young man who found it very difficult to be close to others. His wife was the first person who meant very much to him, and his emotional life was invested in her and the work. The couple's relation to community, friends, in-laws, and even to their own children was mediated by Mrs. Brodsky. By providing emotion, warmth, and the capacity for interpersonal relationships, she permitted her husband the opportunity to function primarily in only two spheres: the marital dyad and his occupational role.

This arrangement was put under increasing stress for a variety of reasons as Mr. Brodsky entered his late thirties and early forties. His career advancement slowed down and then stopped—partially because of economic circumstances and partially because he seemed ill equipped to make the necessary transition from the technical end-of-project development to management. He was not, he tells us, the kind of man who could get the most out of other people or even communicate with them very well. The final blow came when, at age 41, the company he worked for closed down. For several months he underwent the mortifying experience of being unemployed and having to locate a new position. His current job is far less prestigious and well-paying than those he previously held.

In the Brodsky family, too, mother and children have moved together, allied against the father. This alliance is more muted than in the case of the Williamses and has a somewhat different emotional tone. The mother and the two children, ages 17 and 21, are not so much in combat with Mr. Brodsky as they are determined to have warmth and enjoyment despite him. Both children feel that he has always been distant from them, that they were, in effect, raised by their mother. They also identify with her enthusiasm for life, the outdoors, travel, and getting together with people. The mother and children now operate almost as three adults, sharing interests, activities, and friendships. This emergent pattern has left John increasingly alone.

His heavy drinking began when he was in his mid-thirties. In this period the family power structure and coalition patterns were

changing, and it clearly predates the period of occupational stagnation. His increasing reliance on alcohol seemed to be his major
mechanism for escaping the sense of depression and isolation that
emerged as the changes took place. In the absence of any positive
human relationships, occupational achievement appears to have
been insufficient to sustain him.

As career progress became more problematic, his remaining
defenses (and the myths of self in which these were manifest)
eroded rather quickly. He would no longer resist his wife's desire
to return to work. In the past several years she has reestablished
herself occupationally to a point where she runs the adult education program at the local community college. This work keeps
her out of the house all evening while Mr. Brodsky has gravitated
to a pattern of early retiring and early rising. This has effectively
isolated them from one another; they almost never take a meal
together or speak. This is a radical departure from the earlier
years of almost constant companionship. Surprisingly, their sexual
relationship survives this emotional estrangement.

We see, then, a wife who is ascending as her husband declines.
She is, however, gracious in her ascendency, supporting and protecting him from any insult or implication that he is any less than
he has ever been. He seems much older than his 44 years and,
after a couple of hours of contact, becomes palpably depressed.
She behaves much like his eldest daughter, showing respect to
the older man while essentially being his caretaker. He has retreated into increasingly solitary activities but claims that these
provide important rewards.

One poignant example of his isolating compensatory activities
is a routine of rising before daybreak, having breakfast alone,
then walking to a nearby hillside to watch the sunrise over the
skyline. He claims that his family misses half the day by not seeing this sight, thus transforming his depressive early-morning
wakefulness into a "sign" of his energy.

Indeed, Mr. Brodsky attempts to cling to a myth of himself
as successful, vital, and the central force in his family. The resources available to him via his middle-class status and superior
intelligence contribute to his efforts at maintaining this illusion.
It would even seem that he finds some solace in his relative success and affluence. Mr. Brodsky openly harbors ideas of an occupational comeback by which he will recoup all his losses. His
family colludes in the efforts at denial of problems and assertion

of health, but they are aware of the underlying reality of John's condition. Privately, they speak of his anxiety and depression. Their behavior toward him in the interview situation can only be described as "kid gloves" treatment. Any question that might have embarrassed or betrayed Mr. Brodsky produced a family rally to evade or diffuse the issue. In a startling reversal of form, he confided privately that he really wished he had weeks of continuous time to tell the psychologist-interviewer all that was really on his mind. It was as if each segment of the family had to protect the other from open acknowledgment of their shared reality.

In contrast to the earlier cases, on the initial contact and on the questionnaire, Brodsky overtly presents an air of mastery over the stresses of life. The family colludes in supporting this facade when in his presence, protecting him from probing questions that might reveal incongruities. However, when alone the wife and children report a trend toward decline, disintegration, and isolation, although his wife in particular repeatedly asserts faith in his eventual recovery. No one conveys a sense of crisis. Rather they work hard at playing out a version of the American success story, providing only a few passing glimpses of the progressive decline Brodsky is undergoing. The economic and educational resources of the family are important elements in the man's being able to construct myths about himself that negate and disguise his sense of stagnation.

The Working-Class Denial Type

Like Brodsky, Ed Fielding reports satisfaction on almost all the indicators of stress on our questionnaire. He claims to be in good health with a satisfying job and happy home. However, he also scores high on denial. Throughout the interview he maintains the same claim of complacent satisfaction, providing only a few hints at problems when prodded or ridiculed by his wife Joan. It's interesting that his rigidity is reflected in his inexpressive face, monotonal responses, and minimal gesticulation.

We first encountered the Fielding family in the context of a Friday evening home visit. Although the time of the investigator's arrival had been previously agreed upon, the Fieldings seemed unprepared to receive their "guest." Mr. Fielding had not arrived home from work, the house was in some disarray, and Mrs. Fielding was completing household tasks. She seemed congenial and responsive, speaking freely about her life and marriage despite the intermittent presence of early adolescent children. Only the two youngest children remain at home, their only son and eldest daughter having moved out. Mrs. Fielding almost immediately revealed dissatisfaction with most of her married life, describing the early years of being tied down with young children as particularly torturous. More recently, she has "gotten out from under" by finding employment and a set of her own friends she sees without her husband.

Mr. Fielding's arrival led to a palpable change in the emotional environment. The children quieted down and ceased their movement from the TV to their mother's side. Joan became more tense and circumspect while Ed seemed less than delighted about "her" visitor. In the course of that evening, and in subsequent interviews, some of the relationships between Mrs. Fielding's reemergence and her husband's involutional processes became evident.

In the early years of their marriage she had been very compliant to his demands that she remain almost totally enmeshed in home and family. She was young when married, accustomed to personal freedom and to being "pampered" as the baby in her family. She was also several years her husband's junior and, as she now sees it, unprepared to give up her freedom. The first child was conceived very shortly after marriage, and Mrs. Fielding soon found herself anchored to a home and the demands of small children. Ed felt it unseemly to help with such chores and, in fact, demanded care and attention for himself at the end of the working day. He was to be the breadwinner, she the nurturant "mother"—a pattern of expectations which still persists and which he still defends.

This existence, Joan declares, precipitated her into years of depression. She was "sociable" and yearned to visit friends and go out. Ed disliked going out, was generally hostile and suspicious to their acquaintances, and was reluctant to leave the children with anyone else. For many years he prevailed, ruling the family (they all agree) with an iron fist. The couple socialized very little, and Joan was permitted no autonomous activity. A major tool in his control of Mrs. Fielding was the fact that she could not drive. He would not teach her, and they lived in an area lacking public transportation.

Quite suddenly, when Ed was in his late thirties, he developed a number of vague physical maladies, and even began to fear that he might be stricken by a heart attack. He became increasingly phobic about driving, claiming lower back pain after an hour behind the wheel. Rather than resisting, Ed began to demand that his wife learn how to drive. Her newfound mobility soon blossomed into the acquisition of both a job and a set of friends. Joan knew that she was making her husband uncomfortable, but she turned on her tormentor, flaunting her power. She has become aware of herself as an attractive, capable woman and openly fantasizes about the men with whom she works. Joan stimulates Ed's discomfort by making invidious comparisons between him and her boss.

The irony of this cannot be appreciated unless one recognizes the needs and fantasies that fueled Mr. Fielding's long-standing efforts to control and isolate his wife. His distrust of others and dislike of parties and socializing were, in large part, reactions to an almost consuming fear of his wife's possible infidelity. Having come from a background of early object loss and inconstant mothering, he looked to his wife to "always be there," responding to his need for her. This need to have her as his exclusive property was destructive not only to Mrs. Fielding but also to their children. In many respects, he could never accommodate "sharing" her with his own offspring. He lived with this conflict partially by identifying with his children: He would give them the "close family life" that had been withheld from him in his childhood. At the same time, he could bear little real intimacy with his children. He would be with them, but neither talk to nor understand them.

This highly isolated, patriarchal family structure began to erode as the children matured. The wife could not confront Mr. Fielding on her own, but became increasingly vocal in her complaints as she found allies in the two eldest children. They, too, chafed under their father's controlling style and his demands for a family-centered existence. The mother and eldest son became particularly close, often in opposition to Mr. Fielding. As a conflict between father and son escalated, the boy precipitously left school and moved to another town to work. Of all the elements of Mrs. Fielding's current bitterness toward her husband, the issue of his "driving our son from home" evokes the strongest feelings.

The remaining children are rather open (when seen individually) about their negative feelings toward their father. In their view he neither understands nor cares for them, but instead demands that they enact prescribed rituals. Mrs. Fielding is increasingly feeling a sense of her own strength and freedom. She states an unwillingness to hurt her husband by leaving him or acknowledging her growing interest in other men, but seems unable to keep her rage from occasionally surfacing. In joint discussion she is alternately deferential and derisive. (Example: Mr. Fielding says, "I don't like to go out at night and leave the children with a sitter." Mrs. Fielding, voice dripping with sarcasm, responds, "We certainly need to hire a baby-sitter when we have a sixteen-year-old daughter.")

They are now leading almost parallel existences. The Fieldings' mutual sex life is virtually nonexistent. Both mother and children are finding increasing interests outside the home while Mr. Fielding sits at home, drinks beer, curses the neighbors (with whom he has had many open conflicts), and broods. Always withdrawn, he is becoming noticeably more isolated and morose as the years pass. He is disappointed in his work life, where he has neither progressed nor found support and friendship. He has remained in a semiskilled spot for many years, while his age-mates have either become supervisors or assumed more-skilled and higher-paying positions. He feels estranged from and hostile toward the younger workers around him whose values and behavioral styles he finds incomprehensible or repugnant. He reports persistent somatic distress at work that can be relieved only by the use of tranquilizers.

In this context, Mr. Fielding conceives of his wife and children as his last refuge in a hostile world: If his occupational life and peer relations have not worked out, he "at least has (his) family." He thus finds it necessary to deny the anger and familial dissolution that is clearly underway. There are indications that Ed must have registered, on some level of awareness, the nature of his wife's increasing disenchantment with their marriage, but he is unwilling to acknowledge this information. He does, however, speak wistfully of his chance to become a career Marine, rather than marry when he did. He describes this choice as his "big mistake," since he would currently have served enough time to retire. These reminiscences can be seen to have at least two thrusts. The "corps," he implies in much of what he says, would have been a more satisfying family in which to have lived. The above bespeaks some awareness of that which he vehemently denies: Things have worked out badly for him at home. The yearning for retirement in a 42-year-old man is also a barometer of his current degree of verve and energy.

The defining quality of Fielding's response to this pattern of decline is his denial that anything is wrong. He sees himself as "average" and "normal" with no specific problems. He closes the interview on a note of curiosity about why we would be interested in someone like him, "who has no problems."

The Middle-Class Integrated Type

Tom Conley is a respected civic leader in a town south of Boston, a town where his family has prospered for five generations. His father was a local family doctor for forty years, while his uncle, Tim, was town mayor throughout Tom's childhood. Tom idolized his uncle and during his first year at Harvard he began working with him in the area of city planning and renewal.

Through his contacts, Tom got to know many of the local political and business leaders. In fact, he became so heavily involved in the development of a new town master plan that he dropped out of Harvard in the fall of his sophomore year. He continued taking evening courses at another college, but, much to his father's chagrin, never returned to a full-time education. When he was 23 his uncle died, but Tom continued to work actively with his successor. The following year Tom accompanied him to a meeting of urban mayors and was offered an exciting job at the Department of Housing and Urban Development.

He tells this story as if his selection was quite accidental, something which happened over cocktails at a hotel bar. In fact, it is testimony to his rapid self-education, drive, and capacity to engage others instantly and effortlessly. His performance during our interview was truly impressive. He could have gone on entertaining us for hours with humorous anecdotes about local history, interspersed with quotations from Shakespeare, the Bible, or whatever source might add ironic depth to his conclusions about his life and local events.

One of his stories is indicative of both his relationship to his wife and children and his interpersonal style. He delights in a sort of puckishness, a refusal to take himself seriously. At his oldest son's graduation ceremony the boy was the center of attention. He received highest honors and was chosen valedictorian of the class. At the celebration following the ceremony a group of parents gathered around and someone asked Tom what he had done to produce such a successful son. He announced that he had discovered a secret that accounted for everything. "At this," he said, "people gathered in closely. Here was the man who knew! There was the evidence—a valedictorian. What was the secret?" When he had everyone's attention, Tom announced, "The secret is that from the time John was born until he was twelve years old, I stayed away from home and had nothing to do with his upbringing."

Tom's work did, in fact, take him away from his family for much of this period. Aside from his work at HUD, he started a travel agency and developed an interest in the restoration of old buildings. He retained a dual interest in national, long-range planning and local restoration projects, and he was quite successful. His job required him to spend four days each week in Washington, permitting little contact with his family. When he was home on weekends he was continually involved in travel transactions and politics although it is true he was able to show continued interest and affection for his sons. None of them ever doubted their father's love, and time together was treasured. He involved them in activities they all enjoyed and learned from. During the home interview he showed us several pictures of his restoration work. One of the accomplishments of which they are proudest was the restoration of an historic inn in the mountains of New Hampshire which the family now uses as a vacation home.

Over the years he has remained actively involved in urban planning, and recently he was appointed chairman of a commission charged with designing and reconstructing an old section of South Boston. In discussing this project, he seems to engage all parts of himself. He draws on his knowledge of community needs as well as his appreciation for local history. He makes use of his knowledge of construction and renovation, trying to insure that the valuable older buildings are appreciated and preserved, while at the same time being sensitive to the current needs of children, families, and older people. This project represents a vehicle through which Tom is attempting to come to grips with many of the issues we associated with generativity.

As a side project, Tom has decided to complete college, planning to acquire his degree from night school before his son graduates from Dartmouth. However, the obvious competitiveness he feels is but one thread of his motivation for returning to college, for he deeply values the new learning he is acquiring in history and literature. It also cannot be separated from his working through his feelings toward his now-deceased father: his attempts to integrate the values and aspirations that his learned father held for him and which Tom now holds for his own son.

Although he has spent a great deal of time away from home, his relationships with his children and wife, Jean, seem to be warm. His three sons, John, 19, Steven, 15, and Michael, 12, idolize him. In some of the adventures they describe at the mountain inn Tom seems to play the part of an adolescent gang leader. An example is a ski trip last year in which Tom drove the boys to the inn in a near-blizzard, then spent the weekend with them trying to track down deer in snowmobiles. He regularly takes them to Bruins hockey games, where they sit in a box seat provided by one of Tom's friends.

His wife was frank and bitter about the distance that developed between them over the years. But about three years ago they confronted their problems, joined a marriage encounter group, and began rebuilding communication. Since that period she claims that the relationship has improved immensely. And certainly the interviewers had a sense of warm acceptance between them during the home visit.

However, not everything has gone smoothly for Conley. His rapid career start had generated high expectations. When he lost his position through a change of administration and subsequent department shake-up, he became quite despondent. For a long time Tom harbored hopes of finding a comparable position, but his lack of formal credentials became a real obstacle. Conley eventually faced up to the altered circumstances and set out in other directions. He cannot, however, keep from reflecting on the opportunities he might have pursued if given the chance to use the planning and administrative skills gained through years of first-hand experience and increasing responsibility.

The energy expended in his work took its toll on his family life, as did the years of distress and readjustment that followed Tom's career reversals. Married to an Italian wife with strong family ties, he discovered many points of disagreement after the first years of marriage. Tom seems to have been both patriarchal —demanding his freedom and his wife's obedient domesticity—

and somewhat adolescent. He asked his wife to play an almost maternal role in this period, giving him some solidity and control which he could then resist.

The second son, Steven, became embroiled in this relationship when it was at its worst. Physically, he is overweight, like his mother, but he spends a great deal of time with his father working at the travel office. He apparently played a mediating role in some of the conflicts, voicing his mother's cautious stance when with his father on adventures, and defending his father's actions to his mother. Conley has become aware of Steven's role and jokes about it to him. But he has also made efforts to minimize the turmoil and foster both his marital relationship and the son's development by involving him in the travel business.

What seems to characterize Conley's response to life stresses and challenges is an active, confronting style. He is sensitive to the internal and external signals of distress and can respond creatively to them. There is a complexity to the man, apparent in his humor, his multifaceted response to familial problems, and his expansive energy in holding together a diverse occupational life. His educational and familial background have helped a great deal in making him so resourceful. Well-placed friends and family connections have been invaluable at critical turning points. Such assets seem to be present in most cases of transcendent-generatives we've found. However, as some previous cases have shown, they are not sufficient to insure a satisfying middle age. And as the next case shows, they may not even be necessary.

It is important to point out that Tom is not in any sense perfect, either in his eyes or by the criteria of a developmental schema. He remains somewhat the brash, immature jokester, hinting that issues of conflict-of-interest at work had been neatly sidestepped for a number of years. He openly acknowledges some impetuousness and rebelliousness in his choice to end his formal education—a choice which may have limited his career possibilities. We cannot say that time has shown a uniform progression through life issues, but rather that his adulthood has been characterized by an increasing self-acceptance, feeling for others, and capacity to define what is important to him. In the context of such awareness, areas of difficulty or conflict can be worked on or acknowledged as part of the self without evoking feelings of self-hate or stagnation.

The Working-Class Transcendent-Generative

Bill Mayne is a 42-year-old man who specializes in heating and electrical construction work. At one point, his large colonial-style house was a run-down duplex, but he has remodelled it into a single home until now it resembles a cover picture for *House Beautiful*. The living room is furnished with wall-to-wall carpeting and plush colonial-style couch and chairs. A large, color television is the focal point. The large kitchen is completely modern, with built-in appliances surrounding a butcher-block work table. Bill drives a new air-conditioned pickup truck with a closed-in back where he keeps his tools. He recently bought a new Ford Granada for his wife and son.

The home is situated in an old neighborhood near where Bill's wife, Marie, grew up. They have mixed feelings about the neighborhood. Marie can walk to shopping areas and to the subway, and she knows many of the older families. But recently some "minorities" have moved in, giving the Maynes less of a sense of being at home. The public school, Marie claims, is now "99 percent black" so they have moved their children to the local Catholic school. They are particularly wary of the people in a nearby high-rise apartment where "families are always coming and going." But, all in all, they like where they're living. Bill says there are problems everywhere, so there is no sense in moving. Yet as the interview progresses we get the feeling that he would rather live in the country but concedes to his wife's wish to live near her family and old neighborhood. The Maynes appear to be less ethnically prejudiced than conservative, preferring the familiarity of neighboring families they have known for years to newcomers of any sort.

Bill comes across as a careful, shy man committed to a traditional life style with a traditional division of labor at home. At times in the early parts of the interview, he seems to be choosing words carefully, sometimes appearing to use phraseology to which he is unaccustomed so as not to appear illiterate to the interviewer. He sits with his arms resting on his legs, as if not to take up too much space. Marie, in contrast, is expansive and relaxed. One arm rests comfortably on the back of her chair while she scans the room, taking in the whole scene.

Bill first got interested in heating systems after high school, through a correspondence course. He learned more about them while in the Navy, then increased his knowledge through "trade magazines" and learning on the job. Twice he attempted to start his own business but found it wasn't profitable. He says the failures were upsetting, but it's better "not to have to worry about bookkeeping, paperwork, and complaining customers." His wife reports that she is "very glad he got out of it. I didn't like the long hours and the worry. Tension would build up at home." Although he is currently satisfied working as foreman on large jobs with a construction firm, he hopes to go back to running his own business on a "semi-retirement basis" in the future.

Bill enjoys supervising younger men. Rather than order them about, he prefers to work along with them and to set a pace that they emulate. Two nights a week he teaches apprentices in the union school. To keep abreast of new developments in the field, he attends an annual week-long training session sponsored by the union at a nearby college.

The husband-and-wife relationship appears to be both mutually gratifying and very much in balance. Though they live near Marie's family, their friends are people Bill met at work. He seems introverted in relation to her expansiveness, but she portrays herself as dependent on him, having been "pretty naive when we first got married." He pays the bills now, though she has handled finances in the past. Bill can laughingly say, "She thinks her way works better, because she pays the bills on time." But they both seem to find his style of handling the family finances quite acceptable. She is totally responsible for housework, and until recently didn't have employment outside the home. A few months ago, encouraged by Bill, she took a job as a receptionist at a travel agency. Bill is continuously remodeling the house. In the past he has rewired the place and rebuilt the heating and plumbing system as well as having redone the interior. The interviewer comes away with a sense that each partner feels a degree of personal effectiveness.

Bill has pieced together a life structure that works for him. He feels at home in his work. He has a relaxed and organized relationship with his wife. His children respect him and would like to emulate him. And his relationships with younger workers and his students suggest that he positively values himself and the skills he has acquired.

However, two factors differentiate this working-class version of integration from the middle-class version. First, there is a strong tendency to define success in terms of material acquisitions and "buying-power" rather than in work accomplishments, community activities, or interpersonal relationships. These men seem extremely gratified by having achieved the American dream of having enough money to get whatever they want. Their pride is invested in their homes, cars, boats, furniture, and other acquisitions that represent concrete, undeniable evidence of their effectiveness. There is also a defiant element to these acquisitions, an assertion that these men can have all that the upper middle class aspires to without having to be an "organization man" or wear a white shirt and tie. On the other hand, their relationship to their work and family seems rather low-key, even neutral in affect.

Second, they avoid introspection. They do not express doubts, fears, or any sort of ambivalence about themselves or their families. In one extreme case of this type the interview even seemed to be pervaded with a sense of smugness. We asked a successful contractor how he disciplined his son and he replied, "He always got what he wanted." When we prodded further, he repeated himself and asked, "Why shouldn't he? I could afford it." When asked for his feelings about his son's problems at high school involving truancy and defiance of teachers, the father merely shrugged his shoulders and said, "I never finished high school and I did okay."

Conclusions

Looking beyond the quantitative data at the case studies, we have found validation for our typology. Though each man is unique, the expected patterns of disorganization or integration, denial or openness, are apparent in the cases chosen from each quadrant. The reader should not be misled by our decision to present composite cases of crisis, denial, and integration from each social class. We present an upper- and lower-class man from each type in order to make the pattern of experiencing middle age more apparent. However, as indicated earlier, not all the types are equally likely to occur in each social class. The resources of the upper class make comfortable adaptation more probable for that group. The deprivations of lower-class existence make symptom-formation (psychological, psychosomatic, and physiological) more frequent in that stratum, with a common pattern of defensive rigidity and denial being utilized in the attempt to live with and disguise these accumulated wounds.

As the quantitative data suggested, the man's style of response to the midlife transition reflects not only his personality, history, and life circumstances, but also the influence of culture. Social class, in our society, affects education, residence, and style of life to such a degree that working- and middle-class men represent virtually separate subcultures. Membership in either subculture, and its associated definitions of one's self and what is worth valuing, seem to saturate the modes of living we have been describing. Within each subgroup men identify themselves as winners or losers depending on how close they come to that culture's ideals, very few manifest the detachment to define a more unique set of meanings or aspirations for themselves. Within this context, it is not surprising that the most "successful" men by external criteria (highest status, income, education) have the greatest chance of feeling positively about their lives as they enter middle age. Not only does this system produce a great many casualties, it also seems to be distortive of what we normally regard as human values. Most men, middle or lower class, devote much of their lives to acting out stereotypes of what they "should" be—caught up in subcultural ideals of strength, power, control, and competitive success. It apparently requires a rare individual to transcend these issues in order to experience intimacy and selfhood.

This culturally induced one-sidedness also has an internal stimulus. Investment in the relatively impersonal world of work and consumption relieves these men from dealing with painful, personal conflicts. In listening to their biographical accounts and in examining their experiences outside of the work role, we gain a fuller sense of these conflicts and their influence at the midlife transition.

In the next chapters we expand our picture of these areas of our subjects' lives. Making use of both quantitative and qualitative data, we explore the relationships of the different types of men to their wives, children, parents, and friends.

Chapter 6

HUSBAND AND WIFE
RELATIONS AT MIDLIFE

Both cross-sectional and longitudinal studies have found that marital satisfaction declines as couples approach middle age, reaching its lowest point when adolescent children are leaving home.[1,2] Whether the focus is on sexual relations, intimacy, or overall satisfaction, the data point in the same direction: Middle age represents the doldrums of marriage in our culture. However, after the children are gone the relationship recovers, with scores on marital satisfaction tests approaching those of the early stages of marriage.

The distribution of power in the relationship follows a different curve. In the early stage the power relationship tends to be close to egalitarian, with the husband having slight dominance over the wife. When young children arrive, the wife loses ground, reaching her low point in influence over major decisions. But as the children approach adolescence, she begins to gain more power.[3] As the couple advances into middle age, the wife is perceived as the force to be reckoned with in the family.[4] The husband, on the other hand, is seen as a passive, contemplative background figure.

Despite this descriptive agreement, past research has not been particularly illuminating in helping us to understand the changes in marital satisfaction. Pineo, for example, explains the decline at middle age as "regression towards the mean."[1] That is, immediately after marriage, satisfaction is at its highest point because couples choose each other on the basis of affection. Since the score is highest then, later measures of satisfaction have nowhere to go except down. Just as the student who performs at his peak on one test will be likely to score lower (toward his mean) on the next, the couple that scores at their peak on a marital satisfaction test are likely to score lower later. Such regression toward the mean may occur, but it does not explain why satisfaction scores decline steadily as couples approach middle age. Nor does it account for Rollins and Feldman's[5] finding that intimacy and satisfaction increase again after the children have been "launched" (left the parental home).

In this chapter we examine our findings on the changing emotional and interpersonal aspects of marriage as couples enter middle age. Drawing on both our quantitative and qualitative data, we will attempt to better describe and conceptualize these transformations of the marital relationship during middle age.

Quantitative Findings

Close to 90 percent of our middle-aged men were married when we contacted them. The average number of years married was 15.1. Most of these men have children, the average age of the oldest child being 14 years. The fact that most couples have children means that the husband-wife relationship can only be understood in the context of their relationships with their children.

Looking at our quantitative measures of the marital satisfaction, we find support for previous research. Following Duvall's[6] model, we break the life cycle of the marriage into seven stages (see Appendix 2). During the newlywed stage prior to the arrival of children, we find that the majority of men (73 percent) report being "very close" to their wives. With each advance into a new stage of the marriage the proportion reporting feeling very close declines, reaching the lowest point (43 percent) when adolescent children are leaving home. Thus, the general trend in our data is similar to that found by Pineo and Rollins and Feldman.

However, not all our groups show the same pattern of decline in satisfaction. The decline is most precipitous for the lower-class subjects, especially the punitive-disenchanted (Quadrant 4) type. In this latter group only 24 percent report feeling very close to their wives at middle age, and 45 percent believe marriage is simply not rewarding after twenty years. In contrast, among our transcendent-generative (Quadrant 2) group, 80 percent see marriage as rewarding and 55 percent report feeling very close to their wives.

The fact that some groups show more decline in satisfaction than others may provide some clues about the kinds of stresses on the marital relationship that lead to dissatisfaction. How do we understand the finding that working-class deniers report the least marital satisfaction during middle age, and that the transcendent-generatives report the most? What are the stresses that impinge on or alter marriage at middle age? And why are some groups better able than others to cope with them? To answer these questions we turn to our qualitative data.

Qualitative Findings

Looking at our follow-up interviews of twenty families, we find four main shifts that characterize marriages at midlife and that are associated with alterations in the marital relationship:

1. The general increase in the wife's relative power and autonomy;
2. The wives' collusion in protecting their husbands' defensive mythologies about themselves;
3. The habitual utilization of each other in a psychological and attitudinal division of labor, each requiring the other to provide the emotional qualities that they feel they lack or choose not to exercise;
4. The loss of control over adolescent children.

The processes centering around the fourth factor are so complex that we have devoted a whole chapter (Chapter 7) to them. In this chapter we deal only with the first three factors.

The Increase in the Wife's Relative Power and Autonomy

Previous studies have found that the wife's relative power in decision-making declines during the period when she has pre-school children in the home.[6] It is during this period of intensive involvement in the home that she reaches the lowest point of impact on major household decisions. However, as she moves toward middle age a number of converging events result in a relative increase in her power.

First, as the children get older, she is likely to begin moving in wider circles outside of the home. Close to 50 percent of the women in this country return to work during this period. The increased resources that the wife controls in the form of money, sense of competence, and information result in increased influence at home.

Second, the most common family constellation is one in which the wife is the central point in the communication network of the family. We repeatedly hear that both the children and the husband see her as the one who "understands them" and who listens to their central concerns. She is perceived as the primary source of warmth and support in the family unit. Her position also gives her an opportunity to form coalitions with the children that add to her impact on decisions about purchases, moves, vacations, and so on.

As a result of these factors she begins to gain power. Neugarten and Gutmann[7] indicate that this development reaches a point in later middle age where the wife is seen as both a powerful and impulsive figure, whereas older males are seen as contemplative and passive. Implicit in and contributing to this process is the fact that the wife becomes more autonomous during this period. These bids for autonomy are often made concrete in the form of a return to school or work.

Although we did not gather quantitative data pertinent to the distribution of power in the household, our qualitative observations support the past findings. Sixty percent of the wives in our follow-up interviews were working either full- or part-time. Even in those cases where the wife was not working, the majority still showed signs of gaining influence and autonomy. In one such case the husband's failures at gambling were used as a lever to help her increase her own influence and autonomy. The husband's mismanagement of family funds was taken as proof that she should control their budget, doling out an "allowance" to him each week. In another case, the wife's increasing involvement with her extended family and at the V.F.W. Woman's Auxiliary provided her with an undiscovered sense of strength and competence, leading to far more assertiveness in confronting her husband and participating in family decisions.

The changing distribution of power in the home generally

placed strain on the husband-wife relationship, particularly in the sense that the husbands resented the challenge to their power. One hundred years ago a man may have expected to come into full patriarchal authority as he moved into middle age. Such expectations remain a vague and often unstated part of our subjects' concept of ideal family patterns, while in reality the father begins to lose power at this time. As husband and wife negotiate a more egalitarian relationship, there tends to be an escalation of overt conflict. This renegotiating of the relationship, involving a period of changing demands and questioning of the meaning and value of the marriage, often results in reduced satisfaction. Once the transformation of the relationship is complete, a period of restabilization may follow, when the couple once again feels more committed to and happier in the relationship.

The Protective Pattern in Wives of Deniers

As the wife moves toward increased autonomy, she often does so in a delicately balanced climate of deception. Mother and children often form secret alliances—deceiving, laughing about, and simultaneously protecting the husband. The wife recognizes the husband's efforts at maintaining an image of himself as patriarch. She seeks to avoid confrontations that might undermine his belief of being in control of the family and having their support and respect. Consequently, the relationship becomes entangled in a web of deception. The couples seem more intent on not hurting or on protecting each other than on sharing experiences.

This sort of truce is utilized partially to control the anger felt toward the man by his wife and children. No longer fearful of him, as they often reported themselves to be earlier in the family's history, the accumulated resentment can become an explosive force in the family. It is expressed through jokes among the children, half-whispered asides, and an awareness that "the old man" no longer has the emotional strength to stifle them. This very weakness evokes a sense of disdain, but also of pity. The rest of the family tends to tacitly agree on a strategy of helping the father to save face, yet of demanding their rights in those areas they regard as crucial.

The protective pattern is particularly common in our pseudo-developed type. The deniers tend to be either utterly dependent on their mothering wives or overtly tyrannical in their homes. Their behavior seems rarely to fall between the two extremes. In both cases the wife plays a collusive role, aware of how arbitrary the husband's behavior can be, but assisting him in maintaining whatever script he is trying to present to the world. They act as a team, with the wife working hard to play the proper role in assisting her husband to maintain his presentation of self.[8]

Ed Fielding illustrates this pattern in dramatic form. Soon after meeting his future wife, he was driving a group home from a party. He could not see her face because she was in the back seat, but as the group talked and laughed, he felt more and more attached to her. Symptomatically, he "fell in love with her voice." From this early point, he attempted to disembody Joan and attribute to her only those characteristics he craved. Not only his image of himself, but his definitions of his wife and children, are dominated by his fears of isolation and abandonment.

An important facet of Fielding's development was his insecurity in his relations with women. His mother died when he was three. His father remarried but soon divorced a second wife. He has a clearer recollection of his father's third marriage; Fielding feels he was treated as a burden, the tolerated stepchild. His father and stepmother were frequently out of the home, leaving him to deal with managing his stepbrothers. His memories of childhood show clear continuity with his current stance. Having felt rejected and unable to control his world in the past, Ed felt compelled to create a world where he had absolute dominance.

When he married, he vowed to "create for his children the home he never had." Part of what was meant by this vow was, of course, that he hoped to obtain his own ideal mother, giving to himself the nurturance and constancy of which he had felt deprived. In the beginning Mrs. Fielding fit the desired pattern. She maintained the home meticulously and was there whenever the children or Mr. Fielding returned. She had not learned to drive because Fielding "didn't think it was necessary."

However, as she approached middle age, Mrs. Fielding began declaring that she found the arrangement intolerable. Although she would placatingly support many of Fielding's demands and constraints when he was present, covertly she supported her son who, as an adolescent, was in revolt against his father.

As she talks about her early years, one gets the impression that Mrs. Fielding saw herself as a quite dependent young woman.

Fielding's domineering style and isolation of the family may have been experienced as a relief for Joan, even if it was also unpleasant and difficult on other levels. However, as she moved through her thirties, she felt more able to confront the world and her husband in assertive ways. She finally learned to drive, then took a job at a local travel agency. Both steps were of much symbolic importance to Joan, proving to her that she could be competent and courageous. Mr. Fielding's response to his wife's expansiveness was to withdraw from outside friends and social engagements even more. He attempted to rationalize his depression and rage —fury at his wife for escaping his private space—by invoking beliefs about the evils and dangers outside that might impinge on the home. He speaks in an almost paranoid way of malevolent baby-sitters or potential vandalism on the part of a neighbor.

This pattern of marital evolution is repeated in several of the other denial cases. The wife initially accommodates herself to the husband's vision of family life as a circumscribed, patriarchal world. She may even express a sense of losing herself in the demands of her children and husband. However, as the children develop toward adolescence, she forms a close alliance with them. An underground resistance to the father develops. There is open compliance to his wishes while resentments are shared more covertly. Finally, the wife makes bids for autonomy: a job, more contacts with friends, resistance to changing residence, etc. She becomes a more assertive force in the dyad. Usually she will protect the husband's vulnerable facade of patriarchal controls, but sometimes she will ridicule and attack him, or simply ignore him. The precondition to this revolt seems to be a growing sense of freedom and maturity as the wife approaches the end of her child-bearing years.

While changing cultural expectations about women's roles and women's psychology may feed into these shifts, they are also part of a more universal pattern of changes over the life course. Cutileiro's study, *Portuguese Rural Society*,[9] explores the increasing freedom of women as they move beyond their childbearing years. This increasing freedom and social power can only be granted, in terms of the local folklore, because of the diminished threat of women's sexuality. Women must be controlled and confined when defined as young and desirable: Their turn for dominance comes later in the life cycle. These same dynamics seem to operate in many of the couples studied.

The husband's response to these shifts is most typically to avoid conflict and pretend nothing is happening. The Brodskys, for example, arrange a work schedule in which they hardly meet except for a few hours on weekends. Mr. Brodsky tells us that his happiest moments of the day are when he is out walking alone at daybreak. He shows little awareness of the implications of such statements, insisting that his marriage is as good and close as it ever was, despite the fact that he feels most alive when his wife is still asleep, having worked until midnight the night before.

As described in the previous chapter, both Fielding and Brodsky first presented themselves as remarkably free from feelings of dissatisfaction, physical or psychological problems, or difficulties at home or work. In their presence the wives do not often challenge these patently distorted perceptions. But in private, both wives told of serious physical problems and difficulties in the marital relationship or with the children. The husbands are treated as if they were vulnerable, fragile entities that might be shattered if the full truth were openly confronted.

Another form of the protective pattern occurs in one of our open-crisis cases, the Wilsons. Bob makes no effort to hide his sense of physical and psychological vulnerability. He sees himself as a failure, both economically and professionally, and he has recently had health problems. His wife expresses discontent with their failure to achieve those things they wanted and expected from life. However, rather than display anger toward her husband, she finds herself in an uncontrollable rage at her son, who is breaking away from the home and making bids for autonomy.

As is typical of the open-crisis cases, the Wilsons' relationship began in a romantic phase. At least as they reconstruct it, they felt and acted very much like a model couple for the first ten to twelve years of their marriage. They found the process of getting started in their adult lives a sort of adventure. Mild adversity and lack of affluence seemed almost like fun, especially because they were regarded as transitory experiences. Moreover, the other young couples they knew were often in similar straits, making them feel that their problems were "normal." The future seemed endless: Bob would eventually "find his niche." Sarah took pride in making do, and functioning as "super-mom." Her child-centered activities appear in retrospect to have served as a diversion, permitting her to ignore the growing disparity between their joint expectations and the evolving reality of their lives. Thus, as her sons moved into adolescence and began to resent her involvement in their lives, Sarah felt startled by what she began to observe. Her neighbors' and friends' husbands had become established, many of them making double and triple Bob's income. They drove new cars, had saved for their children's education, and took vacations to Europe or Mexico. Not only did the Wilsons lack these things, it was becoming obvious to Sarah that they might never achieve them.

It was about this time that Bob began having great difficulty dealing with the younger social workers at the hospital. Sarah expressed envy at the comparative successes of her middle-class neighbors. But, as we have discussed, her dissatisfaction does not spill over into direct conflict with Bob. Instead she manifests a protective stance toward him. Her bitterness is directed to her son, while her husband is treated with sympathy and support. When she declares, in describing her son, that "your years of help and work don't seem to yield anything," it is clear that she has condensed both father's and son's sins into a single figure.

It is Sarah who "pays the bills" and "sees that the gas tank is filled." In the family interview she acted as the spokesperson. Even direct questions to Mr. Wilson evoked answers from Sarah about how "they" felt. About their relationship Mr. Wilson says, "She and I fit like an old shoe from the start." At least part of that feeling must stem from her willingness to meet his dependency needs and her capacity to avoid expressing any anger or criticism toward him. She seems, both by our observations and Bob's testimony, to be a consistent source of support and uncritical acceptance for him. Moreover, she acts as his link to other people, keeping them from being estranged from their extended families and community. These connections are among the few sources of support and pleasure that have remained viable for them.

Prior to their marriage, Sarah had gone to business school for a year and then worked as a bookkeeper. After the marriage, Bob reports that he urged her not to work, explaining that "A woman shouldn't work if she doesn't have to." However, last year Sarah took a part-time job again doing bookkeeping work for a local trucking firm. She is home when everyone needs her, she says, yet she has found a way to get out and try new things. By adept juggling of her time she attempts to maintain the equilibrium and create the illusion that nothing is changing. Bob's willingness to accept both her employment and that illusion is indicative of his increasing sense of decline. He no longer demands that he be the "breadwinner," requiring only that his altered status is not focused on.

The increased power and autonomy of the wife—either through her assertiveness or the husband's abdication—is one factor that places strains on the marriage during middle age. Among the deniers, the strategy for dealing with the transformation of the relationship is consistently one of avoidance and pretense. In many cases the wives collude in maintaining the pretense that neither the men nor their relationship is changing. The collusive strategy itself may then become a source of strain, as the members of the family alternatively experience and conceal the reality of their situation. They come to resent the inauthenticity required by their shared distortions. The transcendent-generative, who deal more openly with stresses, are more likely to confront the implications of the changing familial structure and adapt in ways that open the possibility of greater satisfaction. At the same time the very openness implies a real willingness to examine the relationship and to risk marital dissolution. There is far less willingness or interest in maintaining a devitalized relationship, but rather an investment in working toward a fulfilling later adulthood.

Psychological Division of Labor

A distinguishing characteristic of the husband-wife relationships at midlife appears in all of our response types. This is a marked division of emotional labor, a mutual utilization of perceived characteristics in the other to complete, balance, or bolster the self. If the husband is adventurous or reckless, the wife is cautious and timid. If the wife "has a temper," the husband is "easy going" and passive. If the husband is a pessimistic "grouch," the wife is an optimist, always seeing the brighter side. Only two of our twenty follow-up cases consisted of husbands and wives who resembled each other in their modes of relating to the world and each other. Both were from the transcendent-generative quadrant and seemed less in need of this sort of stereotyping and mutual utilization.

This finding is unexpected given all the negative findings of studies of need complementarity in mate selection.[10] Aside from Winch's study of 25 couples,[11] there have been only a handful of findings that support his contention that "opposites attract." Most studies of young couples indicate that people who are similar in background, values, and needs tend to fall in love. However, virtually none of the reported studies deal with middle-aged couples. Since the question has been "Why do people fall in love?" the research has focused on engaged and young married couples. If we assume for a moment that these findings are essentially accurate, they suggest an interesting dynamic. People tend to feel more comfortable with, and marry, others who share their view of the world. Conservative men marry women uninterested in risk-taking; people who like to socialize seek each other out and men choose marriage partners who share their values about family, male-female differentiation, and so on. This pattern of reinforcement through shared perspective appears to shift and become far more complex over ten to twenty years of marriage. If our subjects are representative, husband and wife move increasingly toward adopting differing postures. Their relationship becomes an externalization of inner misgivings or debates. Husband and wife both consistently and predictably take the position of being the foil, adversary, or one who "balances" the excesses of the other. In this section we will describe and discuss some of the stylistic and emotional complementarity and suggest a developmental explanation for the finding.

Examples of Complementarity

In Chapter 5 we introduced Tom Conley, an aggressive, extroverted real estate developer. He likes to portray himself as daring and adventurous, in the thick of the action. He describes his wife as his "anchor." In decision-making episodes he is often expansive and tends to overextend himself, while she resists.

They also define separate territories for their activities and dominance. The house is Jean's space; she decides on how it will be furnished, how time will be scheduled, what food will be served. Tom is more comfortable and takes control when the family travels, at his business, or at their vacation home. Both the decision-making process and the territorial preferences underline the reciprocal ideas Tom and Jean have developed in their marriage. A competent, shrewd manager in the outside world, Tom plays out the impulsive adolescent with his wife, inviting her to act out the role of his slightly outraged but amused mother.

Her stoicism in the face of his erratic behavior seems to stimulate Tom's adolescent stance. Jean seems to expect that she will be the matriarch to a houseful of teen-age sons.

Examples of this interactional process are abundant. One afternoon Tom was late coming home from work. Jean reported being worried when she still hadn't heard from him by dinner time. Suddenly he arrived, towing a dilapidated sailboat behind his station wagon.

"I didn't know what to say," reports Jean. "Here we were short of money, having just moved into our new house, and he drives up with a sailboat." Tom involved the boys in fiberglassing the boat and soon after the purchase he announced he was joining the local yacht club. "We shouldn't be doing this," said Jean. "Our budget won't support a yacht and the style of living that goes with it." But they joined, and the club has now become the center for family social life, especially for the adolescent children.

Recently Tom decided to end Jean's complaints about the size and shape of her kitchen. He sent her away over a weekend to her mother's place, and involved the boys in reconstructing the whole kitchen. "I didn't even want her around," he says. "She would only fret and interfere when it came time to knock down the wall or tear out the cabinets."

As Steven, the second oldest son, has moved into adolescence, he has become identified as an extension of the mother's cautious side. His brother laughs when telling of how Steve will walk around and check all the tires before getting into the car. And he simply refuses to go into the sailboat unless everyone is wearing a life jacket. It is interesting that this son, who is the one who works most frequently with the father on his projects, has taken on his mother's "anchor" role vis-à-vis the father. Jean herself reports that she used to be "much more adventurous." But, living with Tom, she feels she has to be "the one to keep a lid on things." Tom's expansive, energetic, and engaging style leaves little space for those in his nexus to express similar traits. His sons decline competition with him in this dimension, appearing more withdrawn and restrained in their own activities.

A second example of such complementarity comes from Ed Fielding, a man more closely fitting our "denial" type. Both Joan and Ed agree that he is the "one with the temper." And indeed, he seemed to be able to mobilize anger at the drop of a hat, even during the interview. At one point he told a story of how an elderly man once asked his wife to dance at the local V.F.W. club.

> *"I was sitting right beside her, . . ."* he said, *"and he never even looked my way. Just took her two hands and asked her to dance."*
>
> *Ed didn't say anything at that point. But then, ten minutes later, the elderly man came over and asked his wife to step out in the hall. In retelling the story, Fielding got up and walked across the kitchen.*
>
> *"I got up,"* he said, *"and walked over to the door,"* his anger mounting as he squared off facing the refrigerator.
>
> *"Hey buddy! How about it, huh?"* he says, with a threatening gesture towards the refrigerator.
>
> *"How about it?"*

Even in the kitchen with the interviewer, three months after the event, Joan seemed to shrink visibly as she watched Fielding dramatize the event.

In disciplining the children, Fielding plays "the heavy" while his wife plays the part of soothing hurt feelings. He acknowledges that he "overreacts" to the children so "they don't have the same kinds of problems I had growing up."

Conversation with Joan reveals that she feels a need to "control her temper because he gets so violent." Fielding only recalls her losing control twice. At those points she retreated to her bedroom where she slammed the closet door repeatedly until she calmed down. Prior to the marriage she had been shy and dependent, almost unable to express emotions. Fielding's needs for support have drawn out her nurturant qualities and led her to be more assertive. He utilizes her relative psychological stability to keep himself in check, while his lability serves as a channel of expressiveness for her, releasing her from the pressure to display her own emotionality. At the same time, his neurotic incapacities and symptoms give her a sense of relative strength, of being needed.

Factors Contributing to Differentiation

One possibility is that this emotional differentiation, or at least a perceived receptivity to playing such roles for one another, was a factor in bringing the couple together in the first place. But, as mentioned earlier, the many studies indicating similarity of needs and defenses leading to attraction make this seem unlikely. It would seem to us more plausible, given this data, that the couple begins the relationship sharing many similar values, needs, and defenses. They also may share similar ambivalences about how to deal with stress and difficult decisions. However, if each responded in the same way to a crisis, for example, breaking

down and crying or losing their temper, they would find themselves in competition and immobilized. There is a certain degree
of efficiency in each member of the couple drifting toward acting
out one side or the other of conflicting impulses. Rather than
both being immobilized by conflict or both competing in expressing the same needs and feelings, both are free to act, and yet
express their ambivalences through the actions of the other. The
presence of the other acting out one impulse (for example, anger)
frees the person to act out a conflicting impulse (for example,
fear). Usually the differentiation process is guided by the stereotypes of male and female in our culture: The male is aggressive
and the female is passive and conciliatory. However, the reduction
of ambivalence and competition can just as well be resolved by
reversing the stereotypes.

A second factor contributing to differentiation may be the role
stereotypes of husband and wife. After marriage, the different
role demands and routines exert a pressure toward different styles
of relating to the world, with one or both of the couple drifting
away from earlier ways of relating. Keniston finds such a pattern
when studying the parents of alienated youth.[12] When the couples
meet they support each others' urges to rebel against traditional
sex roles and move toward artistic occupations. However, economic needs and the demands of children lead the fathers to drift
toward more lucrative jobs while the mothers invest their energies
in the home, with subsequent further differentiation in values and
behavioral style. In Keniston's cases the role demands seem to be
a key factor in the movement from similarity to differentiation.

A third factor that may contribute to the differentiation is the
process of interpersonal negotiation described by Leary.[13] People
are responsible for their own interpersonal environment, argues
Leary. Through coaching, reinforcement, and punishment, one
person leads another to play out a part that is complementary to
his or her dominant needs. Thus the dependent, masochistic
person eventually coaxes people with whom he interacts into
playing an assertive, exploitative role toward him. The spouse
may resist being cast in such a role, but eventually succumbs to
the implied demands of the other. Fielding seems to have created
just such a situation with his wife, recreating his customary interpersonal nexus by evoking the rejection he fears but expects.

A final factor contributing to the polarization of couples is more
characteristic of the denial type. One component of the denial

pattern is a tendency to project undesirable characteristics onto others.[14] This process seems to be more pronounced in heterosexual relations governed by traditional sex-role stereotypes. The stereotypes form a foundation for such mutual projection, drawing sharp distinctions between the "me" and the "not me."

The net result of the interpersonal processes and role demands is that each partner can serve as a projective receptacle for the other. Where the male is seen as dominant and aggressive, the female is seen as dependent and nurturant. Where the male is seen as adventurous and courageous, the female is seen as timid and delicate. Each projects onto the other those traits and urges they deny or find undesirable in themselves, minimizing ambivalence and internal conflict by delegating parts of the self to the other. This process clearly is congruent with the defensive style described in our denial types, who attempt to present a facade of positively valued masculine traits to the world.

Regardless of the factors leading to differentiation, one consequence is that each partner comes to see himself or herself as unlike the other, sometimes to a point where their mutual interdependence becomes a source of anxiety rather than a defense. The process of differentiation can push the partners into an increasing sense of distance from each other and alienation from their own feelings.

In the long run, this differentiation process can lead to an increasing sense of stagnation and a decreasing sense of satisfaction in the marriage. Particularly in denial types, the polarization, coupled with a lack of communication, leads to the man experiencing his wife as alien and dangerous. She cannot be counted on to confirm the view of the world to which he clings. In the transcendent-generative type, open communication and receptivity to the wife's changing needs and perceptions may mitigate the differentiation process and lead to a renewed sense of connectedness and sharing at this stage of marriage.

Conclusions

We have found several recurrent dynamics that contribute to dissatisfaction with the marital relationship in middle age. First, the wife's bid for autonomy at this point is likely to lead to rearrangement of the expectations, power configuration, and emotional infrastructure that has characterized the relationship through the child-rearing years. As the children move from being dependent on her to being her allies, the mother's autonomy and power increase steadily. The changes require renegotiation of the relationship and create uncertainties that may undermine marital satisfaction, particularly for the man. His unchallenged hegemony over the family unit must be relinquished.

Second, the projective pattern most common in our denial types undermines both open expression and mutual respect between husband and wife. As the husband confronts the stresses of maturation by retreating into the denial pattern, his wife colludes with him, supporting his distorted perceptions of himself and his interpersonal world. She often enlists the children in this collusion, supporting the fragile illusion that the father is the potent patriarch, while instructing the children how to get what they need without disturbing the father's attempts to maintain his facade. The distortion of communication and implied disdain and hostility toward the man ultimately undermine the relationship between husband and wife. Each encounter between them becomes an anxiety-ridden attempt not to reveal their feelings and perceptions to each other.

Finally, emotional differentiation results in husband and wife habitually polarizing in their styles of dealing with crises and decisions. As each becomes entrenched in a pattern that is the inverse of the other's style, he or she comes to experience the spouse as alien. Rather than being able to utilize each other in a "balancing" way, each comes to feel increasingly hostile to the other's way of experiencing the world.

Past research has shown that once the children leave home, satisfaction with the marital relationship can recover. On the basis of our findings we suspect that in part the recovery is due to the acceptance of a transformation of the relationship. The encroachment of middle age creates a set of conditions that facilitate this transformation. Besides contributing to the increased autonomy for the wife, the loss of the children may contribute to and even necessitate alteration of the emotional balance of the family group. For example, the loss of Bobby in the Wilson house will upset the emotional economy of the household. When he is no longer immediately available to function as the symbol of this father's shortcomings for Sarah, there may well be more direct confrontations between Sarah and Bob. This could lead either to a more overt sense of disenchantment, or to a more reality-based acceptance of each other. This interplay between marital dynamics, children's maturation, and parent-child relationships will be explored in greater detail in the next chapter.

Endnotes

1. Pineo, Peter C., "Disenchantment in the Later Years of Marriage," *Marriage and Family Living*, vol. 23, 1961, pp. 3–11.
2. Rollins, Boyd C., and Harold Feldman, "Marital Satisfaction over the Family Life Cycle," *Journal of Marriage and the Family*, vol. 32, February 1970.
3. Blood, Robert O. Jr., and Donald M. Wolfe, *Husbands and Wives: The Dynamics of Married Living* (New York: Free Press, 1960).
4. Neugarten, Bernice L., and David L. Gutmann, "Age-Sex Roles and Personality in Middle Age: A Thematic Apperception Study," *Psychological Monographs*, vol. 72, 1958.
5. Rollins and Feldman, *op. cit.*
6. Duvall, Evelyn M., *Family Development* (Philadelphia: J.P. Lippincott, 1962).
7. Neugarten, Bernice L., and David L. Gutmann, *op. cit.*
8. Goffman, Erving, *The Presentation of Self in Everyday Life* (New York: Doubleday Books, 1959).
9. Cutileiro, Jose A., *Portuguese Rural Society* (Oxford, Eng.: Clarendon Press, 1971).
10. Tharp, Ronald, "Psychological Patterning in Marriage" in *Man, Woman and Marriage: Small Group Processes in the Family*, edited by A. Grey (New York: Atherton, 1970).
11. Winch, Robert F., "Another Look at the Theory of Complementary Needs in Mate Selection," *Journal of Marriage and the Family*, vol. 29, November 1967, pp. 756–762.
12. Keniston, Kenneth, *The Uncommitted: Alienated Youth in American Society* (New York: Harcourt Brace Jovanovich, 1965).
13. Leary, T.F., *Interpersonal Diagnosis of Personality* (New York: Ronald Press, 1957).
14. Adorno, Theodore W., Else Frenkel-Brunswik, Daniel J. Levinson, and R.N. Sanford, *The Authoritarian Personality* (New York: Harper & Row, 1950).

Chapter 7

PARENT-CHILD RELATIONS AT MIDDLE AGE

Our children are often the measuring rods that convey to us that we are aging. Psychologically and physically we may not feel any older, but our children's yearly changes in height, interests, and maturity are objective indicators of the years going by. One of the most concrete indicators that a man is reaching middle age is the presence of a teen-age child. It is when the family reaches what researchers have called the "launching stage" of development—that period in which children move from the parental home and begin to establish themselves more or less autonomously—that the parents are most apt to be wrestling with the problems of becoming "middle-aged." In this chapter we examine the evolving relationships between parent and offspring as the child moves through adolescence. These relationships are typically conflict–ridden, involving problems of parental disengagement and adolescent separation. We will be particularly interested in the effect of children on the parents' changing sense of themselves and in the use of children in working through ambivalence about themselves and who they have become.

This aspect of adult maturation is perhaps the most complex that we deal with in our study. The man's experience of his role as father and his relations with his children change as he approaches midlife. At the same time, his children are themselves changing and the family as a group is also undergoing metamorphoses.

Stages of Family Development

A widely used schema for viewing this evolution has been developed by Duvall,[1] who sees the family as going through nine discrete stages. The stages of particular relevance for our study are the fifth through the eighth:

V. Family with adolescent offspring (oldest 12–16, possibly younger siblings)

VI. Family with late adolescent (oldest 16–20 until first child leaves home)

VII. Family as launching center (from departure of first to last child)

VIII. Postparental family, the middle years (after children have left home until father retires)

Most of our midlife respondents find themselves in stages V, VI, and VII, but this variable is class-linked. More affluent professionals tend to marry and have children later in life than blue-collar or unskilled workers. Physicians, for example, may feel that they are just starting their careers in their mid-thirties and hence have young children at home when they are 40 or 45. With these reservations in mind, we can still describe the tasks and issues families typically face during the father's midlife period. These have been described by Barnhill and Longo[2] as they are associated with the transitions from stage to stage in Duvall's scheme.

Problems during Transitional Stages

V-VI: Experimenting with Independence. As the oldest child is moving into late adolescence and young adulthood, the family needs to allow independent, counter-dependent, and adult strivings to emerge. Increased mobility, sexual experimentation, and the need for making initial career plans require a gradual lessening of the primary ties with the family of origin.

VI-VII: Preparations to Launch. Acceptance of the independent adult role of the first child requires several role transitions in order to permit the child to leave the family nest and move toward developing his or her own home.

VII-VIII: Letting Go—Facing Each Other Again. After many

years of family focus on child-rearing, it is a problematic transition for the parents to let go of the children and to face each other as husband and wife alone again. This requires, as well, that the children be able to leave the parents to themselves. In addition, the development of the new roles of grandparent (for the parent) and parent (for the children) in a new three-generation arrangement is generally required.

From the father's perspective, the demands of these transitions can often be emotionally traumatic. The capacity to acknowledge, respond to, and even gain gratification from the child's turbulent maturation is far from universal. Even fathers who have related well to young and pre-teen-age children may find great difficulties in these later stages of parenting. These difficulties can be better understood if we recognize the meaning and psychological functions of the father's role.

Resistance to Loss of Authority

Many men in our culture attempt to utilize the family as a special zone, one in which they wish to feel both in control and loved. This position of dominance and centrality is in sharp contrast to their more usual experience in the outside world: one of being peripheral and dominated by circumstance. The child's maturation and turning outward become a challenge to this arrangement, be it real or fantasized. The father often then reacts as if his last vestige of power and selfhood is being stolen by the growing child. The struggle that ensues is one of ownership and control. The parents may feel that the culture (for example, "the neighborhood," "the school") is the enemy, subverting their child and, through him, the household. They work to keep these alien elements removed from their home. At a later point (the VI-VII transition), the child may come to be viewed as the enemy, either as a traitor to the family group or as a subversive force that is bringing the larger world into the sacred family space.

Some of the general overviews of family life indicate that parent-child relationships are most problematic when children reach adolescence.[3-5] Our own data clearly indicate that both middle- and lower-class fathers become more authoritarian in their attitudes toward child-rearing as their children move into adolescence and the launching stage (see Table 7-1). They express agreement with such items as, "Whatever some educators may say, 'Spare the rod and spoil the child' still holds, even in these modern times" and, "A child should not be allowed to talk back to his parents, or else he will lose respect for them." These increases in rigidity and punitiveness may be indicators of the fathers' emotional difficulty in dealing with the adolescent.

Redefining Family Culture and Parental Identities

These feelings of the father stem from the meaning and uses the family has had for the father in his earlier adulthood. Most observers agree that the modern family has become a highly specialized unit, performing expressive emotional functions for its members rather than being a unit of work or political life. It can be a retreat from the pressures of everyday life where one is able to shed the pretense of external roles and express intense emotions that must be controlled outside the home. Nor is it merely suppressed feelings engendered in the external world that emerge in the family context. The privacy and intimacy of the home also create an environment where parents may gain gratification through temporary regression in play and involvement with young children. Immersing oneself in the play and fantasy of the child can be not only an escape from adult pressures, but also an important means to enhance personality integration through spontaneous self-expression.

Benedek[6] elaborates on this line of thinking by suggesting that parents rework resolution to critical issues throughout the life cycle by actual and vicarious participation in the development of their children. This process can help the parent to achieve a greater sense of self-confidence and autonomy. However, Benedek's analysis focuses on the early preschool stages of life. The possible extension of her theory to adolescence remains to be explored. Some findings suggest that adolescent children and their middle-aged fathers confront similar identity issues. Their simultaneous attempts to confront these issues may exacerbate the difficulties of both, while also creating the possibility of mutual stimulation and support.[7]

In the families studied, this turmoil was partially attributable

Table 7-1 Life Cycle Stage and Attitudes Toward Child-Rearing (low score means high authoritarianism)

Stage of Life	Middle Class			Lower Class			Total		
	Mean	s.d.	N	Mean	s.d.	N	Mean	s.d.	N
I Young unmarried men	2.41	.35	20	2.45	.38	35	2.44	.37	55
II Newlywed men without children	2.29	.48	8	2.31	.35	17	2.30	.40	25
III First child preschool age	2.37	.40	24	2.15	.47	30	2.25	.45	54
IV First child grade school age	2.32	.41	61	2.14	.49	38	2.25	.45	99
V First child high school age	2.31	.48	17	2.01	.40	19	2.15	.47	35
VI First child beyond high school (launching phase)	2.12	.47	44	2.19	.45	51	2.15	.46	105
Total	2.29	.44	174	2.21	.45	200	2.25	.45	374

	F	P
Class	2.54	<.10
Stage	3.20	<.01
Interaction	1.94	N.S.

Note: Single, separated, and divorced older men were not included in their analysis. With regard to the family life cycle, they are "out of phase."

to the consistent parental identification with their children. The parents often attempted to enlist the adolescent child in the re-working of their own resolutions to adolescent life-cycle issues.

The wife of one of our transcendent-generative men illustrates this pattern well. She has six children and in the interview spoke many times of her difficulties in young adulthood adjusting to the sense of siege from the demands of the babies and her sense of feeling "hemmed in by the four walls." In describing her some-what rebellious seventeen-year-old daughter, she states:

> *Jan has no head on her. She crosses us. I'm afraid for her. She is like me, but she can't stand me saying that. 'Let me go!' she says. She wants to take care of herself too much. My mother used to say I was cursed. I was drawn to the anti-hero. Oh, I plead guilty! During the ages of 13 to 19. And I had many riles with my husband. She hates to be told she is like me. But I'm damn glad I was like that. It's healthy. Jan sees me as old-fashioned in the same way as I saw my mother.*

The mother's identification with the daughter is obvious, but whether she approves or disapproves of her behavior isn't at all clear. This kind of ambivalence on the part of parents is part of the confusion generated as the parent identifies with the child, relives that stage of life, and alternates between encouraging the child to escape the fate the parent chose and demanding that the child validate the parent's identity by following the same path.

We observed a fairly consistent unwillingness on the part of the parents to let their children move out of the matrix of emo-tional and symbolic meanings the family had developed. For many of these parents the home and family had become the emotional center of their existence, the terrain in which they felt some control and some capacity to express their own needs and desires. The children were crucial elements in maintaining these feelings, serving as foils, companions, and an obedient and ad-miring audience. The children's growing need and desire to escape this relationship—to become involved with peers and the wider culture—seemed often to engender a sense of abandonment and fear in the parent. The child's attempts to separate himself from the family and from the place assigned to him in the family culture generally meet with parental resistance.

As the adolescent tentatively reaches for individuation and independence, a separate self, he must also confront his own conflicts over continued desires for protection and nurturance. The parent is called upon, despite his own sense of loss, to help the adolescent find the capacity to give up some of his dependency on the family. In order for the child to achieve a sense of separateness and integrity, he or she may show severe opposition to parental values, beliefs, and life style. Underneath this rebellious negation is often a fearful need to remain within the protection and control of the parents. We commonly see a picture of heightened anger, conflict, and mutual disappointment. Both parent and child had expected more love, understanding, and consideration from the other than was forthcoming. This anger and parent/child warfare may be acknowledged or unspoken. It is sometimes a transitional phase and in other instances it becomes a long-term obsession, locking both generations into an emotional morass.

Many children find it most difficult to make the break and may postpone or avoid establishing their own life structures. In some of the families studied, children into their twenties continued to utilize their parents as primary emotional supports and sources of guidance. In so doing, the children avoided the problem of individuation and insulated the parents from the costs of letting go.

Our objective in this chapter is to present some of the common modes of adaptation to the problems of this stage of family development. These modes are illustrated through discussion of our composite case studies. We will first look at the range of adaptation and responses in the pre-launching phase family, then move on to look at types of parent-child relations during the launching phase.

The Pre-Launching Phase

The pre-launching phase of family life is characterized by relatively controlled conflicts between parents and adolescent children, as well as between husband and wife. Changes are clearly emerging as both mother and children experience rapid gains in autonomy and greater investment in the world outside the home. The parents tend to react to these changes with a mixture of gratification, resentment, and alarm. While it is nice to see your children grow strong and effective, these changes raise the specter of "losing them." The initial images of this loss are focused on their corruption by the outside world. Fathers see their children as becoming "too fresh," wearing clothes that are "too tight," and developing "the wrong values." As they fear seeing their children abandon them, psychologically and physically, the father often responds by attempting to close ranks, to see the family as an encampment in a hostile territory. The inside (home, family, ethnic group) versus outside ("strangers," the broader community, social change) dichotomy becomes exaggerated as the struggle intensifies. Working- and lower-middle-class men, particularly, engage in a battle to negate the outside world and all forms of change. This negation seems to represent a denial of their own aging as well as an attempt to forestall their children's independence. They are struggling to retain an image of the patriarchal home, and of their own potency and dominance over wife and children.

General Characteristics

In the families visited, the issues of dominance, autonomy, and dependency held center stage. Most families seemed to deal with each issue in an exaggerated way: mother *or* father being defined as in control; children being given either carte-blanche or no discretion—treated either as infants or as if they should be self-sufficient. This exaggeration is indicative of the conflict and confusion the families were experiencing, the need they felt for unambiguous resolutions to these struggles.

In this poorly understood drive for stability, the process of role differentiation and stereotyping discussed in relation to marital dynamics becomes part of the broader family evolution. Children tend to be typecast as "the good one" or "the troublemaker" and are often identified as being "just like" one or the other parent. Whatever characteristics the adolescent manifests seemed to be exaggerated or distorted in the family's definition of them. Minor rule violations are taken as concrete proof of criminal tendencies; small failures or successes are seized upon as harbingers of the child's future.

A heightened resentment or distrust of the environment is also repeatedly expressed by families in this phase. Some of the fury and repression directed at the child seems to derive from a feeling of impotence in controlling the world he or she is entering. The parents repeatedly expressed preoccupation with the drugs, sexuality, self-indulgence, and delinquency their children were being exposed to. "Growing up" was seen much more in terms of such rebellious experimentation than positive acquisition of skills or resources. Consequently, most of these parents worked to slow down their children's maturation—to keep them at a level of development where they were more home-oriented and dependent. As might be expected, this led as often as not to the rebellious response the parents were attempting to forestall, particularly with sons. In some of the families observed, however, the parents' efforts did seem to produce a prolonged preadolescent stance on the part of at least one child in the family.

Many middle-class couples are likely to move to the suburbs when their children reach school age, if they haven't done so already. They see the schools and neighborhoods there as places where their children can be more insulated from the "corrupting" influences of the city. In this environment they are also more able to institute and maintain routines that reflect their values. In a sense the family culture emerges and comes into full flower in this pre-launching phase.

The Fieldings

Because of his lack of financial assets, Ed Fielding has remained in what he sees as an undesirable neighborhood. He lives a few blocks from a large foundry. He tells us that across the street is a family where "the father drinks all the time and beats the kids for no reason." He says that many divorced women live nearby who "let their children run wild." Delinquency and drugs are common, the Fieldings report, and they see themselves as protecting their children from these influences.

An episode a few years ago with their son John illustrates processes that occur late in the pre-launching stage. As they described him, John seemed to have been immature as a sixteen-year-old, anxiously seeking parental approval rather than actively dealing with heterosexual and peer relations. His father disciplined him with spankings until he was thirteen.

During the spring when John was sixteen, the vice-principal

in the high school called about John's week-long absence from school. His teachers were not worried because he did well in school. But they wondered if he were sick. Mrs. Fielding was puzzled, since she had sent him off to school each day that week.

When questioned by Mr. Fielding, John at first denied skipping school, then admitted what he had done. He had a chance to get a job as a gas station attendant if he came to work every day for a week and learned the routines. He had skipped school to learn the job.

Mr. Fielding told the vice-principal not to worry about punishing John, because he would take care of it. The vice-principal assured him that he did not intend to punish him, but Fielding insisted on it. The punishment—grounded for two months to the house after school and on Saturdays and Sundays. And he was not allowed to have his stereo in his room. The punishment expresses Fielding's desperate attempts to maintain control and keep his son from the temptations of the larger world. As he told the story, Fielding expressed regret that he could no longer use physical punishment and had to resort to less direct means. Repeated episodes of this sort eventually led to the son's exit from the home when he was eighteen.

It may be recalled that the Fieldings now have two younger daughters remaining at home, ages thirteen and sixteen. Fielding would rather watch television each night than go out, because he does not like to leave his children with baby-sitters. "You never know who you can trust," he says. "The newspapers are full of stories of violence and negligence."

His image of himself as protector of the home and his daughters' innocence is expressed as criticism of the neighborhood, where "a lower class of people" is now moving in. They have transformed a peaceful enclave into a hostile, threatening place. This is just another illustration of the evil forces around his family, of people "who don't know how to keep to themselves and respect other people's rights." He complained about a neighbor's car that was blocking his driveway one night. Soon afterwards, he reports, someone had dumped a milk shake on his car. Ed takes such incidents as proof of his many fears and resentments. Aside from being distrustful of his own wife and children, he is quite convinced that he is surrounded by people lacking in morality and self-control. His sixteen-year-old daughter is still not allowed to date. He personally takes her to and from school dances, requiring her to leave by 10:30 P.M. Joan and the girls clearly think these requirements laughable, and try to find ways the eldest can have some social life without directly confronting Ed. It is also obvious that their patience is wearing thin, and that more overt conflict over this issue is in the offing.

At the moment, however, Joan's control is at least partially disguised. She permits the girls social outings Ed knows nothing about, buys them clothes of which he would clearly disapprove, and generally lets them know that their father is unreasonable. It should, however, be pointed out that she shares many of her husband's concerns, albeit in more muted form. Joan, too, believes that the local high school is filled with "potheads" and teen-age pregnancies. Although her techniques differ, she, too, feels a tremendous pressure to give the girls sufficient guidance and control so that they won't wind up in trouble. While Ed wants to see his two youngest as children rather than adolescents, Joan is more clearly conflicted. At times she sees them almost as adult companions, filling some of her own needs, and at other times treats them like her "little girls." In either event, she expresses a real need to keep them close to her, dreading the situation of being left behind with Ed as all the children move on to their own lives and interests.

Mr. Fielding vigilantly attempts to protect his family from the contaminating influences he sees around them. He has attempted to build a nurturant, though rigid, cocoon, and for the most part the younger children have stayed within the closely guarded bounds. The controls generate strains, but the younger children have not yet rebelled against them.

The Pre-Launch Cocoon

The Fieldings, like other families in this stage, illustrate common patterns: (1) The mother is closest to the children and is the most important influence on them. She sets the specific boundaries that enclose their behavior. (2) The father seems to back up the mother's rules, although he is beginning to get more involved in discipline as the crimes and punishments become more complex. (3) Both mother and father express an almost desperate need to "keep" their children. However, the forces that threaten to disturb the cocoon and "overwhelm" the children are located primarily "outside" rather than seen as maturational pressures or demands. Only constant vigilance and strong controls can "protect" the family from them.

Group Processes during the Launching Phase

As we move from the pre-launch to the launching phase of family development, the dynamics of parent-child relationships tend to become more complex and often more dramatic. Direct confrontations and challenges—which may have been simmering beneath the surface—come to the fore and families often seem to be engaged in open warfare. These battles go beyond the level of dominance between family members, and reflect a more profound debate over values, identity, and the definition of their shared reality.

Role relations and family culture have crystallized by the time the children reach adolescence. Procedures for decision-making have been worked out and the grooves are well worn. Through repeated interactions the couple and children have built a shared conception of their social world that is taken for granted by family members. Beliefs about family relations, the neighbors, school, and other community groups are as solid as the walls of the house —and are just as much a part of the taken-for-granted reality as the family members orient themselves to the world. "Stay away from so and so," or "Go to this person if you want that," are prescriptions that are carved in stone in the family culture. These assumptions and guidelines form boundaries around the thinking and behavior of family members. It would take a major anomaly to unfreeze this family paradigm and lead the family members, for example, to seek out a new doctor, grocer, political party, or religion.

However, the paradigm has been largely determined by the parents at an earlier point in their family's development. Since that time changes in the culture and social structure have occurred. The family may have changed their position in that structure by moving up or down on the class hierarchy or simply by moving to a new neighborhood. For example, parents who are children of immigrants may find themselves now living in a world quite different from the ghetto they grew up in. They formed their images of husband-wife relations, politics, religion, and so on in response to the beliefs and characteristics of that setting. Now, as their child goes through adolescence, they are in a very different social landscape—perhaps in a suburb, a small town, or a high-rise apartment.

Boundary Testing

As the adolescent child wrestles with the problem of finding a place for himself in that social landscape, he may act as boundary tester for the family culture. In adapting to the new environment, he takes on and brings home values, ideas, dress patterns, and hair styles that are not accepted in the family culture. Although he may feel himself as a separate person simply trying to find a place in the world, he is still a member of the family group. And as he tries on new identities, he is likely to become more or less deviant in relation to the family culture.

The parental response to the boundary testing is critical to their own development at this stage as well as to the adolescent's. As the child brings home new ideas about sex, religion, or art, the parents may respond defensively or they may go through a healthy reevaluation of their own conceptions. If they are able to openly sort through the new patterns being fed into the family, they may enrich their culture and find wider opportunities for fulfillment for themselves and for their younger children. At the very least, open consideration of alternative life styles may lead to a deeper appreciation of and commitment to their own values. If they respond defensively and actively try to suppress any signs of deviance, they not only squelch the adolescent's development of a sense of identity, but also reduce their own chances for growth through new inputs into their culture.

Deviance

Essentially, we find that the boundary-testing adolescent can serve the same positive functions for the family that the deviant serves for other social groups. Rather than being a sign of family decay or disorganization, a limited amount of deviance can serve positive group functions. The conflict over the behavior brings members of the family out of the ruts of everyday life and into communication with each other, shared feelings of outrage and hostility bringing the rest of the group closer together. Through communicating about the behavior and expressing shared values, the members replenish understanding of and commitment to old values. The confrontation with the "not us" makes "us" more clear. Thus a limited amount of deviance ultimately contributes to family organization and vitality.

The constructive effects of deviance can be even more profound under some conditions. By acting out shared but suppressed impulses in a family or group, the deviant may contribute toward the members working through anxiety-provoking ambivalence or conflict. For example, the adolescent deviant may act out the shared wish to be more independent of an oppressive mother or father. On one level, the other family members may be outraged, while, on another level, they identify with the deviant. The other children may respond to the behavior, reconsider their own timidity to parental domination, and by vicariously participating in the conflicts, they work through their ambivalence about the constraints in question. In this process many parents may also begin to grapple with the ambivalent needs that require them to behave in certain rigid ways and engage in ritualistic conflicts with their children.

In the families studied the adolescent child often served such a function for the family group. He or she acted out desires suppressed by the parents. Overtly, the parents acted to control him; covertly, they identified with an encouraged the behavior. In some cases the situation may lead to classic double-bind communication,[8] the parents saying both, "If you do it, I'll punish you," and "If you don't do it, I'll punish you." Finally, the parent says, "If you try to talk about this dilemma, I'll punish you. Now go to it!"

In other cases this split in levels of communication may lead to the kinds of mystification and "efforts to drive the other person crazy" that Laing[9] and Searles[10] describe so well, where parental injunctions and definitions are pressed on the child but unacknowledged for the adolescent.

Scapegoating

These tensions over the integrity of the family boundaries are manifest in several prominent issues and dynamics that recurred in the families in our study. The first of these dynamics is scapegoating, the use of one or more of the children to symbolize or divert conflicts from within or between the parents. The parent, that is, experiences an undesirable trait or unacceptable feeling of his or her own as if it were coming from the child. The child then becomes the target of parental hostility which he cannot escape. He is induced by the parents to behave so as to justify their anger. As a number of writers have discussed,[11] this process of scapegoating can become a central facet of the family's culture. This is especially true when the child is used to stabilize relations between the parents, as when all the anger they might evoke in each other is instead focused on one of their offspring. The parents may then reinforce and validate each other's distorted view of the scapegoated child since he is serving common needs for them both. In this context, other siblings are easily induced to join in the aggression toward the victimized child. The family's stability as a system can come to depend on this definition of one child as "bad" or "different," and the concomitant illusion that all other family members are well and harmonious.

More commonly, the scapegoating process is less extreme and more fluid, different children occupying the position at different points in their development. The process, moreover, is not entirely negative or destructive. In projecting onto and then battling with their children in a relatively controlled, loving context, the parents may rework neurotic positions and gain a sense of closeness with their offspring. The scapegoated child may gain a greater sense of autonomy in the difficult process of differentiating his own intentions and feelings from the attributions of his parents.

Idealization

A second dynamic may be characterized as the opposite to scapegoating—idealizing the adolescent child. In our cases the child was sometimes viewed as an agent of redemption by one or both parents. In this role the adolescent became the agent charged with fulfilling dreams that had been shattered or left dormant in the parents. The child's successes can be defined as a vindication of the parent, as providing compensation for a marred or incomplete identity. Again, identifying with the child may strengthen the parent. The parent who dropped out of school may vicariously return, or one who abandoned interests in art or business may gain new inspiration.

In both the scapegoating and idealizing relationship the parents are relating to the child through projective identification. However, in the latter case the child is seen as possessing positive traits and crossing desirable boundaries. In both cases the parental identification with the child may generate positive change in the parent's sense of self. Old aspirations, fears, and urges are reawakened and may lead to attempts at altering the self. Of course, the resulting turmoil may also lead to defensive withdrawal. Our primary points are that such projective identification is more or less ubiquitous and that it represents a stimulus for parental self-examination and change.

Transformation of Role Relations

A third group level process that occurs during the launching phase is the transformation of the parent-child role relationship. As the child moves toward independence, the parents must relinquish their authority. This process often does not unfold with ease. Parents are ambivalent about giving up their dominance, and children are often ambivalent about giving up dependency. The ambivalence leads to vacillation and overreaction on both sides. The child may become counter-dependent, attempting to prove he or she does not need guidance or support by openly staging confrontations and deliberately doing what the parents forbid. The parents, in turn, may stage their own confrontations over money, attitudes, or behavior, attempting to prove they are still in control, "not just another pal." The ambivalence on both sides may continue into young adulthood, until the child is established in the adult world.

Taken together, these processes generate a great deal of conflict during this period. Disengagement from intimate relationships is never easy. Disengagement coupled with individual and family dynamics that lead to reconsideration of the self-concept can be particularly problematic.

The Dynamics of Disengagement

Before grounding these issues in our case studies, it may be helpful to discuss some of their general manifestations in a number of families. Launching-phase parents continue to regard the family as a sanctuary, but express greater acceptance of the idea that their children must now involve themselves in the outside world.

If, in the previous phase, parents generally fought against their childrens' demands for autonomy, we are now just as likely to hear the opposite complaint: They are "too clingy" or "hanging on too long." Both parent and child wish to set the timetable and terms for the child's separation, believing that they can avoid the pain of this transition through such control. In terms of midlife issues, the launch phase is far more poignant than the earlier parental stages. Parents tend to see a kind of summarizing or index of their own success in their childrens' adjustment or accomplishments at this point. If the children are somehow "doing well," the parents feel vindicated. If they are having difficulties, the parents are often bitter (blaming the children), guilty (blaming themselves), or both. While all parents know these emotions, there is a sense of finality to them in launching-phase families, as if they are seeing a final outcome. Once again, these exaggerated perceptions are linked to a need for closure, as if the parents can no longer tolerate the upheavals and ambiguities of their childrens' movement into adulthood. Unable to control their offsprings' fate, they seem to crave an answer: How will it turn out? The need for such an answer further stimulates the tendency for stereotyping the offspring. An extreme image of each child as strong or weak, mature or immature, is further crystallized, and the family acts to lock each sibling into the assigned role. The fathers seem to have become more emotionally involved in these dramas as compared to earlier phases, as marital tensions become increasingly intertwined with issues of the children's separation.

Perhaps unexpectedly, the midlife father displays greater emotional difficulty in letting go of his children than does the mother. These families' homes and clutter graphically illustrates that this period is indeed transitional for them: Children's bedrooms are left intact although unoccupied for a couple of years; pets and hobbies of earlier years lie about; pictures of younger families remain on pianos and den walls. The general sense conveyed by men in this period is one of slightly stunned loss. Old patterns of puttering around the house, or coming quickly home from work to be with "the family" persist, although there are no longer children nor so many tasks that require this attention. In contrast to the men's presentation of sadness and semi-pointless puttering, the wives seem ready and eager to begin a new phase of their lives with enhanced freedom and possible marital closeness.

Identity Threats and Strategies of Identity Maintenance

The compromise that emerges in many of the families between the mothers' push to move on and the fathers' nostalgic clinging to earlier patterns is the definition of the home environment as a harbor rather than the "fortress" of the previous stage. The home represents, that is, a place where the maturing offspring can return to find acceptance, nurturance, and a temporary respite from achievement pressures. The interaction between most parents and children is markedly different at this point, taking on a quality of adult-to-adult interchange. It becomes clear that parents are identifying much more directly with children in this phase, seeing themselves as young adults reliving earlier choices and struggles. This process of identification may combine with certain key events —like the engagement or marriage of the eldest daughter—to trigger a reawakening of earlier marital conflicts. If the women were, in the previous stage of family development, beginning to reassert themselves, their reemergence is now accelerated. In a number of families this evoked a sense of being thrown back in time. The marital tensions and unresolved issues of the pre-parental phase were remembered vividly, and the couples felt almost as if they were back where they had started in forging a relationship. However, this time around, the wives were far more determined to stand their ground.

This identification with the children and reworking of early adulthood choices tend to provoke heightened self-consciousness. Parents in this phase are much more likely to engage in reviews of their own identities, thinking through occupational choices, relations to their own family of origin, life styles, and their own definition of what is appropriate or possible for their generation. There is often disdain or derision expressed for "dirty old men" or for people who compete with their children rather than accepting their maturity gracefully. These tirades suggest a conflict over relinquishing the view of one's self as young and an effort to find a new generational self-definition that does not feel demeaning.

A second aspect of this close identification is the direct use of one or more of the offspring to relive the parents' unsatisfactorily resolved identity struggles. We were presented with numerous examples of situations contrived by the parents that virtually forced their children to reenact portions of their own biographies.

This might come out in the form of pressure to choose certain schools or occupations (money being used as the carrot and stick), pressures for daughters to marry early or not at all, or simply the attribution of certain characteristics to the selected child.

Quite frequently, this designation of one child as "just like mother" or father was tied to a process of scapegoating. To be "just like" is to be seen as a reincarnation of all the bad or problematic aspects of that person, often in magnified form. As an observer may recognize, parents can induce their children into playing out just such roles, as with the daughter who is told simultaneously that mother envies her attractiveness, freedom, and capacity to enjoy herself, but also that she is too wild and had better settle down. Despite the overt conflict associated with scapegoating, it may have an almost magnetic appeal to both parents and the designated child, the conflict between them representing the riveting emotional issue in their lives and a powerful bond between them.

In several instances the sexual tension behind the conflict and scapegoating was manifest. This can be a highly problematic and unspoken issue between fathers and their young adult daughters, producing ambivalent and contradictory paternal responses: Flirtatiousness, avoidance, anger, and protectiveness alternate and collide. This mixture of provocative battles (as a means of getting close) and mutual withdrawal (to sidestep the issue and the associated guilt) is an almost standard sequence between fathers and their maturing daughters.

Once again, the collapsed time perspective is characteristic of this dynamic, the fathers experiencing their daughters as remarkably similar to the wives they had courted some twenty years earlier. The sense of "reliving" the courtship feeds into the reemerging husband-wife confrontation, enhancing the likelihood of both overt conflict and rapprochement between husband and wife. Unfortunately, the scapegoated child may well be used, and induced to adopt extreme behaviors, as a way of relieving some of this marital tension. If husband and wife can both be angry with (or even obsessed over) the misdeeds of just one child, they can continue to avoid a possibly divisive showdown between themselves. The child must implicitly agree to serve this function, taking on some central characteristic of one or both parents and relieving them of responsibility for it. In this section we elaborate on two of the case studies introduced in Chapter 5 to illustrate some characteristics and variants of the interactional patterns in launching-phase families. The first is the Williams family, Tony Williams being representative of the working-class denial pattern. The Williams case is somewhat uncommon in terms of the continuation of male dominance. Bob Wilson, it will be remembered, is the middle-class social service worker in the midst of an overt midlife crisis.

The Williams Family

Tony Williams's efforts to maintain a stoic facade in the face of the stresses of midlife were described in Chapter 5, along with his tendency to see the source of his problems as outside himself. In this section we examine his relationship with his children, especially his second daughter, who seems to be a target for the tensions of this period. The dynamics of this scapegoating process are made more complex because of a tightly interwoven extended family, coupled with the nuclear family's pattern of avoiding confrontations with Williams. As we shall see, the tensions between the mother and mother-in-law as well as those between husband, wife, and older children are symbolized and played out in the relationship to the younger daughter.

In the husband-wife relationship the Williamses show a typical working-class pattern with the man presenting an image of complete dominance in the home. He handles the money, making major decisions, and handles difficult discipline problems. He presents himself as if he is imitating a "tough cop" or army sergeant, taking no nonsense or backtalk from the children.

Though Tony reports no problems with his son, we find that he recently dropped out of college. His father does not see this as problematic since the son soon found a job at a local delicatessen and has bought a new car. Currently, the family tells us with a mixture of annoyance and amusement, he uses the house as a "dormitory"; he has his own apartment in the basement where he comes home to shower and sleep, then goes off with his friends or girlfriend. His mother describes her son as "easy going, nice looking, doesn't like to be corrected, but he doesn't answer back." Not being oriented toward education or any career, he may be destined for a work life like his father's—scrambling from one low-skilled job to another to make ends meet. The parents seem tolerant of his current identity diffusion and occasional rebelliousness, as long as it doesn't lead to trouble outside the home.

The relationship between the daughters and the parents is more problematic. Mary, the oldest, is working as a secretary and making payments on her own car. She lives at home and pays rent, though she still shares a room with her younger sister. She reports that her father is a tyrant to live with. He picks on his wife for watching too much TV or sitting down to do a crossword puzzle. He dominates the downstairs with unpredictable moods that intrude on everyone. "He picks at everything." Consequently, Mary says, she gets out of the house as soon as possible in the evening. She used to sew after dinner, but Tony stopped her because it interfered with his listening to his police radio. One of his more annoying habits was to have her sit down while he read her crime stories from the newspaper.

As Mary explores the outside world and moves toward building an adult identity, she finds she must avoid her father. His attempts to intrude in and control her life seem connected to a reluctance to give up the patriarchal father role as well as a resistance to new cultural influences she might bring home. However, the concern with maintaining the father role appears to be most salient with this man. At one point the interviewer asks Tony how he disciplines his children. He dramatically extends his arm with his thumb pointing down, "The rule of thumb," he explained. His older children don't even attempt to get beyond the thumb to begin a dialogue about their deepest concerns. Instead they avoid him and seek means to keep the tension under control.

One factor that contributes to keeping the tension under control is the use of the younger daughter, Debbie, as a scapegoat. We first got an indication of Debbie's relationship to the family in the initial family interview when Debbie, unfortunately, was not present. Williams was fielding a series of questions about his illness in a bored, nonchalant manner. The interviewer then asked if his being around the house was a source of conflict now.

Williams shook his head to indicate "no." He started to say, "We don't have much conflict," when he was interrupted by Mary's sarcastic comment, "Except when Debbie comes home." For the first time mother, father, and daughter talked over each other with animation:

"She gets the house in an uproar."

"She only has to be home five minutes."

"She's different!"

Later, when we probed further, we discovered more about her meaning in the family. Debbie is identified as a "little biddy." As a young girl she spent a lot of time with her grandmother, Mr. Williams's mother, who lived in the apartment attached to the back of the house. Mrs. Williams reports that this grandmother kept wanting "to run both sides of the house." And now that she has died, the family seems to see Debbie in this intrusive role. The parents complain that after they have gone upstairs to bed Debbie asks them, "Did you lock the door?" or "Did you check the gas?"—the very anxieties her grandmother displayed. Another "problem" that marks her as different is that she never saves her money, but rather spends it on gifts for the rest of the family. These gifts only make them angry and uncomfortable.

To illustrate a typical episode of how "hopeless" this daughter is, her father tells a story of her recent accident. It was after Tony's health problems developed, and she went to the store to get him some cokes, potato chips, and other groceries. A few doors down some neighbors had their sidewalk pulled up and a trench dug to work on a water pipe. As Debbie was walking home with the groceries, lost in thought, she walked right into the trench. A bottle broke and a piece of glass cut her hand. The lacerated hand required surgery and stitches to repair, and a period of time in a cast. Her accident and debility during this period was a continual subject of ridicule.

When the mother and father were alone, the interviewer asked if they could elaborate on what they meant by Debbie being different from the other children. At first they described her physical differences—she is bigger-boned and heavier than her sister. They also described more of her intrusive pattern. "She sleeps with her eyes and ears open." During her operation for her hand, one eye popped open and couldn't be closed. This incident became another family joke: Debbie couldn't even mind her own business during surgery.

But, then surprisingly, they described a number of traits that might be construed as positive, though the family saw them as undesirable. Debbie works part-time as a clerk in a grocery store. Part of her being different involves her pattern of spending her earnings on gifts and surprises for the family. In fact, they point out, the night of her accident she was returning from making purchases for her father. One of her "problems" is that "she always worries about everyone else."

Debbie's place in the family is thus built around their primary conflicts. First, she is consciously identified with Tony's mother, an identification helped by her closeness to her grandmother. Mrs. Williams, as we have indicated, had a number of problems in adjusting to living in her husband's parents' house. Her mother-in-law continually criticized her housekeeping and child-rearing. The mother-in-law maintained her influence through her control of her son, Tony. Marie reports that, "When Tony came home from work, she always had a list of things to do waiting." Even now Marie tells us that Tony likes a spic-and-span house because that's the way his mother was. Now that the mother-in-law is gone, Marie seems to be displacing these feelings to her daughter. Her daughter is seen as constraining, the stranger and intruder in the house, one who is both a clown and a threat.

There is much evidence that the mother resents her husband's dominance—a version of the male patriarch that he acts out despite his inability to earn enough for them to set up their own home. The accumulated tensions from this relationship have been displaced onto the daughter. Certainly the characteristics of intrusiveness are also attributed to Tony. Debbie is being used as a surrogate mother against whom Marie and Tony can express resentments never fully shown to their parents. But the fact that other family members also engage in the scapegoating behavior suggests that Debbie's role serves multiple functions now, the pivotal one being a focus for the tensions generated by their efforts to appease Tony. She acts as the lightning rod attracting the hostility engendered by Tony's tyrannical demands. For the older children Debbie seems to represent the immaturity they are striving to leave behind as well as the intrusive "nosiness" of their father.

Whatever the source of the attacks, they are taking their toll on Debbie. Besides showing multiple signs of anxiety and social withdrawal, she makes repeated attempts at appeasement that only become the occasion for further attack. Debbie seems unable to alter her stance, or even realize what is happening to her.

We can only speculate on the long-range outcome of this process. The pattern of seeing Debbie as the family "loser" has already led to a poor academic career. And no one in the family expects her to do well on the marriage market, a negative attribution she has internalized. Once again the parents' need to involve their adolescent child in working through old tensions and controlling current strain are likely to greatly impede her development.

In the Williams case, the relationship to the younger daughter seems to be part of a pervasive tension centering around the mother and father's failure to achieve independence from their families of origin. Mr. Williams has had a disorganized and unsuccessful occupational career. Early failures forced him to remain dependent upon his father, whom he still idolizes. His disappointing career has been capped by an injury which, though not completely debilitating, he is exploiting for whatever gains are possible by refusing to go back to work until his lawyer has obtained the maximal benefits.

His complacency about his son's lack of ambition seems to be based on an identification with him. The son is being tacitly encouraged to reiterate the experience of his father. If the son is able to maintain self-esteem without seeking a sense of identity or fulfillment in work, then the father can see his own life pattern as validated. If the son were more successful than the father, it would be interpreted as an aggressive victory over him, one that the family could not tolerate.

Williams's major compensation in his own career failures has been his role as father. Here he maintains a facade of ruling patriarch. He attempts to use the sense of power derived from keeping his wife and children "under his thumb" to compensate for his inability to achieve independence from his own parents and fulfillment in the work sphere.

His wife's development parallels his. After being the "youngest child" in her family, she established a conflicted relationship with her mother-in-law, characterized by dependency and resentment. The tensions manifested in this relationship are now being focused on Debbie, the daughter who is identified with that mother-in-law. The use of this daughter as a surrogate mother has sharply skewed her development.

In this case, it is even more difficult to grasp Debbie's investment in enacting the highly negative identity she has in the family. In offering herself as a sacrifice and target for their aggression, she surely becomes the emotional center of their collective universe. This role also gives Debbie a sense of purpose and destiny. Her life as a "nag" and "loser" has been mapped out for her, relieving her of the tension of choosing her own existence. Debbie represents, then, a side of most of the adolescents in these families: a wish for parental cues as to who they are and who they should become. What is not evidenced by Debbie is the usual counter-wish not to be dominated by parental prescriptions.

The Wilson Family

The reader will recall that the Wilsons' oldest son was born just before his father made the decision to go to graduate school with the "great and glorious dream" of getting a degree in philosophy and becoming a college professor. His inability to meet the requirements led him to shift to a career in social service because "It was practical." It would provide him with a means to support a family. His early work in an employment agency was frustrating because of a limited income. He finally drifted into counseling at a children's hospital where he hoped to help disabled young people avoid the mistakes he had made.

When we met them, the Wilsons seemed confused and desperate. He has lost his job, having been fired because he and his younger supervisor have "different philosophies." To make matters worse, Mr. Wilson had a heart attack this year. But in spite of these difficulties, he and his wife see as their most serious problem the rebelliousness of their son, Bob, Jr. It was this son who appeared to be the emotional center of the home after Bob's early setbacks. His precocious development and successes as a youngster compensated for many of the disappointments. "He was number one," Mrs. Wilson reports.

In retrospect, it is obvious that this reliance on Bob, Jr. as the compensation for a lifetime of disappointments has become increasingly problematic in the last four years. At work, a younger man came into the office and Bob was asked to be his "guiding light." Prior to this he had been on his own: counseling families, running the evaluation program, "the chief cook and bottle washer." In the emerging team structure Bob found he had more and more differences with his co-workers. "I was the only one there who had on-the-job experience. I didn't want to overshadow this kid who had his first job as director. But his and my philosophies didn't get along." The conflicts finally culminated with Bob's dismissal. One of the factors still holding Bob back from looking for a job is a sense of being trapped. "Practically," he says, "I'm committed. In terms of pension I'm stuck with state civil service for the next ten or fifteen years." At the same time he feels strongly that he "has had it with counseling." He's reached a point where he has stopped believing in the values and goals he tried to instill in his adolescent clients. Bob speculates idly on becoming an assistant director of a charitable organization, a secure job not subject to political whims and where he could try to work in a number of administrative domains. But realistically he doesn't see much chance of obtaining such a position.

But the most disturbing problem to emerge at this time, we are told, was that young Bob began to rebel, to "change his personality." He had been a model child, an outstanding student, very religious, president of the local youth organization, even an active door-to-door campaigner in the previous elections. He was good at public speaking and it seemed he was inclined toward politics. In this period, their relationship was rewarding to both father and son. Mr. Wilson "always tried to encourage him to be independent and creative." And Bob, Jr. describes his father as "firm and effective" and reports that they have had "amazing intellectual discussions." Father and son spent many hours together each day. Bob deliberately arranged his work schedule so that he finished at four o'clock, rushing home to play chess or have a catch with Bob, Jr. while they discussed the day's events. While Mrs. Wilson and their younger son, Brian, often criticized and teased them about their closeness, it continued to be an important element of their lives. After young Bob turned 16 and obtained a driver's license, his interest in girls and his peer group began to grow, and he sought ways to avoid the obligation of spending late afternoons with his dad. His father, however, had great difficulty finding another center to his interests, and worked frantically to keep his son interested. He understands now that he was deliberately blind to his son's changing needs, although the boy continued to try to oblige him.

But as Bob, Jr. moved into his later teen-age years, things began to change. He let his hair grow long, began talking back, and "walked around moody all the time." He developed the ambition of becoming an actor and playwright—a profession that his parents fear because of its "seamy side," its association with drugs and sex, and its economic uncertainties. Bobby says his parents would rather have him be an insurance salesman, something concrete. He says they're trying to "squelch" him. He has developed an intense interest in existentialist philosophy, which he says his parents find a direct challenge to their deeply held religious beliefs. His mother says the things he reads now are "not nice anymore." His father favors the classical philosophers and claims therefore not to be interested in his son's readings. Last year, as a senior in high school, Bobby produced and acted in a Sartre play. He has been accepted into a six-year program in a dramatic arts college, and during this summer he worked there as an apprentice on some productions. He says he thought he'd hate the remote area, but has grown to love it. Bobby feels that the prospect of going into drama is "scary," but he is certain he wants to do it. Both his prospective major and choice of college are quite alien to his parents' urban, religious, and career-oriented values.

He has been dating a girl that his mother considers a "loose woman." He responds by saying that his parents are old-fashioned and exceedingly strict about sex; his mother is described as a "wicked prude." In the home interview his mother expressed disdain for "this woman" who drives over with her car to pick him up. However, Mr. Wilson quickly pointed out that when they were dating, she often picked him up in her car. It was unclear to the interviewers whether Mrs. Wilson's anger over this issue was directed more toward her son or her husband. Sexual freedom or constraint represents one issue over which the Wilsons are split in their expectations for Bobby.

Bobby sees his mother as the instigator of attacks on him. At one point he told her she would have made the best director of drama there ever was. She didn't know whether to be complimented or insulted. His father is described as "cool" and "holding his feelings in." But his mother seems to be in a rage against Bobby; at times she seems to view him as dead, as if a stranger is dwelling in her son's body. Bobby relates the story of their visits to a family counselor. His mother urged it. At one point the counselor asked her, "Do you love your son?" She said, "Yes," and he asked, "Do you like his school?" She said, "No."

"His clothes?"

"No."

"His hair?"

"No."

"What do you like about him?"

She couldn't say. After a while Bobby tells us they stopped going to the counselor because Mrs. Wilson thought he "wasn't too bright."

The growing rift in the family reached a culmination during the previous winter. Bobby was president of the youth organization at his church. They met on Saturday afternoons in a church-owned house that happened to be next door to the police station. In addition to discussing business the members also smoked marijuana at these meetings. One afternoon a police officer caught a whiff of what was happening and raided the place. Bobby was booked and placed on parole. His father was calm and controlled throughout the episode, but his mother just "yelled and yelled," repeatedly asking herself and anyone who happened by, "Where did I go wrong?"

The next week Mr. Wilson was sitting at home in the living room reading the paper when he felt the classic heart attack symptoms, pain moving up the left arm and settling in his chest. Mr. and Mrs. Wilson now interpret this event as the culmination of their struggle with Bobby, believing that he has symbolically destroyed his father. What he has destroyed is his parents' attempt to mold him into the vehicle for their deliverance. Both had implicitly believed they could achieve through their son the greatness that had eluded them. Mrs. Wilson, who treated Bobby almost like the "good husband" she should have had, now reacted like a woman scorned as he found outside interests. Bob's unwillingness to look for a job is another outcome of these beliefs. If their dreams are ended, there is no use trying to go on.

Analysis and Summary

In the launching-phase families studied, we generally see the children's continuing enmeshment in parental conflict and family mythologies. Midlife men attempt to recruit their sons into a reworking of earlier issues, either implicitly asking them to compensate for the father's disappointments or to relive earlier phases of the father's history.

These frequent attempts to create virtual identity between fathers and sons contrast with the complex relationships with the daughters. The emotional and symbolic utilization of older daughters, both before and after marriage, is obvious and dramatic. Through them the mother's earlier selves are often seen as being reincarnated. This gives the mothers a chance for vicarious participation in a new beginning, helping to articulate an emergent redefinition of their own identities. Although unacknowledged, the middle-aged man looks to this "rebirth" of his wife as a source of emotional and erotic renewal.

It is important to note that the father's role in this drama at first seems peripheral but that his emotional involvement is often intense. He both acts as an extension of the mother and replays his earlier role as suitor. He may struggle to control his late adolescent daughters physically and ideologically, just as he attempted to control his wife. In both instances he feels morally righteous, simply encouraging what he sees as proper values for a young woman and prospective wife. The man typically doesn't see the jealousy and possessiveness behind these efforts.

In the Williams case we see the son identifying with and imitating the father. Instead of ambitiously striving after long-range goals as many of his friends are doing, he drops out of college and takes a job near home that provides him with enough money to buy a car and sustain an active social life. His father is pleased with his son's short-range orientation vis-à-vis work and his acquisition of the new car. Tony feels this son poses no problems for him. However, we hear that the situation is structured so that the boy avoids the family continuously. He has his own apartment in the basement and uses the home as a dormitory. Thus, the strains inherent in the son's individuation and acquisition of new values are dealt with through avoidance.

The older daughter, Mary, shows a similar pattern of avoidance. Although she is close to her mother, she minimizes contact with her father. She sympathizes with her mother's plight in dealing with her intrusive and dominating father, but she avoids the situation as much as possible. She pursues friends and activities outside the family boundaries in secrecy, with occasional eruptions when friends encounter Tony.

The tensions built into this situation, both historically and currently, are expressed in the frequent confrontations with the younger daughter. Debbie's pattern of sharing and concern for others might be viewed as an attempt to introduce new ways of relating in this narcissistic family culture. On one level, Debbie is attempting to act as therapist for the family, to absorb their aggression and help them find ways to relate to one another. This need to "cure" the family is a kind of symptom. Unable to help them change, Debbie cannot separate herself from them or her sacrificial function. In fact, her preoccupation with the familial drama hinders Debbie's ability to cope actively with the external world and her own emotional maturation.

In the Wilson case the father is more obviously and directly involved in the son's adolescent struggles. We hear about his misguided compromises in life, from high school through adulthood. Now we hear of his disillusionment and alienation, of his inability to believe in the dreams he offers to clients in his role of counselor. His wife speaks with disturbing admiration of successful neighbors—self-made men who made the right moves in life. Together, the Wilsons invested their hopes for redemption in their son. They chose to see Bobby as a symbol of hope, as a second chance at succeeding in a world where they had failed.

Bobby has seemingly responded to their disillusionment more strongly than to their requests that he achieve their vindication. Like his father, he studies philosophy, but unlike his father he values the disillusioned existentialists over the faithful classicists. Rather than settle for the secure, moderately ambitious life style of his father, he chooses the insecurity and anti-institutionalism he associates with a career in the theater. As the pressures toward a conventional life mount, along with the guilt his doting parents have induced, he retreats into moody, passive resistance and lets his hair grow long. Finally, he gets into trouble in the outside world over marijuana.

His bids for individuation, for disengagement from his parents' fantasies of using him as "compensation" for their own wounds, are interpreted as "craziness." Their son has inexplicably gone astray. The mother, at least, expresses the urge to disown him: All that she has invested in him is being squandered. She cannot appreciate him as a person with desires and goals of his own, but feels only that her ticket out of the gray world of compromises into the shining world of conventional success has been destroyed.

What the Wilsons cannot appreciate is the relatively healthy adaptation their son has made to the confusing, contradictory messages they've been sending. On the one hand, the world is a heartless place where you compromise away your dreams. The father implicitly says, "If you act like me, you'll wind up in a meaningless life of alienation." On the other hand, he urges the son to stay on the conventional path, because the alternative to meaningless alienation may be something even worse. The son's compromise is to opt for a career that has the potential of conventional reward, but allows him to express his alienation from the conventional.

The father seems alternately to smile on this choice and feel that it is killing him. Perhaps at some level he understands the ingenious synthesis his son is attempting. Perhaps he is vicariously involved in this young man's adamant commitment to his dream in the face of obstacles. The primary feeling one gets is that Bob remains confused and ambivalent, that he is no more prepared to help his son choose a life than he is to advise his clients. Perhaps the father's reliving of this phase of life through his son will rekindle hopes of fulfillment and give him a greater capacity to help others find their own paths to adulthood.

The mother's sense of betrayal is more manifest. Her husband having failed her, she invested in the son. And she worked hard to pound him into the conventional mold: "Dress nicely, date nice girls, go to church, go to college." During his childhood he was "number one," and she was the "best director he ever knew." Now, as he breaks free of his role in her life and she must deal with disengagement, she finds herself unable to let go. Rather than simply allowing her son to find himself, she feels abandoned and retaliates by rejecting him. Bobby is also the recipient of pent-up anger over her husband's failures; the anger is directed at the father's namesake. In a more general sense he is receiving the brunt of the anger of a woman whose planned escape from life's torments has been closed off.

The levels of enmeshment between mother and son are remarkably complex. Almost as an aside, Brian (the younger son) mentions his mother's early interest in amateur productions. Possibly her son's involvement in the theater will rekindle the self she was when she first met her husband, working on props and lighting in the college theater. Being forced out of her total investment in her first son may enable her to reinvest in a relationship with her rather needy younger son and her husband, or in a new sense of her own purpose. There is clearly a need for the Wilsons to find a new sense of purpose not so dependent on their son, or they may be locked into a sense of bitterness and defeat.

Midlife parents show a variety of responses to their children's bids for individuation, depending on marital dynamics, father's midlife response, and family developmental phase. The responses vary from avoidance, to demanding recapitulation of their own biographies, to entanglement in old conflicts, to encouraging growth and development. Most of the twenty families we examined in depth were in various stages of launching their children. In virtually none of our case studies did the parents show an easy, unconflicted reaction to the children's evolving individuation. As the children sought to discover something about themselves and the outside world, the parents played the part of policemen and judges. In the earlier, pre-launch phase, they commonly resented their children's attempts to move outside the family's boundaries and the parents' definition of who they were. We feel that our case studies are typical in this regard; turmoil and resentment are common responses to this stage. The literature on interpersonal relations in other settings[12] has shown that the termination of relationships is usually problematical, generating an upheaval of unresolved tensions and anxieties about loss. The family is probably the context in which this dynamic is most pronounced. If the children are a part of the defensive mythology that defines the parents' life structures, then the disruption of that mythology must be emotionally wrenching. It may be that the more positive inputs into the parental culture do not appear until after this stage, when parent-child relations are reconstituted on a more fully adult-to-adult basis.

Endnotes

1. Duvall, Evelyn M., *Family Development* (Philadelphia: Lippincott, 1962).
2. Barnhill, Laurence R., and Diane Longo, "Fixation and Regression in the Family Life Cycle," *Family Process*, vol. 17, no. 4, 1978.
3. Blood, Robert O., Jr., and Donald M. Wolfe, *Husbands and Wives: The Dynamics of Married Living* (Glencoe, Ill.: Free Press, 1960).
4. Rollins, Boyd C., and Harold Feldman, "Marital Satisfaction Over the Family Life Cycle," *Journal of Marriage and the Family*, vol. 32, February 20, 1970.
5. Reiss, Ira, *Family Systems in America*, 2nd ed. (Hinsdale, Ill.: Dryden Press, 1976), p. 163.
6. Benedek, Therese, "Parenthood as a Developmental Phase," *Journal of the American Psychoanalytic Association*, vol. 7, 1959, pp. 389–417.
7. Levi, L. David, H. Stierlin, and R.J. Savard, "Fathers and Sons: The

Interlocking Crisis of Integrity and Identity," *Psychiatry*, vol. 35, February 1972.

8. Bateson, Gregory, D. Jackson, J. Haley, and J. Weakland, "A Note on the Double-Bind," *Family Process*, no. 2, 1963, pp. 154–161.
9. Laing, R.D., *Self and Others* (London: Tavistock, 1961).
10. Searles, Harold F., "The Effort to Drive the Other Person Crazy—An Element in the Aetiology and Psychotherapy of Schizophrenia," *British Journal of Medical Psychology*, vol. 32, no. 1, 1959, pp. 1–18.
11. Farrell, Michael P., and Peter Curtis, "Scapegoating in Families," paper presented at the Annual Conference for the Alliance of Family Therapy and Family Research, Tallahassee, Florida, April 1981, and Farrell, Michael P., and Stanley D. Rosenberg, "Parent-Child Relations in Middle Age," in *Understanding the Family: Stress and Change in American Family Life*, edited by C. Getty and W. Humphreys (New York: Appleton-Century-Crofts, 1981).
12. Farrell, Michael P., "Patterns in the Development of Self-Analytic Groups," *Journal of Applied Behavioral Sciences*, vol. 12, no. 4, 1976, pp. 523–542.

Chapter 8

EXTENDED FAMILY RELATIONS IN MIDDLE AGE

In recent decades social scientists have been announcing the death of the extended family and arguing whether it was basically a desirable event. Parsons[1] was among those arguing that it was all for the better, while such viewers as Ogburn[2] and Zimmerman[3] saw in it portents of the decline of civilization. Lurking in the background of this debate was the suspicion that the image of grandma and grandpa, mom and pop and the kids in the big old house was all a myth, an image projected onto the past that reflected today's wish more than yesterday's reality.[4]

Beginning in the late 1950s, some researchers began carrying out serious examinations of the question of how much damage had been done to kinship networks by industrialization.[5-7] To many people's surprise they found the extended family, especially the parent-adult-child tie, very much alive and well. People may not be living in three-generation homes, but exchanges of resources and emotional support are common for the majority of the population. Family ties become especially important during crises and holidays, but many parents and their adult offspring maintain continuous contact with each other, at least on a weekly basis.

Before the theorists could regroup and make sense out of these findings, a whole set of new historical findings emerged that further complicated the picture. Combing through old church and state-house records to obtain demographic data for pre-industrialized Europe, historians found evidence that the three-generation home never was common. In fact, Laslett's extensive research[8] showed that it was about as uncommon in England in 1650 as it was in 1950. (Approximately 15 percent of family households were extended in both periods.) To make matters more complex, it became apparent that when the three-generation home did exist, it was characterized by strain and conflict. It seems that the younger generation was usually kept around or stayed around more for reasons of economic necessity rather than for emotional ones.[9,10]

The explosion of new information has raised questions on industrialization's impact on family relations and on the quality of contemporary parent-adult-child interaction. In this chapter we draw on our family interviews in order to contribute to the understanding of these relationships, arguing that the midlife male is still very much engaged emotionally with his family of origin. While our focus is on the changing relationship of middle-aged men to their own parents, we have also found it necessary to include the man's involvement with in-laws and his wife's relationship to her parents. It is this latter relationship that emerges as the major link between adult generations. Past research has focused on frequency of contact and other external connections between generations. In this analysis we emphasize internal, subjective processes in men: not only their actions in regard to extended family, but the meanings that these ties have in their own experiences of themselves and their lives.

In our interviews with the twenty follow-up cases, we obtained information about past and current relationships between the men, their parents, and their in-laws. We asked the men to talk freely about this aspect of their lives; to provide concrete episodes as well as overall evaluations of the relationships. In looking at the histories these men produced, we decided that intergenerational processes can best be described as falling into three phases: early adult ambivalence, post-marriage drift toward the wife's family, and, at midlife, the resumed dialogue with father. Just as separation from children reawakens early marital issues, impending middle age and parental decline reevoke memories and feelings from late adolescence concerning obedience to or rebellion against father.

Early Adult Ambivalence

In accord with past researchers[11,12] we find that a predominant concern of our subjects in their late adolescence and twenties is getting away from their parents. However, we find a strong undercurrent of ambivalence in their descriptions of this phase. While there are often lurching moves toward autonomy, the men also report episodes of drawing on parental resources during this period and being anxious about the parents' evaluation of their choices and behavior. In their opening performances as adults their parents are still a major part of the audience.

Tony Williams's description of this period of his life illustrates the process in detail. After returning from the service when he was 22, Tony borrowed $2,000 from his grandfather to start a trucking business. He hoped to marry his childhood sweetheart after the business became "established" and sufficiently profitable. It took considerably more digging before Tony revealed that some of his hesitancy was based on his parents' lukewarm feelings toward this girl. Although she came from an acceptable family, they saw her as cold and aloof. She was employed and quite willing to suffer some of the lean years with him; her parents even offered to rent them a second-floor apartment at a nominal fee. Tony capitulated, however, to his parents' demands that he wait while he established a partnership with an equally young and inexperienced friend. They bought two earth-hauling trucks and started taking contracts. The business failed within a short period. Tony says it failed "because my friend didn't want to work. When things came apart, he was down in Florida with a girl."

Tony then went to work as a machinist, working nights and during slow periods as an undertaker's assistant. During this period of holding two jobs to pay back his grandfather, he saw little of the girl he was hoping to marry. He related to the interviewer the dialogue on the evening he called her up after not contacting her for several months. He called from a phone booth, and her mother answered:

"Hey, is Marie there?" he asked.

"She's not here," said her mother.

"Well, when is she coming home? What is she, out with her sister?" asked Tony.

"No, she got married," said her mother, "she doesn't live here anymore."

"Oh," said Tony, "Okay."

He reports being shattered at this point. He lived with his parents, worked, but did nothing else. His mother would tell him to go out and, having no destination, he'd go for long drives up the coast.

A few years later Tony met another girl who was also recovering from the disappointment of a broken engagement. When Tony found out about the previous entanglement, he simply said, "Hey, that's why pencils have erasers. So what?"

They dated for a few months, then Tony decided to bring her home for Thanksgiving to meet his relatives. Aunts, uncles, brothers, and sisters were all there when Tony walked in with the girl. They all liked her, then Tony's mother pulled him aside and asked about her. Tony told her about the prior boyfriend. His mother gave him what is remembered as a withering look, muttering, "That's great. A secondhand girl! A secondhand girl for my boy!" she moaned. Tony broke off the relationship.

The episode is extreme, but it illustrates themes that are more widely shared by the men in our study. First, we see Tony's early bid for financial independence in the trucking business, a bid financed by his family. When this failed, he worked doubly hard to pay off the debt and be free, neglecting other relationships in the process. He became increasingly isolated except for his involvement with the extended family, where he was treated like an adolescent son. Unlike an adolescent, however, he had no peer group to counterbalance his reliance and focus on the family. His earlier friends, if still in the area, were involved with wives and young children, making Tony feel even more behind and inadequate. Having been battered, he apparently was unable to mobilize the confidence for another bid at adult autonomy. Throughout this period he continued to live with his parents and draw on their resources. Thus, we see a mixture of striving for autonomy (or at least claims of such striving) with a protracted period of dependency and parental domination.

We see the extent of his emotional dependence on his parents in the episode with the second girl. When asked why he didn't continue to see her after they disapproved, he simply said, "I couldn't. I couldn't." The loss of his parents' esteem couldn't be tolerated. Marriage would have no meaning if it did not serve to elevate him in their eyes.

Many of our respondents seemed, during this period, to view their parents as being somehow larger than life. Bob Wilson, whose father died when Bob was 20, describes his father as a "colorful," powerful man. Bob recalls straining to keep up with him as they walked through town, almost having to run to keep up with his father's "Boston strut."

After his father died, Bob admits, he was afraid to try to take over the family printing business. He felt his father kept back some "inner secrets" about the essence of the business, so he could never step into his shoes. However, even before his father died, Bob was working to break away from his domination, choosing English as a major in college and aspiring to be a college teacher.

In general, the men portray one or both parents as powerful external forces they attempt to come to terms with in this early period of adulthood. The styles of responding to this image range from dependence and compliance to defiant rebellion. However, the usual pattern is a mixture of the two responses, one being overt and the other covert. Tom Conley is an example of this mixture, dropping out of college against his father's wishes, but making a success of himself by working with a much-admired paternal uncle.

The Post-Marriage Stage

Marriage marks a turning point in the relationship of the man to his family. Pressures toward autonomy increase at this point, and most men respond by setting up their own home. Only two moved back into the husband's parents' home; and four moved into the wife's parents' home. In all but one case the situation was viewed as temporary and problematic, ending with the couple or the parents moving into separate quarters as soon as possible.

The Drift toward the Wife's Family

However, that four of these six cases moved into the wife's parents' home reflects the general trend among the men. The strongest extended-family ties after marriage are with the wife's family. For many men moving into middle age, this tie becomes so strong that the wife's father seems to supplant the husband's as the central patriarchal figure for the extended family group.

Tony Williams again illustrates the general trend. After giving up his second potential mate because of parental disapproval, he went into another period of isolation, finally meeting and marrying his current wife. During the early years of their marriage when she was generally either pregnant or nursing an infant, Tony relied on her family for financial help as well as for baby-sitting. Since they could not afford a car, his in-laws transported her weekly to do the family shopping. Throughout this period he grew closer to his father-in-law, a retired policeman. He respected the older man's resourcefulness in maintaining his home and dealing with a wife who had chronic physical problems. In more recent years his father-in-law has retired and moved to New Hampshire. Excursions to their lake-front home represent the Williamses' sole form of vacation. Tony has adopted the same set (dependency, awe, admiration) toward his father-in-law that he feels toward his own father. At this point they visit frequently and the two men enjoy an easy camaraderie—perhaps the most satisfactory relationship in Tony's life.

The pattern is repeated in several other cases. For example, one subject began his career as a building contractor by working for his father-in-law. Eventually, he felt a need to start his own firm because of the strains of mixing family and work: "You have to do what he says even when he is wrong." However, the break was made without animosity, and they still maintain strong ties of mutual respect and help, sometimes sharing crews and equipment. Feeling independent, he can appreciate his father-in-law more. On the other hand, relations with his own parents have deteriorated to the point where he maintains minimal contact. Being the most financially successful and upwardly mobile of his siblings, he is uncomfortable with and even a little embarrassed by his own family. "I only see them when they want money."

In this process of shifting allegiance to the wife's family, the men seem to idealize their styles and values, coming to view their own families of origin in a very negative light. For some of the men this perspective was partially attributable to efforts to move up the social ladder. Men chose, that is, to identify with their wives' more middle-class background when marrying "upward." Several of our subjects clearly used their fathers- and brothers-in-law in such instrumental ways, being introduced by them into the Lions or local country clubs which enhanced their social standing and career opportunities. Of course, this turning away from their own parents can't be understood simply as status-seeking. Men are as likely to marry women from a similar or lower socioeconomic background as a higher one and will become more engaged with the wife's family in either case. Rather, this idea of the in-laws as providing "connections" seemed to be only one of several possible rationalizations men could use in establishing separateness from their own parents. The effort to find autonomy apparently required them to find alternative sources of support and strength: wives, in-laws, professional identifications, and so on. Moreover, the men could not acknowledge their use of the wife's family as a way to deal with ambivalent ties to their own. It was obviously important to them to see their own actions in moving away as responses to objective pressures: My parents are "too domineering" or "too old-fashioned" or "my in-laws understand us better."

The shift away from the husband's parents and toward the wife's seems also, at least in part, to be the consequence of the wife's more reliable efforts to maintain familial ties and integrate her husband into the extended kin network. The result is a tendency toward a growing relationship or even intensive identification with the wife's father, with increasing coolness or openly negative feelings expressed toward one or both of the husband's parents.

Both the closeness to the wife's family and the hostility toward the man's are amplified through husband-wife interaction. It has been pointed out[13] that after marriage, the "dominant conversation" in a person's life is with the spouse. This continuous conversation about everyday life leads to the construction of a shared, taken-for-granted reality for the couple. Through repeated discussions of events involving their parents, they build and reinforce shared images of them. Such phrases as, "You know how mother is," or "She is at it again," are indicators of such a shared belief system or common set of assumptions. In the construction of these images the wife is likely to play a more active role than the husband. Past research has shown that she continues to interact with her parents more often, a pattern that is socially approved. While it is not "manly" to rely on one's parents, it is certainly "womanly" to retain such bonds. Indeed, the wife will find much of value in utilizing her mother and sisters as sources of companionship, help with children, and information, thus leading her to define her family in more positive terms.

The couples' allegiance is dramatized each year as decisions have to be made about whom to visit during holidays. On these critical days the wife's strong ties to her family may shift the balance of loyalties in her family's direction. This permits the husband to "comply" passively, disowning any guilt he might feel in abandoning his own family. Such imbalance often creates hurt feelings that eventually lead to further division.

The point to be made is simply that both husband and wife have reasons for defining her family as "their" family in this life phase. For the wife it permits the continuance of a more comfortable closeness with her family of origin, for the husband a means of separating from his parents while still garnering support. The couple often justifies these needs by blaming his family, defining them as impossible and idealizing hers.

Regardless of why this drift occurs, it is commonly linked to a growing and open sense of antagonism toward the man's parents. As the couple have young children and move to establish themselves as a functioning unit, they often attribute any possible failings or undesirable traits to the husband's family. Like the scapegoating process with their children, this serves to remove the couple from unwanted aspects of themselves and gives them a shared target against whom they can unite. Men who feel undertrained for their work may, for example, blame this problem on their parents' lack of foresight in directing their schooling, or even to parental malevolence. One of our subjects expressed the feeling that his mother "wanted me to fail. She made it impossible for me to go to college, and my father just went along. Besides not helping, they tried to take credit for everything I did. They led my brothers to believe they had given me the down payment for our house, but they never gave me a cent."

Ambivalence and Withdrawal from Parents

In this period of post-marriage disengagement from his own family, the man generally articulates a set of grievances against his parents. He will emphasize their negative qualities and attempt to see himself as very different from "them." Interaction with the man's parents often becomes stressful and conflict-laden. His sense of his own history may become tainted by these feelings, the man remembering his development as a process of coping with distant, intrusive, or non-understanding parents. While some of these characterizations are based on real incidents, they have a quality of being exaggerated or one-sided. The need for anger at and a felt distance from the parents may serve the same function as his growing attachment to his wife's family. They are both devices to help the man separate from his parents and feel more like an independent adult. This process is made easier if the negative aspects of the relationship are heightened in his perception, and the sense of identification denied.

As we have attempted to illustrate, most of the men report a protracted period of difficulty in breaking away from the parental nurturance and influence. They continue to feel, at some level, anxious to gain autonomy and effectively confront the world. For many of them, there is an implicit competition with father whereby achievement has no meaning unless it surpasses his. For others, there is a belief that father holds the keys to the kingdom, that unless he bequeaths it to them they will be unable to progress. Along with these feelings is a wish to be free, to stand alone and show the father that they are potent without his help. Also, external, cultural expectations make it somewhat "shameful" for the young man to cling to or idealize his parents.

These forces combine to make emotional and physical withdrawal from parents the modal response for men in their late twenties and thirties. This withdrawal may be more or less absolute and may have a variety of emotional shadings. For some men, it is like the journey of a prodigal son: They will go out to prove themselves and return transformed, an object worthy of admiration and pride. For others, it is a bitter renunciation: Not having found love or strength at home, they go out into the world to seek it elsewhere.

This withdrawal does not eliminate the ambivalence that fuels it; instead, it tends to engender guilt. Attachment to the parents remains along with the need to keep them away. The negative perceptions of the parents serve to justify and rationalize the emotional distance and anger the man feels in excluding his parents from his day-to-day existence. He generally finds a willing ally in his wife in formulating these defensive beliefs.

Parental Decline and the Renewed Dialogue with Father

The drift toward the wife's family was not a solution for our subjects, but rather a stage in their working through of conflicting feelings of dependency, love, resentment toward parents, and the desire to feel independent. Even in the period of behavioral withdrawal it was not uncommon for the man's concerns about his parents to have escalated. The man, that is, may become preoccupied with thinking about one or both of his parents, usually father, while interacting with them very little. The man's image of his father takes a prominent place in his ideational life, usually being endowed with exaggerated qualities of either a positive or negative sort. In either event, this parental image is seen as having had a seminal influence on the man's life. Much of his striving in the early or middle adult years represents—at least in part—an effort to break free of this influence. When we examine the range of cases of men in their early forties we find them spread out at a variety of points in this process. While a few still seem to regard their parents in these larger-than-life terms, others have moved on to a more congenial relationship with either their own or their wife's parents. Still others are encountering a third stage—dealing with their parents' decline and death.

Death or a sudden illness yanks the middle-aged son back into the family of orientation. In the intensive interaction with relatives old emotional issues may be rekindled. The son may feel an undertow of guilt about the decisions he made to break free of his parents' life style and their dreams for him. Adult sons are called upon to manage financial and emotional turmoil at this point, and the urge to be a good son, to build a final bridge of solidarity, may reawaken memories of episodes in which either parent or son disappointed the other.

Sons dealing with a declining parent often speak as if their image of their parents has gone out of focus. The reality of an enfeebled, dependent person who needs care and support is difficult to reconcile with the memories of the powerful parental figure. This fragmentation of the image and the reality is associated with an internal process of reworking identifications that may lead to a somewhat altered self-concept at this time, an acknowledgment of earlier distortions and a recognition of their origins.

Dialogue with the Father

One pattern that appears to be widespread in middle-aged men is the use of the larger-than-life image of their own father in their attempts to understand themselves. That is, in explaining themselves and how they have come to be who they are, they make implicit or explicit references to dramatized images of parental figures, using these images as either positive or negative reference points in accounting for what they have become. This process of self-justification and reworking of identity issues often takes the form of an imaginary dialogue with the father. Although they may have long ago established a truce or even a peer relationship with their own father, and although that parent may now be dead or enfeebled and dependent, the middle-aged man continues to wrestle with the powerful parental image and makes use of it in the maintenance of the self. What we find characteristic of mid-life males is both the heightened significance of this internal dialogue and the fact that it begins to shift out of old patterns. While it is true that the dialogue is with the remembered father of the men's youth, at midlife they begin to see this figure in more multifaceted ways. Anger may give way to more complex remembrances of father's caring or concern; awe is tempered by an awareness of their father's weaknesses or pain. As they become, vis-à-vis their own adolescent children, the father of their remembered period, they become more aware of the unexpressed subtleties of the role. They become aware, for example, that their children's view of them as ogre or weakling may be quite fanciful. In this context, they begin to question assumptions about their own parents, and come to some new conclusions. The relevance of the dialogue with father about life choices, and its alteration at midlife, is well illustrated by a case not previously introduced.

Robert Smith is a college professor, although his career has never really "gotten off the ground." He prides himself on his radical humanistic perspective on American society, a view that caused him difficulty in his academic work at a small, conservative college. He won disfavor with the school's administration by coming to the aid of a student suspended for publishing what were considered obscenities in the school newspaper. Smith felt the student's language accurately portrayed the subculture he was describing. At a second school he claims that his critical stance toward the administration during the protest movements of the late 1960s resulted in his dismissal. He liked working at each of these schools but felt that his understanding of the issues and his principles compelled him to speak out. He prides himself on not being simply a political ideologue; he finds fault with the smugness and prejudice of young radicals as well as the behavior of those in authority. His intellectual work and private life reflect a complex and highly differentiated response to the culture and social life around him.

In the private interview with Smith we found that these seemingly self-destructive acts have complex roots in his dialogue with his father. He describes his father as a "sad guy," an engineer who came into hard times during the Depression. He was a skilled carpenter and plasterer and built several houses, but he was ashamed of physical labor so he never said much about these accomplishments. In reconsidering his father's life, Smith describes feelings of pride and pity, seeing his father as a victim of economic and cultural forces that robbed his life of dignity. Circumstance robbed him of his profession, but even when he was working, his internalized image of success made him devalue what he was doing. Moreover, Bob's father conveyed many of these same middle-class standards to his children. Bob also defined his father as a sort of shameful failure, and tried to hide him from friends and fellow students. In getting a Ph.D., he was self-consciously avoiding becoming, like his father, a "failure" and a "nonentity." In college and graduate school Bob had virtually no contact with his parents. After marrying a woman from a much more prosperous background and moving to the East, he often went two or three years at a stretch only sending birthday cards or calling his family on holidays. At the same time, many of Bob's actions represented attempts to atone for his own shame (and consequent guilt) about his father.

His intellectual redefinition of the American economic system casts his father as an heroic victim rather than a failure. Smith's efforts to maintain and assert his own integrity amount to a personal struggle against being devalued, against becoming a captive of external standards as his father was. His efforts to correct the unjust "system" that does not recognize the individual's inherent dignity represent an effort to vindicate his father's honor.

As Bob enters midlife, all these feelings are mellowing. He is less angry at the college he now works for. He has finally found a secure position as a well-liked teacher at a small school, and can even play the role of mediator between factions. He can now visit his parents, as he recently did for their fiftieth anniversary, without feeling embarrassed by them. He plans to fly them out for his own son's high school graduation. These changes accompany a shifting perspective on his father and on his own adolescent reactions to his father's dilemma. Bob is beginning to understand that the tragedy of his father's life was not his slippage on the status ladder, but his definition of that slip as diminishing him. Bob also sees that this was not the only basis of his father's unhappiness, but a focus and family excuse for everything that went wrong in their lives. He sees now that his shame of his father's work was part of a more general adolescent self-consciousness that said as much about his own self-doubts as anything shameful in his father's blue-collar status. As Bob becomes more sure of himself, as he absorbs his son's jibes about college professors as "useless dreamers," he is able to define his father less as a tragic figure and more as another man simply coping with life as best he can. Bob no longer wishes to vindicate his father through his own stellar achievement. He can now speculate on the idea that he has, in fact, sabotaged his own career, through taking unpopular positions, as a repetition of his father's job setbacks. He had great difficulty being successful while defining success as a betrayal of his father's identity. Only as he reaches midlife is Bob able to begin disentangling these issues.

Bill Mayne is less articulate, although equally engaged in reworking his feelings about his father. As we discussed in Chapter 5, Bill is generally managing the midlife transition with minimal disruptions. A major source of satisfaction to him is his material prosperity, which is taken as a symbol of achievement. Just as this affluence is a defining feature of his relationship to his children, so it reflects his feelings about himself and his father. Having grown up in a family where every cent was watched, Bill decided early on that financial security and prosperity were necessary for him and for his children. Although he won't condemn his father for the family's near-poverty as he grew up, he does make continual comparisons. "My kids" (in contrast to himself) "never go without anything. And always the best. They even lay around the house in La Coste shirts and Calvin Klein jeans. When I was growing up, if I asked for a pair of $38.00 jeans they would have laid me out."

Although Bill tries to be fair, to recognize that the obstacles may not have been the same, he still seems to feel some disdain and bitterness toward his father. He cannot grasp why his father could not have done more for all of them. Bill's long-term ambition of starting his own business is part of his continuing dialogue with an image of a lazy, unremarkable father: an image he must disprove as applying to himself. Aside from showering his children with the things he never had, he has instilled in them the same values of ambition, hard work, and high standards which differentiate him from his image of father. The midlife change for Bill in this dimension has been a growing security that he is not like father, that he needn't fight such traits as hidden weaknesses in himself.

Bill is not particularly introspective about these issues. He is aware of strong feelings about his father, about working to be different from him, but does not look at his own biography as an expression of this wish. Rather, he has accepted the occasional awkwardness between them at family gatherings as "just one of those things." The feelings of tension and not wanting to be identified with his father persist, but they are far less acute than when Bill was younger.

Finally, we return to the case of Tom Conley. We referred to the fact that Tom's family had been well established in the same town for a number of generations, and that his father was a physician. Although there was much love and closeness in Tom's family, there were also rather demanding and broad expectations of the children. The boys were to go to Andover and then to Harvard. Credentials in law or medicine, plus marriage to a girl from the right sort of family, were implicit parts of this package, as was the adoption of a tasteful life style. This included a family preference in dress (conservative three-piece suits), a proper home, and so on.

Tom had always loved and respected his father, but also found him intimidating and overbearing. He has expended much energy in his life seeking possibilities to do things his own way, to feel less slavish to these parental edicts. His dropping out of college, his adolescent style, his financial wheeling and dealing are all ways of thumbing his nose at familial expectations.

Tom's recent return to school to finish his degree is one outgrowth of his renewed dialogue with his father, one which followed his father's death several years ago. Tom is finding more to admire in what his father stood for, and less need to prove that he won't be dominated. His own dress has become more like his father's, and he finds himself wanting the same things for his sons that his father wanted for him. He is beginning to realize that "it is not easy to be a father, to help your kids find the way without looking like a tyrant."

Conley's case illustrates the trends we have been discussing. As the dialogue proceeds, the exaggerated image of the parent (for example, as ogre or all-powerful guardian) begins to be tempered, a process often stimulated by the parent's aging and disability. At the very least, that earlier image is no longer perceived as representing the actual person of the parent. As the image and person become partially disentangled, many of these men begin thinking of their late adolescence, the point at which they began to define themselves and make life decisions with long-term implications. Vicarious participation in the lives of their now-adolescent children and the search for standards to evaluate and guide their behavior feed this reexamination process.

This reexamination generally leads in one of two directions: The man may feel that "he had no choice" in these events because of the father's influence, or he may be startled by the idea that he chose as he did. In the former instance, the sense of bitterness and stagnation is enhanced. In the latter case, the middle-aged man looks upon his past behavior with an almost shocked disbelief. He wonders at the exaggerated image he held of his parents and at his own extreme responses to that image, responses which have had a profound impact on his life. This shock can give way to a sense of freedom. He need no longer live in fear, slavish devotion, or opposition to some remembered figure who defines and limits what the man must be.

Conclusion

In this chapter we have attempted to describe some salient aspects of the changing relationship between the middle-aged man and his parents. We have found a number of processes at work as a man moves into middle age. Some men continue to move away from their own parents and toward greater closeness with their wives' parents. For some men, this process goes so far that they come to idolize and emulate their father-in-law, drawing invidious comparisons with their own family. Frequently one or both of the man's own parents are described in negative terms. As men reach the full maturity of middle age, many seem to resurrect the image of their father and renew a dialogue with that image. The dialogue becomes an important psychological focus for them, representing part of a larger process of explaining themselves to themselves. The father-son relationship is but one axis of this explanation, but seems to be the most common focus for it in midlife men. The man tends to regard himself as the product of that imagined father, as his antithesis, or as a living vindication of him. This image has pervaded his life experience, and as he reaches full maturity, he may come finally to understand and articulate it, checking against his own experience as both son and father. This may lead him to begin to recognize its metaphoric, unreal quality, permitting him to live outside of the possibilities defined by it.

Endnotes

1. Parsons, Talcott, "The American Family: Its Relation to Personality and to the Social Structure," in *Family, Socialization and Interaction Process,* edited by T. Parsons and R.F. Bales (Glencoe, Ill.: Free Press, 1955).
2. Ogburn, William F., *Technology and the Changing Family* (Boston: Houghton Mifflin, 1955).
3. Zimmerman, Carle, *The Family of Tomorrow: The Cultural Crisis and the Way Out* (New York: Harper & Row, 1949).
4. Farrell, Michael P., and Madeline H. Schmitt, "The American Family: An Historical Perspective," chapter 4 in *Family Health Care,* vol. 1, edited by D. P. Hymovich and M. U. Barnard (New York: McGraw-Hill, 1979).
5. Sussman, Marvin B., "The Isolated Nuclear Family: Fact or Fiction," *Social Problems,* vol. 6, 1959, pp. 333–340.
6. Litwak, Eugene, "Extended Kin Relations in an Industrial Democratic Society," *Social Structure and the Family: Generational Relations,* edited by E. Shenas and G.F. Streib (Englewood Cliffs, N.J.: Prentice Hall, 1969).
7. Adams, Bert, "Isolation, Function and Beyond: American Kinship in the 1960's," *Journal of Marriage and the Family,* vol. 32, November 1970, pp. 575–597.
8. Laslett, Peter, and R. Wall (eds.), *Household and the Family in Past Time* (Cambridge, Eng.: Cambridge University Press, 1972).
9. Shorter, Edward, *The Making of the Modern Family* (New York: Basic Books, 1975).
10. Gould, Roger L., "The Phases of Adult Life: A Study in Developmental Psychology," *American Journal of Psychiatry,* vol. 129, 1972, pp. 521–531.
11. Levinson, Daniel J., Charlotte N. Darrow, Edward B. Klein, Maria H. Levinson, and Braxton McKee, *The Seasons of a Man's Life* (New York: Alfred A. Knopf, 1978).
12. Berger, Peter L., and H.F. Kellner, "Marriage and the Construction of Reality," in *Recent Sociology,* vol. 2 (London: MacMillan, 1970).
13. Berger and Kellner, *op. cit.*

Chapter 9

FRIENDSHIP GROUPS AND MALE DEVELOPMENT

Friendship groups, like the family, can be the focus for intense feelings and needs. Such groups can play a significant part in identity development and in the formation of beliefs and values. It has long been noted, for example, that delinquent behavior is learned and encouraged in adolescent peer groups, as is sex-role behavior more generally.[1,2] It is in their cliques and gangs that boys learn in detail how men are expected to think and behave. However, research on friendship in later stages of life remains scanty. How does involvement with friends change as men move toward middle age? Do friendship groups continue to have parallel effects on personality development? Is the experience of friendship different for men situated at different points in the class structure? These are some of the questions addressed in this chapter.

Functions of Friendship Groups

Recent studies of friendship show that men become more isolated from friends as they approach middle age.[3,4] The relative withdrawal of men during middle age may either reflect their distress or help to stimulate it: Persons who are involved in friendship groups tend to manifest better psychological health than those without friends.[5,6] It appears that friends contribute to psychological stability by providing nurturance, support, and ongoing demands which can help to alleviate depression or anxiety. Friendship groups provide a feeling of connectedness and shared strength, allaying men's self-doubt or hopelessness. As the relevance of parental models and advice declines, friendship groups become sources of information on how to deal with work-role problems, how to raise children, how to deal with a "too liberated" or "too traditional" wife, how to navigate through bureaucratic structures, and so on. Current experiences of individual group members are fed back into the group, providing information relevant to day-to-day life problems and major life decisions. The norms of reciprocity in such groups also can be of benefit to the members. In some of these groups men exchange economic resources, "connections," or skills, helping each other to maintain a life style that would otherwise be impossible.

Besides these instrumental functions, there are more intimate, expressive functions performed by male friendship groups. In such groups men express and work through doubts, disappointments, and feelings of alienation generated in other settings.[7,8] The man's self-esteem is likely to take a battering at work or in struggles with his family, for example. He may either distract himself from these traumas or rework them in the context of a poker game or a hunting trip with friends. Men count on each other for sympathy and reassurance around such events, sharing the feeling that "we've all been there."

In addition to this relief from immediate day-to-day strains, the group also can play a part in reducing some of the strains built into the process of cultural change and shifting identity demands. As adolescents, our middle-aged subjects were socialized into an image of masculinity that is increasingly being defined as unacceptable in current male roles. Instead of being encouraged to build an identity around the traditionally male values of strength, aggressiveness, and suppression of emotion, men are currently expected to be more gentle, more expressive of feelings, and less aggressive interpersonally. When complying with these demands, middle-aged men may feel uncomfortable or diminished in the roles of father, husband, and worker. However, as many popular works of fiction dramatize,[9,10] it is in the male friendship group that the earlier masculine identity, the one formulated in adolescence, is often preserved and acted out. In the local bar, on the fishing trip, or on the bowling team men can feel free to drop their polite, restrained demeanor. They drive too fast, exchange stories of old exploits, make comments about passing females, and attempt to recapture some of the feelings of freedom, strength, and spontaneity they treasured as adolescents. The friendship group is thus used to pursue gratifications prohibited the adult man in other contexts.

Of course, not all friendship groups perform all these functions.[11] The culture, structure, and effects of friendship groups vary with the man's position in the social structure and his stage in the life cycle. In this chapter we test a number of hypotheses about the functions of such groups for men in these different positions. First, we will focus on the midlife transition as it relates to changes in involvement with friendship groups. After briefly reviewing current ideas about the social isolation of men in contemporary society, we examine our own findings on changes of male involvement with friendship groups. Next, we will look at theories of the effects of friendship on personality in adulthood, comparing and contrasting these to our findings on the effects of involvement in friendship groups.

Theoretical Perspectives on Friendship

Three current theoretical perspectives are highly relevant to our examination of friendship patterns in midlife: mass society theory, fund of intimacy theory, and midlife crisis theory. Each would lead us to predict patterns of change in the midlife transition, and a different meaning to friendship in the men's lives.

Mass Society Theory

Theories of modern mass society argue that men are becoming increasingly isolated from intimate primary group ties outside the nuclear family. Parsons[12] and Slater[13], two leading proponents of this school, portray men living out their lives with only superficial and segmented contacts with bureaucratic officials. In consequence, they feel alienated from themselves and their neighbors. For Parsons, the only relief from this Kafka-esque existence is in companionate marriage, which has evolved as a haven of nurturance to compensate for the impersonality of the world outside. Slater's argument, though quite different, leads to similar conclusions. Socialization into a culture that values independence, competition, and individualistic striving for success leads to isolation and loneliness. Mass society theorists see intimate, meaningful friendships as a dead or dying institution regardless of the man's position in the adult life cycle.

Fund of Intimacy Theory

Another group of theorists[14,15] has argued that each person has a stable and limited fund of intimacy to expend and receive. The more intimacy needs are gratified in one context, the less desire or energy available to search elsewhere for outlets. This would lead us to expect that friendship groups are important to young men, but would fade in significance after marriage, particularly if the relationship to the wife is companionate.[16] We would also predict that friendship contacts would decline even further when children are added to the home, increasing again after children begin to leave.

Midlife Crisis Theory

Finally, stage-oriented developmental theorists[17,18] see the entry into middle age (early forties) as a crisis period. In this stage there is an increased likelihood of a depressive withdrawal from friends as a man attempts to cope with the crisis and do the internal work of revising his sense of self. This view would lead us to expect a noticeable drop in friendship involvement at middle age, followed by a recovery as the men move onto a new plateau.

Research Findings

Past research, we might note, has not clearly supported any of the theorists. There is some evidence[19-23] that mobility and the companionate family are not associated with isolation from primary group ties, especially not from extended family ties. These findings call into question the predominant theories that portray men as isolated, suggesting instead that primary group ties continue to play important parts in the lives of people in contemporary society. Although some relevant data has been reported, we have very little reliable information on how friendship relations change through the life cycle.

For example, Nelson's findings[24] indicate that companionate marriages are associated with less involvement with friendship groups. However, his data come from working-class women's reports about their husbands and may not provide an accurate picture of male friendship behavior.

Lowenthal *et al.*[25] investigated the changes in friendship behavior at different stages in the life cycle, finding that newlyweds list the largest number of friends and midlife men the least. This is just the opposite of what would be predicted by the fund of intimacy theorists, and it contradicts other recent findings.[26] To make matters more perplexing, Lowenthal cautions that the findings may be artifactual. These couples may have listed both husband and wife of another couple as friends, whereas in fact only one is a friend. In any event, these couples' friendships are quite separate phenomena from male friendship groups, focusing on different activities and serving other functions.

Current theory and research findings thus leave us with a less than clear picture of male friendship behavior. Although Parsons' critics have dispelled the image of the isolated man in contemporary society, we are still left with these questions:

1. Under what conditions do men become more or less isolated?
2. How is degree of isolation related to the life cycle?

For the answers, let us look at the findings from our survey questionnaire responses.

Findings from Survey Questionnaire: Life Cycle and Friendship

In our original questionnaire administered to 500 men, we asked questions relevant to four aspects of friendship: (1) whether or not the subject has a friend (or friends) he sees on a regular basis, (2) how often he has seen those friends over the past month, (3) how often he discusses "difficult personal problems" with these friends, and (4) what types of activities he engages in with these friends.

In order to assess the pertinence of our data to the theories discussed (mass society, fund of intimacy, and crisis), we examined the relationship between the life cycle and friendship behavior. Since each perspective has different implications for how such behavior will vary with the life cycle, such a comparison will help us to estimate their relative feasibility. Table 9-1 pre-

Table 9-1   Stage of Development, Men's Mean Age, and Mean Years
Married

Stage		Mean Age	Mean Years Married	N
I	Young unmarried men	24.75	0.0	55
II	Newlywed men without children	29.36	2.17	25
III	First child preschool age	31.15	5.84	54
IV	First child grade school age	37.27	11.57	99
V	First child high school age	41.31	16.79	35
VI	First child beyond high school (launching phase)	44.97	21.54	105
	Total			374

Note: Single, separated, or divorced older men were not included in this analysis.

sents the life stages along with information on our men concerning
the average ages and number of years married at each stage. We
have dropped from the analysis those older men who have never
been married, since their pattern is somewhat unique. After
dropping these men we are left with 374 subjects. Of these men,
79.6 percent report having friends they see on a regular basis
(see Table 9-2). The size of this percentage certainly does not
support the mass society theories of isolation, the majority of
men maintaining regular friendships.

However, looking at the relationship between stage of life and
number of friends, we do find a distinct pattern of change. In
the young unmarried group 90.7 percent report having friends.
This percentage drops sharply with marriage to 76 percent.
Moving into the next two stages, we find a slight recovery in

Table 9-2   Percentage of Men Having Friends, by Stage of Life

Stage		Percent	N
I	Young unmarried men	90.7	55
II	Newlywed men without children	76.0	25
III	First child preschool age	83.3	54
IV	First child grade school age	84.8	99
V	First child high school age	69.4	35
VI	First child beyond high school (launching phase)	71.2	105
	Total	79.6	374

$X^2 = 13.31$
$P < .01$

Note: Class has no effect on whether or not person has friends.

Table 9-3   Mean Number of Friends by Class and Stage of Life

Stage		Middle Class	s.d.	N	Lower Class	s.d.	N
I	Young unmarried men	2.20	1.33	20	2.14	1.20	35
II	Newlywed men without children	1.63	1.11	8	1.94	1.94	17
III	First child preschool age	1.79	1.32	24	1.10	1.10	30
IV	First child grade school age	1.70	1.30	61	1.37	1.37	38
V	First child high school age	1.59	1.35	17	1.05	1.05	19
VI	First child beyond high school (launching phase)	1.52	1.32	44	1.11	1.11	61
	Total	1.71	1.32	174	1.21	1.40	200

	F	P
Class	5.73	$<.05$
Stage	4.36	$<.001$

friends. But then as the children move into adolescence, close to one third of the men report having no friends. The trend seems to be that marriage tends to diminish male friendship commitments, and movement into middle age leads to even more isolation from friends.

Even those who do maintain friendships report a sharp decrease in the number of friends they see regularly after marriage (Table 9-3). And, again, we find that the middle-aged men report having the fewest friends they see regularly. It is interesting to note that although this pattern holds for both middle- and lower-class men, the lower-class men tend to have fewer regular friends.

We find the same pattern when we look at the rate of contact between friends and the degree to which they discuss personal problems (Table 9-4). There is a sharp decline in rate of contact after marriage, then a trend toward even less frequent contact as men move toward middle age. Likewise, intimate discussions are less likely among friends after marriage, reaching their lowest point as men cross the threshold into early middle age. However, with both contact and intimacy we find a slight upswing in men's involvement with friends as their adolescent children begin to leave home (Stage VI).

Finally, if we look at the types of activities men engage in while together (Table 9-5), we find that young men are more likely to participate in all-male activities (hunting, fishing, etc.), while

Table 9-4   Stage of Life, Rates of Contact, and Degree of Intimacy in Male
             Friendship Groups

Stage		Rate of Contact*	% Often or Sometimes Intimate	N
I	Young unmarried men	4.49	81.3	55
II	Newlywed men without children	3.55	75.0	25
III	First child preschool age	3.29	59.7	54
IV	First child grade school age	3.18	54.7	99
V	First child high school age	3.08	48.1	36
VI	First child beyond high school (launching phase)	3.45	53.9	105
	Total	3.49	61.1	374

* 1. Once or twice per month   4. Five times
   2. Three times   5. Six or more times
   3. Four times

Table 9-5   Types of Activities Shared with Friends

	Younger Men (23–33)	Older Men (37–50)	Total
All-Male Activities (hunting, sports, etc.)	82.42% (75)	65.16% (159)	69.85% (234)
Couple Activities (dinner, movies, etc.)	17.58 (16)	34.84 (85)	30.15 (101)
Total	100.00% (91)	100.00% (244)	100.00% (335)

$X^2 = 9.31$
$P < .01$

Note: Men without any friends are not included in this test. Figures in parentheses
indicate number of subjects.

older men are more likely to participate in couples-oriented activities (dinner, bridge, movies).

In summary, young men are very likely to have a friendship
group that they see often. When together they discuss personal
problems and participate in all-male activities. With marriage,
involvement in friendship groups declines sharply. Even those
men who do maintain friends see them less often. This trend
toward less involvement with friends is most evident in early
middle age when children are moving into adolescence. When
older men do see friends, they are likely to see them in a heterosexual rather than an all-male context. Finally, after children

begin to leave home, there are indications that involvement with friends increases again.

The low point of involvement at middle age supports Lowenthal's research. However, the sharp drop in involvement among newlywed men is directly contradictory to her conclusions. Apparently Lowenthal's finding of relatively high involvement with friends among newlyweds was an artifact of her data. At least for men, marriage leads to greater isolation from friends.

The pattern of findings certainly does not, on the surface, support the mass society theory of isolation of men. Overall, 79 percent report having friends they see regularly. Even at the point of least involvement in middle age we find 69 percent reporting that they at least have friends they see regularly. The quality of these relationships may become less intense, but they are nonetheless maintained. Aside from the fact that the majority of men do have others they define as friends, we do come away with a sense that there is some genuine intimacy in these alliances. Although the friendship groups described to us may never recapture the involvement and loyalty of the adolescent group, these relationships often persist over many years. Some of the men do open themselves up to their friends and care for one another. This is not often expressed directly, but more often in acts of mutual help or sacrifice. If these relationships are not profoundly intimate, they are obviously far more than plastic encounters between strangers.

Nor does the research strictly support the midlife crisis theory. Rather than finding an abrupt decline in involvement with friends during early middle age, we find a gradual decline after marriage. It is true that the low point of involvement occurs at the time when crisis theorists predict, but this appears to be the result of a gradual erosion in friendships rather than a sudden crisis. As with our findings in other dimensions, this suggests a modified view of the midlife crisis as an evolving stage, one that reflects the emergence of long-developing problems. Our crisis men were indeed the most socially isolated, a state of affairs with complex roots. The underlying difficulties that led them to drift away from friends and family of origin were an integral part of their crisis. At the same time, friendship involvements (had they been maintained) could obviously be helping Bob Wilson or Tony Williams to cope better with the career and family stresses they are undergoing. Bob's job dilemma, for example, is far from unique. He states, however, that he "has no one he can talk to about it" and thus feels even more isolated and stigmatized. Tony's growing disenchantment with his friends, and pulling back from activities with them, has resulted in their loss of interest in him. His current bitterness at the world and irritating demands on his family for attention are outgrowths of this process.

Our findings appear to fit fairly well with the limited fund-of-intimacy paradigm. Before marriage, men meet intimacy needs in their friendship groups. After marriage, involvement with friends declines as a man's wife begins to meet these needs, and he experiences demands to give primary loyalty to the marital dyad. As their children move into adolescence, involvement with friends declines further. As we have seen, adolescent children are a powerful emotional focus for midlife men. They often try to isolate the entire family from the outside world, to freeze it in time. Ed Fielding is one example of this phenomenon. At midlife he turns all his emotional energy toward the attempt to control and infantilize his children, finding the outside world inhospitable and threatening. Tom Conley also turns from peer group interests to an investment in his sons, but there is a different flavor to this transition. Tom had always gotten much more gratification out of "being with the boys." Especially while he was working in Washington, hard drinking (and perhaps a bit of womanizing), elegant dining, and golf had all been mediums for close and meaningful friendships. As Tom's sons have grown older, he has become fonder of them and their company. He sees this period of their lives as his "last chance to really get to know them," and most of his leisure activities include them. His outside friendships are now less actively pursued, but it is easy to see them being revived as Tom's sons leave home and establish their own families. As our statistical data indicate, men do reinvolve themselves with friends in the post-parental phase of midlife proper.

Our data suggest that friendship groups are a less significant force in the lives of middle-aged men. To the extent that such groups provide support, a sense of belonging, and a component of self-definition for younger men, these functions must be shifted to work and family by midlife. At this stage, men have fewer friends, see them less often, are more likely to see friends as couples, and in general are less intimate with them. The implications of this diminished involvement in peer friendships will be explored in the next section.

Effects of Friendship Networks

The nature of friendship group involvement is not only a function of life cycle stage, but it also reflects social class differences. Dunphy,[27] for example, has argued that men at the bottom of the social structure have less access to power and other resources needed to manipulate their environments, and are more likely to have encounters that lower self-esteem and increase frustration. When men in these circumstances meet, they are likely to communicate their resentments. We know from our studies of adolescents and young men that such communication typically leads to a group culture that articulates and amplifies their feelings of alienation. Under the right conditions the group culture may legitimize antisocial activity and encourage illegal solutions to the common problem of deprivation.

Ed Fielding, the factory worker described earlier, illustrates some of these processes. When asked if he had any friends, he at first indicated that he no longer maintained any real relationships and disliked his younger co-workers. When pressed further, he said he had a few friends at the factory. He goes into work early in the morning to have some coffee before his shift begins. At lunchtime the group assembles in an unused warehouse at the back of the plant.

> *It's this huge dark room, like a gymnasium. While we eat, we sit around a picnic table and play cards. We're like a pack of rats gathered together in the corner of a cellar.*

What makes them like a "pack of rats," aside from the setting, are the sentiments they convey to one another. They share anger and bitterness at management, at the government, at their children, and at their co-workers. The inequity of life is one of their major themes, and they have responded to the feeling of "being shafted" by helping each other pilfer from the plant. The group is also a place where TVs, stereos, and bicycles can be bought for very little money, no questions asked. Ed conveys the feeling that greed is less the motive for these men than defiance. Their larceny is the only thing that makes them feel even slightly potent. They are left, however, with a pervasive sense of alienation, defining themselves (as they are defined by the system) as losers.

Middle-class men, in contrast, are likely to engage in friendship groups with a more optimistic quality. Enjoying resources and identity inputs that make them feel better about themselves and their social environment, these men need not stress anger or self-justification. On the other hand, middle-class men may bring qualities of competitiveness or ambition to the social setting, limiting possibilities for closeness and acceptance. They tend to use friends and acquaintances in efforts to wheel and deal, to seek contacts or professional advancement. To the extent that this is true, middle-class friendship groups become little more than an extension of the work place, serving nothing in the way of intimacy needs. Middle-class friendship groups may, then, either reduce or have no impact on the man's alienation, depending on whether the group is genuinely intimate or merely an expedient alliance.

Findings on Friendship and Alienation

Using Nettler's Anomie scale as a measure of alienation, we find that the pattern Dunphy hypothesizes holds for younger but not older men (Table 9-6).

For young middle-class men, the more often they see their friends, the less alienated they are likely to be. The reverse is true for younger lower-class men. Furthermore, we find that young middle-class men who have friends they see on a regular basis are more likely to have received a raise or promotion last year and see their chances for advancement as good (Table 9-7). For the younger lower-class men, the trend is just the opposite, though only the relationship between getting a raise and having friends is significant ($r = -20$).

Thus, there is evidence that friendship group exchanges for

Table 9-6 Correlations Between Frequency of Interaction with Friends and Anomie Scale

	Younger Men		*Older Men*	
	Middle Class	*Lower Class*	*Middle Class*	*Lower Class*
Correlation	−.23	.28	—	—
Number of subjects	(40)	(71)		

Table 9-7 Correlation Between Having Friends and Job Success

| | Younger Men | | Older Men | |
	Middle Class	Lower Class	Middle Class	Lower Class
Received a raise last year	.23	−.20	.05	.08
Received a promotion last year	.23	−.03	.09	.08
Feels he has chances for advancement	.36	−.06	.19	.20
Number of subjects	(40)	(71)	(157)	(168)

younger middle-class men tend to reduce alienation and increase beliefs in and chances of success. For younger lower-class men, friends tend to amplify the feelings of alienation generated by occupational and economic frustrations.

With older men the picture is different. We have already seen that older men are less involved with friendship groups. Now we find that friendship is not related to their degree of anomie or their perceptions of opportunities at work. In general, at least with this data, it seems that friendship plays a small part in shaping attitudes or self-conceptions of older men.

Summary and Discussion

It appears that friendship groups serve different purposes for men at different stages of the life cycle. As men move through adult maturational stages, they experience different problems, concerns, and priorities that color their relationships to friends.

For unmarried men in their twenties, friendship groups serve important functions. The majority of these men spend a good deal of time with friends and appear to rely on them to meet complex emotional needs. As these men confront the life cycle problems of gaining a sense of identity and intimacy, the group provides a degree of support and validation of self-worth. For lower-class men, the group culture amplifies their sense of alienation from the larger system. Our data suggest that involvement in the group also undermines their chances of doing well in that system. For middle-class men, involvement in the group appears to reduce their sense of anomie and increase their chances of material success.

With marriage, friendship groups begin to become less important to men. Men gratify intimacy needs inside the family. Old friends get separated as they seek out jobs and homes. Within the marriage, maintenance of old friendships often creates strains. A man's wife may become jealous of the time spent away from home. Or the man himself may become jealous of his wife's attractiveness or attraction to his friends. Finally, the demands and expectations of husband and father roles lead men to feel that they have less time available to spend with old friends or acquire new ones. We see a number of consequences and corrolaries to this reduced involvement. The midlife male generally exhibits a narrowed focus, family and work being the defining elements in his life. This is associated with some stickiness in regard to his wife and children, the father clinging to them and fighting their efforts to move out of the familial system into the larger culture. For those men who do maintain genuine friendships outside the family, there appear to be positive gains in maintaining a sense of perspective. Our findings also underline earlier observations of the impersonality of contemporary culture. Friendship groups are, by middle age, dominated by issues of status, acquisition, and mutual use, surely corruptions of what we normally regard as intimacy. Mass society theorists may have overstated their case, but our culture does appear to encourage a gradual de-personalization of self and an impoverishment of relationships outside the family.

Endnotes

1. Thrasher, Frederick M., *The Gang* (Chicago: University of Chicago Press, 1926).
2. Dunphy, Dexter, *Cliques, Crowds and Gangs* (Melbourne, Australia: Cheshire Publishing, 1969).
3. Weiss, Lawrence, and Marjorie F. Lowenthal, "Life Course Perspectives on Friendship," in *Four Stages of Life*, edited by M. Lowenthal et al. (San Francisco: Jossey-Bass, 1975).
4. De Hoyos, Asteria, and Genevieve De Hoyos, "The Amigo System and Alienation of the Wife in the Conjugal Mexican Family," in *Kinship and Family Organization*, edited by B. Farber (New York: John Wiley, 1966).
5. Blau, Zena Smith, *Old Age in a Changing Society* (New York: New Viewpoints, 1973).
6. Lowenthal, Marjorie F., and Clayton Haven, "Interaction and Adaptation: Intimacy as a Critical Variable," in *Middle Age and Aging*, edited by Neugarten (Chicago: University of Chicago Press, 1968).

7. Farrell, Michael P., "Artists' Circles and the Development of Artists," paper presented at the American Sociological Association, New York City, August 1980.

8. Cohen, Albert K., *Delinquent Boys* (Glencoe, Ill.: Free Press, 1955).

9. Dickey, James, *Deliverance* (Boston: Houghton Mifflin, 1970).

10. Kesey, Ken, *One Flew Over the Cuckoo's Nest* (New York: Viking, 1962).

11. Laumann, Edward, *Bonds of Pluralism* (New York: John Wiley, 1973).

12. Parsons, Talcott, and Robert F. Bales (eds.), *Family, Socialization and Interaction Process* (Glencoe, Ill.: Free Press, 1955).

13. Slater, Phillip E., *The Pursuit of Loneliness* (Boston: Beacon Press, 1970).

14. Schutz, William C., *FIRO: A Three Dimensional Theory of Interpersonal Behavior* (New York: Rinehart, 1958).

15. Nelson, Joel, "Clique Contacts and Family Orientations," *American Sociological Review*, vol. 31, 1966, pp. 663–672.

16. *Ibid.*

17. Erikson, Erik H., *Childhood and Society* (New York: W.W. Norton, 1950).

18. Levinson, Daniel J., Charlotte N. Darrow, Edward B. Klein, Maria H. Levinson, and Braxton McKee, *The Seasons of a Man's Life* (New York: Alfred A. Knopf, 1978).

19. Axelrod, Morris, "Urban Structure and Social Participation," *American Sociological Review*, vol. 21, no. 1, February 1956.

20. Litwak, Eugene, "Extended Kin Relations in an Industrial Democratic Society," in *Social Structure and the Family: Generational Relations*, edited by E. Shamos and G. Streib (Englewood Cliffs, N.J.: Prentice Hall, 1965).

21. Sussman, Marvin B., "The Isolated Nuclear Family: Fact or Fiction," *Social Problems*, vol. 6, 1959, pp. 333–340.

22. Booth, Alan, "Sex and Social Participation," *American Sociological Review*, vol. 37, April 1972, pp. 183–193.

23. Laumann, *op. cit.*

24. Nelson, *op. cit.*

25. Lowenthal et al., *op. cit.*

26. Schulman, Norman, "Life-Cycle Variations in Patterns of Close Relationships," *Journal of Marriage and the Family*, November 1975, pp. 813–821.

27. Dunphy, Dexter, "The Subsystem and Supersystem of the Primary Group," in *The Primary Group*, edited by D. Dunphy (New York: Appleton-Century-Crofts, 1972).

Chapter 10

CONCLUSIONS

With our male midlife study, we have attempted to build on and reexamine past findings, assessing the adequacy of existing theories in light of our data. Obviously, no single study can provide definitive answers in such a complex area. We feel, however, that our investigation has been far more comprehensive than most, both in terms of sample size, representativeness, and the various levels of data gathered. It is from this vantage point that we have been able to show the limits and biases of some existing formulations, and to draw the outlines of a more diverse model.

We find aspects of both uniformity and uniqueness in the ways men respond to the midlife transition. The commonalities in experience reflect, we would argue, the pervasive effects of cultural expectations in shaping men's lives and their self-perceptions. That is, most men strive to conform to a limited range of cultural stereotypes of masculinity. The attempt to shape their lives in accordance with such images tends to become increasingly burdensome, particularly in relation to work and family. While the problems of "mid-career" have been previously recognized, the intensity, ubiquitousness, and complexity of family dynamics vis-à-vis midlife changes seems to us to be a crucial area of study. Our own findings suggest a virtual merging of individual and familial development at midlife. Any understanding of the man's altered experience of himself in the world must take into account his changing self definitions, interactions, and reception by others as father, husband, and son. These are not merely roles, but forms of connection to others through whom he has lived vicariously, reciprocally, or in opposition. These central relationships, both in fantasy and in reality, are used as psychological divisions of labor; they are parts of what we normally regard as his personality.

In some instances the shifting family matrix, in creating "burdens" or upsetting earlier adaptations, precipitates a heightened
awareness of self. The midlife male becomes vulnerable to re-
experiencing longstanding conflicts, unfulfilled aspirations, and
profound self-doubt. The typical response to this sense of vulnerability is increasing conformity to the class-linked stereotypes
discussed earlier.

In relation to work, marriage, children, parents, and friendship,
most men appear to drift toward behaviors and sentiments seen as
"normal" for their particular age group and social class. The
similar reactions we described among unskilled workers, for
example, demonstrate their absorption of social definitions of
what they should be. These men feel and act like stereotypes of
themselves: bitter losers. While people are vulnerable to the effects of such typecasting from childhood, midlife represents a
finalization of these definitions: the man trapped in the prison of
his faulty identity.

Intertwined with, and often disguised by, this conforming
aspect of aging in our culture is the expression of the individual
self. The men studied were dealing with their own personal
projects, desires, conflicts, and dreams, although they were often
able to only partially articulate them. While the content of these
individual processes shows much variation, their intrusion into
consciousness at midlife was common. Early adulthood functioned
as a distraction for many of our subjects, a period in which they
could ignore or unselfconsciously play out these feelings by
plunging into work life and family formation. The midlife transition does appear, like adolescence or retirement, to call for a halt
in this total social role involvement, to stimulate heightened concern with issues of identity and personal history. We do not find,
however, that these concerns themselves are translated into a
predictable "passage," "plateau," or "crisis." Rather, a variety of
reactions appear, ranging from heightened awareness of self to
increased rigidity and defensiveness. The resurgence of old
memories, conflicts, and aspirations is generally not a welcomed
experience, but one that intrudes itself in situations of personal
disruption and vulnerability. The only exception, and a relatively
rare one, is among upper-class or well-educated middle-class men.
These men may, in the context of positive self-esteem, utilize the
midlife transition as an opportunity to reexamine and change
earlier choices and solutions.

Familial Dynamics and the Self

One of the striking characteristics of the midlife transition is the man's heightened emotional investment in his family. This shift can be appreciated only in the context of the male pattern of early adulthood, one dominated by occupational concerns. As our quantitative data implied and our case histories confirmed, young men are generally quite absorbed by work role demands. While such striving may be seen as part of being a good husband and father, it also tends to take them outside the family sphere. The workplace represents a more major arena of identity striving for younger men, an arena where defeat is as likely as victory. Men often feel pressure to commit themselves to poorly understood work roles and struggle to cope despite an absence of skills, economic resources, or emotional integration. Under the normative pressure to become economically and emotionally autonomous—and the immediate demands of supporting a wife and children—most young men find compromise solutions that permit them to "get by." There is, however, a cost to these compromises. Young men suffer a sense of alienation and emotional distress. They may move toward a crystallized sense of themselves, but rarely one that fulfills an inner sense of identity.

By the time they reach middle age, most men feel committed to both the work and family roles evolved through early adulthood. While the external routine of shuttling back and forth between the two domains persists, both the man's persona (social self) and his self experience come to be focused increasingly on his family. Even men who withdraw behaviorally or become enmeshed in conflict with their families exhibit this changing self-definition. They neither act nor perceive themselves as enclosed psychological entities, but rather as part of a family group that forms their identity.

We have seen how the wife, children, and material characteristics of the home are used to express and compensate for aspects of the man's self that have been frustrated in the work role. Some men fill their homes with objects that validate their dignity and worth, counteracting the mortifications of self they experience in the outside world. Others enlist wives and children in a script that casts the man as a potent leader and protector, even though the supporting actors do not believe in the script. Alternatively, they may enlist their children as projective vehicles—either as redeemers of their flawed identities or as scapegoats. These uses of the family are brought into relief during middle age, when the children's bids for individuation and the wives' increased autonomy disrupt the attempted compensations. It is at this stage that the middle-aged man's narcissistic investment in his family is challenged and he must grapple with giving up objects he has used as part of himself. This surrender is made all the more difficult by the man's sense that the family is his final refuge, the place where he can find relief from the battering or stress often associated with work.

A complex interaction is precipitated at midlife between shifting role expectations, self-concept, family dynamics, and individual psychological issues developed earlier. The way the men studied handled these shifting aspects of their lives was very much dependent on social class. Different levels of education, income, and occupational attainment led to different midlife experiences.

Combining these social class, family, and individual dynamics into common patterns of response, we have attempted to describe what we see as the major paths of development displayed by men at midlife. Though we do not find "crisis" in the sense of a conscious disruption of identity to be a common pattern as men confront middle age, we do find a range of responses, some of which may be just as problematical as a crisis.

The styles that men use in responding to the developmental demands of middle age can be described in a two-dimensional space. The first axis is the Alienation-Integration dimension; the second is the Denial-Openness dimension. For the sake of clarity we have divided this space into four quadrants and constructed descriptions of the types of men that fall into each quadrant. The four types illustrate points on the spectrum. They are representative portraits of the limited number of styles that men exhibit as they enter middle age. The types also can be seen as points on four different developmental paths in our culture. While we can hypothesize about the development of each of these types from the historical data they and their families have provided, such inference is somewhat speculative. Nor do we know where they are likely to go from here. Future longitudinal research will have to inform us about the process of recovery or change that follows for those affected by the midlife upheaval.

Paths of Development

Development has been conceptualized in a number of ways. Some see it in epigenetic terms—the evolution of an increasingly differentiated and integrated structure of personality. This is a hierarchical metaphor. Others use less daring metaphors to conceptualize development, seeing it as "seasons" or episodes in time. Each season has its characteristic panorama of attitudes, behaviors, and problems, and the characteristics of one season may blend into the next. This view is less explicit, seeing a cumulative hierarchical structure underlying the changes.

Our data suggest that what passes for "development" is a multilayered process. Men in our culture appear to adopt behavioral forms, build skills, and assume "mature," responsible roles without necessarily going through concomitant emotional growth. This is a process of persona building, a process which can carry one through many of life's demands. One concomitant of this strategy is self-estrangement. Men tend to become increasingly defensive as they move from young adulthood to middle age, shutting out feelings, internal conflicts, or confusion that would challenge the image of self they are enacting. This mode of adaptation leads to an increasing discrepancy between the controlled, competent self shown to the world and the confused, adolescent-like self which persists into middle age. The conflicts with and over adolescent children, as well as the vivid remembrances of paternal influence, are the most common indicators that this less-developed substratum of personality continues to be part of the man's midlife struggles.

As these dynamics are described by each man, it becomes obvious that the specifics of many of his life decisions (for example, choice of mate, job, or residence) are expressions of the unresolved conflicts of youth. Careers are, at least partially, ways of rebelling against or appeasing parents; wives may be props in the achievement of some youthful fantasy of success or dominance. The connections are not in themselves remarkable. What we find striking is that our subjects appeared to be almost totally unselfconscious about their meaning. The midlife transition can precipitate a reopening of these issues, leading men to attempt some reexamination of themselves or to seek defensive closure once again. It is often the exigencies of midlife, rather than some newly found existential openness, that mitigates against closure as a solution. The stresses we find associated with this life stage are not particularly surprising. Our subjects were reacting to health problems and concerns, to job pressures and dissatisfactions, to parental death or demands, and to frustrations with maturing children. It was not necessary for these issues to "come to a head" simultaneously in order for them to have impact. The experience of midlife seemed to heighten an awareness of and sense of vulnerability to such changes. When morale begins to slip at midlife, the man may feel as if the bottom has fallen out. This feeling is expressed in the reactions of Bob Wilson and Tony Williams—men who had coped all their lives and who became strangely passive in the face of a deteriorating set of circumstances.

Rather than develop, most men move through a series of adaptations, coping with social expectations to the best of their abilities. This permits them to function adequately in their major life roles and may gradually enhance more basic self-esteem and a sense of human relatedness. However, such internal shifts are not inevitable. Many men invest themselves entirely in the external forms of success: good job, nice home, an attractive wife and kids. These badges of identity are not necessarily correlated with sensitivity, self-awareness, or other features we associate with the idea of emotional maturity. It is a limited kind of fulfillment, but one our culture seems to encourage.

Ironically, these badges of success appear almost to be prerequisites for more profound psychological work. It is the more educated and affluent (even at the blue-collar level) who seem able to transcend social definitions or social forms in order to examine their own lives and make human contact with wives, children, and parents. As Sennett has argued,[1] the "injuries of class" go much deeper than material deprivation. For the middle-aged man to define himself as a vocational failure seems, in our culture, to devastate his self-conception and lead him to estrange himself from others.

This connection of self-concept to occupational achievement was almost universal in the biographies of our subjects. The entrance into manhood was seen as a process of breaking away from parents and becoming economically self-sufficient. The latter was perceived as the precondition for the former, a belief which proved psychologically naive. Although this period of young adulthood was stressful in many ways, it is occupational adjustment that men recollect when speaking about it. The younger cohort used as a comparison group (ages 25–30) does, in fact, exhibit more signs of dissatisfaction, alienation, or "crisis." Although well beyond the age of the adolescent adjustment problems, they score higher than the older men on our measures of anomie and identity diffusion. They are more likely to be dissatisfied with their work, feel a sense of alienation from politics and religion, and show signs of psychological stress. These younger men are still grappling with the problems of finding a place in the occupational hierarchy, finding it difficult to exist at or near the bottom of the economic scale. As both producers and consumers they feel deprived and uncertain about future possibilities.

In our case studies we find that many men experience failure and frustration during this stage of life. In striving to establish themselves quickly or rise in the social class structure, they attempt projects that do not work out. Several of our working-class men, for example, failed in their attempts to start their own businesses, while those of middle-class background failed to achieve their desired occupations. Many men report interpersonal conflicts during their twenties or frustrations in dealing with their parents, wives, or fiancees. Although in retrospect the middle-aged men may miss their years of freedom from familial responsibilities, their reports of actual events from this period reflect episodes of depression, loneliness, and frustration. Eventually, after some compromises, most men piece together a situation that meets their needs, while a few thrive. They develop a personal "way of life," a set of routines and beliefs that enable them to meet the demands placed on them by life in our culture.

The majority of men eventually establish solutions to their work-role problems that are acceptable, only a minority finding real gratification or fulfillment in their work. Family comes to loom larger as the emotional center of the man's universe. It appears that the problem of establishing intimate relationships is, in comparison with career issues, even more complex and difficult. While the men wish to see the home as a sanctuary from a world filled with conflict and struggle, the home turf is as likely to become another battleground for them.

The fantasies and expectations men generate about their families are often unrealistic and narcissistic. Wives may be asked to totally submerge their own autonomy, living cheerfully to serve the husband; children may be required to show loyalty and obedience that make them extensions of the father's will. These expectations often have a bullying or demanding quality, the men having developed little in the way of interpersonal skills or the capacity for warm, intimate relationships. Brodsky, Fielding, and Williams are all variations of this characteristic, demanding that their wives and children serve them whether they like it or not. None of these men shares of himself or gives those around him a sense that he cares for them as human beings. The "love" they express for their families is perceived more as possessiveness and need.

Intimate relationships with parents and siblings fare no better, most men becoming emotionally distant from their families of origin by midlife. Old resentments, competitive struggles, and issues of dominance continue to simmer, making interaction tense or conflictual. Parental images and adolescent conflicts continue to be salient parts of the man's emotional landscape, tending to keep fresh the memories of wounds suffered earlier in the relationship. The introjected images make it difficult for the middle-aged man to see parents or relatives as they now are, and to reveal his adult self to them. For most men, members of their family of origin have the quality of being familiar strangers.

For the middle-aged man, friendships, too, tend to recede in both quality and significance. What friendships remain tend to become more superficial or expedient. Unlike the intense relationships of many young men—who are genuinely concerned about one another's welfare and welcome each other's companionship— midlife friendships are often ritualized or routine. The Thursday poker game or Saturday morning round of golf requires or facilitates little in the way of self-revelation.

For most men, then, the movement toward midlife is a process of self-insulation. Through work achievement, material affluence, the raising of children, and maintenance of marriage they come to be reassured about their capacity to cope with external demands. They take pride in achieving these benchmarks, and tend to become both more inward and less aware of their own limitations and desires. At either end of this statistical norm are the psychological casualties and the more fortunate or exceptional men, those for whom adult life has meant a growing self-awareness, increased acceptance and closeness to others, and a sense of their own competence. Our transcendent-generative type characterizes this path of development.

Path One: The Transcendent–Generative

The transcendent-generative men, as we suggested earlier, are in no sense perfect, nor need they exhibit all those signs of maturity that Erikson describes. Rather, through circumstance or effort, midlife finds them experiencing adequate solutions to major life problems. Work, marriage, parenthood, extended family relations, and friendship all provide rewards and are perceived as worthwhile. These are often men like Tom Conley, who started adulthood with a wealth of resources because of relatively high social status, family backing, and a capacity to overcome internal conflict so as to act and learn from experience. The sense of self he experiences at midlife is not a marked change from that of early adulthood.

Some men who eventually reach this point have not been as fortunate as Conley. They have a history of struggle, failure, and searching, a crucible which makes them more exceptional. Such men show greater sensitivity and a more articulate sense of how they have become who they are. It is for these men that midlife can be a true renaissance, a chance to consummate a kind of inner work they have accomplished over many years. Individual idiosyncrasies and limitations clearly exist, but these are either encapsulated or mild enough so they do not sabotage day-to-day living. Although they may suffer disappointment or misgivings, such men do not appear to have a midlife crisis. Rather, they steadily confront the new problems of middle age with the inherent confidence and multiple coping styles developed earlier. Their capacity to respond and adapt is linked to an openness to their own distress, an openness which differentiates them from their cohort.

Path Two: The Pseudo-Developed Man

The pseudo-developed man attempts to cope by adopting the persona of the successful middle-aged man, a pose which hides feelings of desperation, loss, and confusion. He denies both the internal and external demands that impinge on him, pretending to have everything under control. He initially reports that his work is satisfying, yet his anecdotes about work indicate he has no commitment to it, sees no real value in it, and gets little satisfaction from it. When we elicit details, these men tell us of boredom, conflict, or a sense of having been passed by. They harbor fantasies of starting a new career or regrets about not pursuing earlier opportunities. However, these urges to escape are only vague dreams, not believed in as possible blueprints for change. The sense of stagnation or discontent is only dimly perceived, overtly unacknowledged, and fictionalized as "part of life."

At home the pseudo-developed man claims to have a typical happy marriage and family, a perception maintained by systematic distortion and denial of reality. He is unaware of the inner lives of his wife and children and their feelings toward him, while they experience him as a troublesome force to be avoided.

He maintains his facade through adherence to rigid ways of thinking and behaving. He avoids new experiences and people. He maintains rigid rules of behavior for his children, and interactions with them are based on conveying these rules, enforcing them, or giving examples of the consequences of deviation. He works hard at maintaining a conventionally respectable self-presentation. Information that calls into question his myth of success and happiness is dismissed. He sees himself as a leader; others are simply not able to understand the wisdom of his ways, or else they are people whose views can be discounted because of their race, religion, or some other characteristic that marks them as "inferior."

We refer to him as pseudo-developed because, while he presents himself as having solved basic developmental problems, other evidence indicates that the presentation is based on denial of failures and stresses that surround him. As this type enters middle age he shows few signs that the myth about himself will dissolve. As long as some external calamity does not puncture his adaptation, he will continue his pretense supported by a culture in which his behavior is seen as typical.

Path Three: The Midlife Crisis Type

While our findings have shown the midlife crisis to be atypical, there is a subset of middle-aged men who exhibit many signs of disintegration. They report a sense of being confused, overwhelmed, and alienated as they confront the demands of midlife. Our in-depth interviews indicate that the difficulties they experience have their roots in conflicts and problems of earlier origin, problems covered over during active phase of early adulthood. These men have, for example, maintained highly dependent orientations to their parents, made major life commitments on the basis of compromise and expediency, or maintained a family life based on only superficial degrees of intimacy.

As midlife approaches, the fragility of these temporary solutions becomes evident, leading to a sense that their whole world is collapsing. While they may have known that change was necessary or desirable, they tended to drift through earlier adulthood, procrastinating about basic decisions. These men convey a sense that the approach of middle age is a shock to them, a closing in of time before they have really had a chance to get started. This leaves them feeling quite unable to deal with the growing demands of wives, children, and parents. Experiencing themselves as in need of opportunities, help, and support, they are overwhelmed and bitter when asked to provide these to others.

While it is possible that this midlife crisis is a transitory reaction, we come away with a sense that most of these men are starting a more general process of depressive decline. While tenuous or unsatisfactory careers, marriages, or friendships were maintained as long as these men could hope for a different future, the realization of diminished possibilities disrupts these props. Rather than having domains to fall back on, problems in one sphere resonate with and exacerbate problems in the others. Bob Wilson's occupational dissatisfactions stimulate conflicts with his son, whom he needs to achieve for him. The continued distress over both issues may well have been a contributing factor in his coronary attack, which now makes him even less able to handle the other issues. It is difficult to envision these men regaining the level of functioning and hope that characterized them in their middle thirties. The acute sense of stagnation and depressive symptomatology might well pass, however, and be transformed into a more muted acceptance of their disappointments.

Path Four: The Punitive-Disenchanted Type

Our final path is most strongly associated with pathology. Though these men also exhibit the symptoms of crisis, it would be misleading to describe them in those terms. Rather than suddenly falling off the edge of a plateau of positive adaptation established in their thirties, these men have been in the state of upheaval and unhappiness for most of their lives. They are likely to begin life as sons of semi-skilled or unskilled laborers. They report deprivation, neglect, and brutality in their homes during childhood. Although they may attempt to escape this environment, catastrophic failures in young adulthood, early marriages based on the need to escape, followed by a trend of drifting from job to dead-end job, losing friends, and drinking have led to a repetition of their parents' circumstances, attitudes, and life styles. Having begun life "in the hole" in terms of psychological, social, and economic resources, the subsequent frustrations of adult life have produced the psychological and physical morbidity associated with these deficits.

As they enter middle age they continue to exhibit the symptoms developed in early adulthood: complaining about illness (real and hypochondriacal); distrustful and hostile toward others; isolated, bigoted, depressed, and unable to act effectively to alter their lives. Rather than being in a discrete crisis, these men have been and are in a state of chronic discontent.

Although we feel these four paths of development roughly characterize the lives of most men in contemporary American society, we make no claim for the universality of the paths across cultures and time. It is the current state of our culture and social structure that these men are attempting to come to terms with; and it is that culture and structure that influences the timetable, expectations, and conditions for their development.

The Stratification System

As we survey the life histories of men in our culture and the psychological impact of their movement from adolescence to midlife, we are struck by the casualty rate. One dimension of this destructiveness is clear. Our society establishes expectations and criteria for success that most men will never attain. Moreover, men internalize these expectations and regard their nonachievement as the sign of personal defects. While other writers have noted this phenomenon, its impact on midlife adjustment and family dynamics has not been traced previously.

At a second level, our culture appears to skew male maturation by demands for external conformity. In the process of trying to appear and feel normal, men plunge into school, work, and marriage in uniform and rote ways, often having little inner commitment to or understanding of these choices. Encouraged by cultural ideals of masculine strength and effectiveness, they strive to treat themselves and others mechanically, and become increasingly unable to understand their own motivations. They do not, however, eradicate their own desires and conflicts in this process. The conflicts return to confuse and haunt them as their life circumstances change at midlife. In having to deal with themselves, their wives, their parents, and children, middle-aged men in our society find that much of their maturity is no more than a veneer. Only a fraction of the men—perhaps a quarter to a third —avoid falling into the traps of material failure, lost self-esteem, or extreme self-estrangement. The correlation of social class origins to midlife outcomes also suggests the injustice of the system.

In our society the resources necessary for external success are distributed unequally. Those at the top are at an advantage, and they are more likely to follow a developmental path that leads to the transcendent-generative style in middle age. They generally grow up in homes that provide the psychological resources and values that enable them to cope with the demands of adult life. Years of education are required for most of the more prestigious and rewarding positions; men from the highest social strata are more apt to get that education. These same men are also more likely to receive direct help from family and friends in establishing themselves. The result is that they have better chances to build adequate solutions to the basic economic demands of life in our society. This is not to say that every man who starts life in a middle- or upper-class home is going to become a transcendent-generative. However, those who begin life in a higher social class have a far greater opportunity to avoid some of the destructive effects of the social class system.

In contrast, men who begin life and remain at the bottom of the hierarchy tend to develop in the direction of our punitive-disenchanted type. For them the resources and opportunities necessary to establish a sense of identity in their work are limited. These impediments as well as the lost self-esteem and emotional legacy associated with them are tied to an inability to establish a satisfying relationship with a wife and children. When these men reach middle age they often feel trapped in a situation they dislike, their only consolation being to blame others for their problems or vent their anger on persons or groups weaker than themselves. If for most men "finding yourself" is hard enough, when life is plagued with deprivations it can seem impossible.

In between the transcendent-generatives and the punitive-dis-enchanted are the other two types: the midlife crisis and the pseudo-developed. Both of the intermediate types have failed to achieve internally satisfying solutions to basic life problems. Through a lifetime of compromises the crisis type has reached a point at middle age where he feels overwhelmed by multiple problems. He is dissatisfied with many aspects of his life and he knows it. The pseudo-developed man experiences many of the same difficulties, but refuses to acknowledge them to himself or others. He reports a sense of satisfaction but he also shows many signs of denial, rigidity, and avoidance of potential conflicts. He seems to strive to keep in step with the transcendent-generatives, but his sense of being among them is an illusion. These inter-mediate types are most likely to be found in the middle range of the class structure.

Conclusions

Our research has led us to propose that there are several styles of response to the stresses of middle age. Rather than finding a single universal developmental course, we have found four paths. We have speculated how and why men take different paths, seeing a complex interaction between individual psychological factors, cultural influences, and family dynamics in producing midlife reactions. Our conclusions are based on comparisons of two age cohorts as well as biographical accounts of men and their families. Some of the differences between the two groups may be due to profoundly different life experiences that have led to different internal states and ways of relating to the environment. Only longitudinal research will enable us to untangle generational and developmental effects and to know what lies on the other side of the midlife transition.

Endnote

1. Sennett, Richard, and Jonathan Cobb, *The Hidden Injustice of Class* (New York: Alfred A. Knopf, 1973).

Appendix 1

THE MIDLIFE CRISIS SCALE: PHYSICAL HEALTH QUESTIONS

Midlife Crisis Scale

Unless noted otherwise, all questions are answered with a six-point Likert scale:

1. Strongly Agree   2. Agree   3. Slightly Agree
4. Slightly Disagree   5. Disagree   6. Strongly Disagree

1. Marriage is as rewarding and enjoyable after 15 or 20 years as it is in the earlier years.
2. Many men I know are undergoing what you would call a change of life or a middle-age identity crisis.
3. Almost any job or occupation becomes routine and dull if you keep at it for many years.
4. I am still finding new challenges and interest in my work.
5. In some ways, I wish my children were young again.
6. When your child grows up, he is almost bound to disappoint you.
7. Many people claim that middle age is one of the most difficult times of life. Has it been (or do you think it will be) that way for you? (1. Very Much So; 2. Somewhat; 3. Perhaps; 4. I Doubt It; 5. Not at All)
8. I wish I had the opportunity to start afresh and do things over, knowing what I do now.
9. Many of the things you seek when you are young don't bring true happiness.
10. I find myself thinking about what kind of person I am and what I really want out of life.

11. A person must remain loyal to his commitments if they do not turn out the way he expected.
12. How would you characterize your relationship to your wife now? (1. Very Close; 2. Close; 3. Neither Close Nor Distant; 4. Distant; 5. Far Apart)

Physical Health Questions

1. Do you have any particular physical or health trouble?
   If yes, what is it?_____
2. Have you ever had the following diseases?
   Asthma
   If yes, when was that?_____
3. Hay fever
   If yes, when was that?_____
4. Skin trouble
   If yes, when was that?_____
5. Stomach ulcer
   If yes, when was that?_____
6. Do you feel you are bothered by all sorts of pains and ailments in different parts of your body?
7. Have you ever felt you were going to have a nervous breakdown?

Appendix 2

COMPARISONS OF FOUR TYPES OF MIDDLE-AGED MEN ON SCALES AND SELECTED ITEMS

Table A2-1   Selected Comparisons of Mean Scale Scores of the Four Types of Middle-Aged Men

	Mean Scores for Each Type			
	Anti-Hero or Crisis	Tran-scendent-Generative	Pseudo-Developed	Punitive-Disen-chanted
(N)	(38)	(104)	(85)	(95)
Percent	12%	32%	26%	30%
Social Desirability (Ford)	1.43	1.55	1.61	1.56
Tolerance of Ambiguity	3.93	3.87	3.58	3.55
Authoritarian Child-Rearing (Levinson)*	2.37	2.43	1.97	2.10
Work Satisfaction*	1.93	1.57	1.58	1.90
Nettler's Anomie	1.44	1.30	1.31	1.40
Attitudes Toward War	1.73	1.78	1.93	1.75
Midlife Crisis Scale*	3.27	3.73	3.55	3.21
Depression	1.82	1.50	1.63	1.92
Psychosomatic Symptoms	1.78	1.47	1.50	1.77
Physical Health	1.85	1.93	1.91	1.86
Bigotry*	4.44	4.50	3.12	3.06
Hypochondriasis	1.37	1.31	1.39	1.34
Anxiety*	1.50	1.68	1.65	1.52
Denial*	1.51	1.64	1.55	1.48
Identity Diffusion	3.12	2.39	2.47	3.18

Note: Since the factors used to construct the typology are based upon the scales, it is not meaningful to compare the types with statistical tests. Therefore, we have simply reported the mean scores on our scales and the percent agreeing with selected items.

* A low score on starred scales indicates the concept measured is high (i.e., scale is reversed).

Table A2-2   Selected Item-by-Item Comparisons of the Four Types of Middle-Aged Men

	Percent of Each Type Agreeing with Items			
	Anti-Hero or Crisis	Tran-scendent-Generative	Pseudo-Developed	Punitive-Disen-chanted
(N)	(38)	(104)	(85)	(95)
Shortness of breath	18	5	8	24
Heart beats hard	18	6	11	16
Drink too much	39	35	22	49
Dizzy	13	4	4	17
Nightmares	13	1	8	11
Losing weight	3	5	8	16
Hands tremble	5	3	7	18
Sweaty palms	22	8	6	23
Felt I couldn't go on	43	5	13	41
Might have a nervous breakdown	24	5	1	29
Feel blue	8	1	4	10
Morning best time*	64	53	56	62
Cry	3	1	0	3
Sleep trouble	11	2	12	10
Do not eat as usual	47	28	41	42
Enjoy sex*	9	9	27	24
Constipation	5	1	2	3
Fast heartbeat	0	3	1	4
Tired	13	1	5	11
Clear-minded*	19	14	35	43
Easy to do things*	27	20	39	54
Restless	13	10	7	27
Hopeful*	24	8	21	48
Irritable	65	29	30	59
Fast to decide*	21	13	29	52
Feel needed*	21	4	12	39
Do not feel life full	25	2	16	32
Better dead	0	1	4	6
Do not still enjoy things	16	6	16	38
Thinking about life	84	66	57	80

* Reversed item.

Table A2-2 (continued)

	Percent of Each Type Agreeing with Items			
	Anti-Hero or Crisis	Tran- scendent- Generative	Pseudo- Developed	Punitive- Disen- chanted
Loyal to commitments	33	23	16	12
Ever have wife trouble	56	44	28	65
Friends have middle-age crisis	58	30	40	60
Job dull	62	35	52	80
No new challenges in work	16	7	12	27
Marriage not rewarding	17	7	4	26
Wish kids young	34	23	51	52
Kids disappoint	20	7	9	33
Middle age difficult	57	21	18	57
Start afresh	86	47	51	80
Health trouble	39	17	15	26
Asthma	5	4	7	4
Hay fever	21	12	12	10
Skin trouble	24	10	15	14
Ulcer	19	6	6	15
Pains	5	4	5	13
Sleep trouble	14	5	8	24
Fidgety	35	7	7	33
Headaches	64	40	39	56
Appetite change	0	0	1	13
Stomach problems	19	7	8	22
Waking problems	36	14	16	34
Illness leads to missed work	18	7	16	18

Table A2-3   Items Differentiating Deniers (Pseudo-Developed) from Integrated (Transcendent-Generative)

	Percent Agreeing with Each Item	
	Deniers	*Integrated*
Not always clear-minded	35	14
Feel tired	5	1
Sex not as good	27	9
Don't eat as usual	41	28
Sleep trouble	12	2
Felt I couldn't go on	13	5
Heart beats hard sometimes	11	6
See friends having middle age crisis	40	30
Job dull	52	35
No new challenges at work	12	7
Wish kids were young	51	23
Get ill at work	16	7
Drink too much	22	35
Ever have trouble with wife	28	44
Not hopeful	21	8
Not easy to do things	39	20
Not fast to decide	29	13
Don't feel needed	12	4
Don't feel life full	16	2
Don't still enjoy things	16	6

Table A2-4   Husband-Wife Relations

		Middle Class	Lower Class	F	P
	Closeness to wife:				
I	Young unmarried men	4.25	4.60	Col 7.69	<.01
II	Newlywed men without children	5.75	5.73	Row 4.66	<.025
III	Men with first child preschool age	5.79	5.27		
IV	Men with first child grade school age	5.44	5.32		
V	Men with first child high school age	5.55	4.88		
VI	Men with first child beyond high school (launching phase)	5.35	5.15		
		5.46	5.20		
	Percent very close to wife:				
I	Young unmarried men	—			
II	Newlywed men without children	74			
III	Men with first child preschool age	69			
IV	Men with first child grade school age	54			
V	Men with first child high school age	47			
VI	Men with first child beyond high school (launching phase)	43			

Mean years married: 15.01
Mean age of oldest child: 14.18

Table A2-5 Results of Analysis of Variance Comparing Young and Old Men from the Middle and Lower Classes, Rural and Urban Areas, on Factor I (Alienation) and Factor II (Egalitarianism)

URBAN   Factor I: Alienation

	Young	Old	Total	F	P
Middle Class	−.80	−2.45	−2.17	10.875 C	<.01
Lower Class	.34	−1.29	− .78	8.172 R	<.01
	−.05	−1.90	− .45		

URBAN   Factor II: Egalitarianism

	Young	Old	Total	F	P
Middle Class	.55	.64	.63	2.289 C	N.S.
Lower Class	.45	− .55	− .23	14.379 R	<.01
	.48	.09	.18		

RURAL   Factor I: Alienation

	Young	Old	Total	F	P
Middle Class	−.96	−1.96	−1.62		N.S.
Lower Class	.06	− .99	− .71		N.S.
	−.36	−1.31	−1.03		

RURAL   Factor II: Egalitarianism

	Young	Old	Total	F	P
Middle Class	.12	− .27	− .14	2.87 C	N.S.
Lower Class	−.62	−1.39	−1.19	7.03 R	<.01
	−.32	−1.02	− .82		

Table A2-6 T-tests Comparing Urban-Rural Factor Score Means on Factors I and II

	Rural	Urban	t	P
Factor I: Alienation	−.45 (4.30)	−1.03 (4.45)	1.05	N.S.
Factor II: Egalitarianism	.18 (1.93)	− .82 (2.19)	4.38	<.001

A SELECTED BIBLIOGRAPHY

The books and articles in this bibliography are some of the sources that have influenced our thinking about the experiences of men entering middle age. It is not exhaustive, but it does provide an overview of the range of important theories and research findings in the field. The reader interested in a more comprehensive selection may want to consult the following bibliographies: Men's Studies Bibliography, Massachusetts Institute of Technology, Human Studies Collection, Humanities Library, Cambridge, Massachusetts 02139 and Bibliography of the Committee on Work and Personality in the Middle Years, Social Science Research Council, 605 Third Avenue, New York, New York 10016.

Block, J., and N. Haan. *Lives Through Time.* Berkeley, California: Bancroft Books, 1971. One of the few longitudinal studies of development, but limited because of its focus on gifted children. The study traces boys and girls from early adolescence to their middle thirties and finds evidence for "unity or consistency of personality." They emphasize the importance of early family experiences for development.

Blood, Robert O., and Donald M. Wolfe. *Husbands and Wives.* New York: The Free Press, 1960. Based on structured interviews with over 900 Detroit-area wives, this study finds that wives report more satisfaction in the post-parental stage of life than in any previous period except the honeymoon. The low point in satisfaction is in early middle age. The wives' decision-making power is lowest when young children are in the home, but gains steadily as the couple moves through the rest of the life cycle.

Brim, Orville G., Jr. "Theories of the Male Mid-Life Crisis," *The Counseling Psychologist 6,* 1976, pp. 2–9. An excellent critical review of theories of adult male development, focusing on the works of Levinson, Lowenthal, and Neugarten, but also drawing on other relevant theorists such as Jung, Jaques, and Erikson. Brim highlights distinctions among these theories, isolating those that see crisis and change as determined by external status changes and those that see it as the result of intrapsychic development. He criticizes the latter group for not specifying causes of change.

Cuber, John F., and Peggy B. Harroff. *The Significant Americans.* New York: Appleton-Century-Crofts, 1965. The study reports findings from interviews with 107 husbands and 104 wives who have never considered divorce. They find five types of "satisfied" middle-aged couples: the Conflict-Habituated, the Devitalized, the Passive-Congenial, the Vital, and the Total. The findings point out the need to go beyond surface reports of satisfaction and to examine the history and quality of marital relationships.

Daedalus. Adulthood. Spring, 1976. A special issue on adulthood, with articles by Erik Erikson and others, dealing with maturation in a variety of cultures (Christian, Islamic, Confucian, Japanese, Indian, and Russian). Besides these cross-cultural studies, the issue contains an interesting article by Robert N. Bellah analyzing how the active-secular and the contemplative-sacred polarities have been combined in ideals for adulthood during different periods in history.

Elder, Glen H., Jr. *Children of the Great Depression.* Chicago: The University of Chicago Press, 1974. This book reports one of the few longitudinal studies of development over the years of adolescence through middle age. The study began during the Depression when the 156 Oakland Growth Study subjects were preadolescents and adolescents. The author compares the adult developmental paths of men and women who came from middle- and lower-class, deprived or non-deprived homes. Making use of sophisticated techniques of data analysis, the author looks at the impact of class and family backgrounds on the careers, family relations, values, and health of the subjects as they enter middle age.

Erikson, Erik. *Childhood and Society.* New York: W.W. Norton, 1963. This classic book presents Erikson's highly influential theory of ego development across the life cycle, which proposes a necessary sequence of subjective issues that must be confronted and resolved in a relatively positive manner in normal development. The issues in sequence are trust/mistrust, autonomy/shame, initiative/guilt, industry/inferiority, indentity/role diffusion, intimacy/isolation, generativity/stagnation, and integrity/despair. For a more detailed treatment of the issues of the later life cycle, see Erikson's more recent *Gandhi's Truth* (New York, W.W. Norton, 1969); "Reflections on Dr. Berg's Life Cycle" in *Daedalus,* 105:2, 1976, pp. 1–28; and *Dimensions of a New Identity* (Jefferson Lectures, New York, 1974).

Estes, Richard J., and Harold L. Wilensky. "Life Cycle Squeeze and the Morale Curve," *Social Problems* 25:3 (Feb. 1978), pp. 277–292.

Though this study focuses primarily on 230 employed and unemployed professionals, it also provides a good review of the life-cycle squeeze literature. The evidence from several studies shows that men experience their lowest period of morale when their wants and needs outdistance their income and job status. This period occurs in the early stages of family building when children are young and the man is between ages 25 and 40. As the children leave and the man moves into middle age, he experiences a sharp rise in morale. A minority of financially secure professionals do not show this pattern. Their level of morale is relatively high across the life cycle, with a slight drop when children leave home.

Gould, Roger L. "The Phases of Adult Life: A Study in Developmental Psychology," *American Journal of Psychiatry* 129:5 (Nov. 1972), pp. 33–43. Working with a small sample of patients in group therapy assigned to homogenous age groups, Gould isolates common concerns at seven stages of life. The concerns are used to develop a questionnaire that is given to 524 non-patient friends or acquaintances of eight medical students and hospital volunteers. The method of data analysis is not clearly presented, but a series of curves shows seven age periods: 16-17, 18-21, 22-28, 29-36, 37-43, 44-50, and 51-60. The late teens and early twenties are spent in getting away from parents and establishing oneself as an adult. In the early thirties there is a questioning of one's life, with increased acceptance of one's parents, an increased desire to be accepted for what one is, and an increased attempt to accept children for who they are. There is a negative cast to the forties, with an emerging sense of finite time and a resignation to reality. Orientation towards children is more critical. Friendship has a competitive cast. Around age fifty a mellowing occurs, accompanied by warmer feelings toward parents, children, and friends. The spouse is seen as a companion rather than a parent or a source of supplies. The imminence of death leads to a narrowed time span and renewed questioning about the meaningfulness of life. The stages seem based more on the clinical analysis of patients than on the larger sample.

For a more detailed treatment, see Gould, *Transformations* (New York: Simon and Schuster, 1978).

Gutmann, David L. "The Post-Parental Years: Clinical Problems and Developmental Possibilities," in *Midlife: Developmental and Clinical Issues*, edited by William H. Norman and Thomas J. Scaramella. New York: Brunner/Mazel, 1980, pp. 38–52. Based on his extensive cross-cultural research on aging and development, Gutmann proposes a theory to account for the polarization of the sexes in the early stages of adulthood (men aggressive, women nurturant) and the breakdown of the polarization in later life. After the emergency of the demands of parenthood, middle-aged adults experience a "return of the repressed," with men becoming more nurturant and less competitive, and women becoming more aggressive. Both redirect narcissism from their children to themselves.

Jaques, E. "Death and the Mid-Life Crisis," *International Journal of Psychoanalysis 46*, 1965, pp. 502–514. Based on an analysis of the life histories of great writers, composers, and musicians, this paper argues that a midlife crisis occurs around age 37. The crisis is precipitated by an awareness of mortality and often results in a reworking of childhood conflicts centering around destructive and aggressive urges. Over the life course the artist moves from an impulsive, spontaneous style to a more reflective and mature style.

Jung, Carl G. "The Stages of Life," in *The Portable Jung*, edited by Joseph Campbell. New York: Viking Press, 1971. Jung's thoughts about development in middle age are found throughout his work, but this is one of the more compact presentations of his observations of increased tenderness in men and aggressiveness in women during this period and a crisis centering around renewed confrontation with issues of individuation.

Kohlberg, L., and R. Kramer. "Continuities and Discontinuities in Childhood and Adult Moral Development," *Human Development 12*, 1969, pp. 93–120. This paper contains a good discussion of developmental stage theories, contrasting them with learning theories and the life stage task theories. The authors attempt to extend Kohlberg's theory of moral development into middle age. In contrasting the stages of morality of young men to their middle-aged fathers, they find the middle-aged men slightly lower on stages 5 and 6 thought. The older men show a trend toward increased consistency of thought and behavior, but the authors attribute this stabilization to the pressures of external socialization rather than to internal maturation or integration.

Lehman, H. C. *Age and Achievement*. Princeton, N.J.: Princeton University Press, 1953. A classical study of the age at which men are likely to peak in their careers. Making use of expert evaluations of the works and accomplishments of "dead greats," the author charts curves describing the points in the life cycle when men in different occupations are likely to do their best work. The occupations include science, mathematics, medicine, music composition, philosophy, literature, poetry, art, acting, business, and government.

Levinson, Daniel J., in collaboration with Charlotte N. Darrow, Edward B. Klein, Maria H. Levinson, and Braxton McKee. *The Seasons of a Man's Life*. New York: Ballantine Books, 1978. Begun in 1966, this study has had a major impact on research and on the theory of stages of adult male development. It is based on biographical interviews with forty men ages 35 to 45—ten each of hourly workers, business executives, biologists, and novelists from diverse ethnic, religious, and social class backgrounds. Each man was interviewed for 10 to 20 hours over the course of 5 to 10 visits at home, work, or the researchers' offices.

After inductive analysis of the interviews and biographies of noted public figures, the authors argue that development is closely linked to age. Development proceeds through a predictable series of transitions and plateaus during which a man builds or transforms a "life structure" that has socio-cultural, psychological, and behavioral components. The stages are Early Adult Transition (17-22), Entering the Adult World (23-28), Age 30 Transition (28-33), Settling Down (33-40), Mid-Life Transition (40-45), Entering Middle Adulthood (46-50), Age 50 Transition (50-55), Culmination of Middle Adulthood (55-60), and Late Adult Transition (60-65). As men approach 40 they are likely to be climbing the occupational ladder, breaking free from mentors, and becoming their own men. Whether they have been advancing within a stable structure (55 percent of the men) or manifesting a less stable pattern, all men go through a transition phase between ages 40 and 45. In this period the individuation process involves coming to terms once again with four polarities: young/old, destruction/creation, masculine/feminine, and attachment/separation. Middle-aged men usually move to a more balanced position on these polarities.

Lidz, Theodore. *The Person: His Development Throughout the Life Cycle.* New York: Basic Books, 1968. A comprehensive text on development, drawing on the psychoanalytic perspective.

Lowenthal, Marjorie Fiske, and David Chiriboga. "Transition to the Empty Nest," *Archives of General Psychiatry 26* (Jan. 1972), pp. 8–14. The data for this study are from in-depth interviews with 27 men and 27 women approaching the empty-nest stage of family development (average age 51 for men, 48 for women). Subjects were asked to rate each year of their life from "absolute tops" to "rock bottom." They find that the lowest point for men is likely to be young adulthood, a period described as particularly frustrating. Only one fourth of the men reported work as a current source of satisfaction. Men spoke positively of their wives and reported that their sex lives were about the same or better than in the past. But the women were more likely to view their husbands in negative terms and to report a decline in frequency or quality of sexual activity. Though neither men nor women seemed particularly troubled by the impending empty nest, the authors suspect that men have a tendency to suppress or repress negative affect.

Lowenthal, Marjorie Fiske, Majda Thurnher, and David Chiriboga. *Four Stages of Life.* San Francisco: Jossey-Bass, 1975. This book is filled with a wide range of empirical findings on the emotional states, behavior, friendship patterns, stresses, time perspectives, marital relations, and values of men and women at four pre-transitional stages of life. The sample consists of 216 subjects, with about 25 men and 25 women from each stage of life: high school seniors, newlyweds, pre-empty nest, and pre-retirement. The sample was drawn from one upper-working-class school district. Initial contacts were made with seniors who were the youngest members of their families; other contacts were made through referrals. In general, they find that middle-aged men seem to move into a constricted mode of living. They report the least complex round of roles and activities, the least involvement in friendship, the fewest life events in the recent past. The expansiveness of the younger men is replaced by orderliness and caution in middle age. Their self-concepts become less diffuse, and they are less likely to report psychological problems. Their main stresses center around work. However, the authors suspect denial is characteristic of this group. Wives report most dissatisfaction in middle age and are most critical of their husbands. Wives are becoming more aggressive and are gaining in power. Though rich with empirical findings and suggestive insights, the book lacks theoretical integration.

Maas, Henry S., and Joseph A. Kuypers. *From 30 to 70*. San Francisco: Jossey-Bass, 1974. A longitudinal study of 95 mothers and 47 fathers from the Berkeley Institute of Human Development Study. Subjects were interviewed 40 years after initial contacts made when they were in their thirties and were middle- and upper-class parents. They find remarkable continuity in the life styles of the fathers. The four types of life styles were predictable from data gathered when subjects were in their thirties. The types are family-centered, remotely sociable, hobbyists, and unwell-disengaged. Though life styles are continuous, men show personality changes, filtering toward three types: person-oriented, active-competent, and conservative-ordering.

McGill, Michael E. *The 40 to 60 Year Old Male*. New York: Simon and Schuster, 1980. A popularized self-help guide for middle-aged men. Though without references or clear presentation of the method of data analysis, the author claims the book is based on contacts with over 2,500 people during a four-year period (500 questionnaire responses, 200 interviews, and hundreds of letters from people in crisis). The book argues that male midlife crisis is a pervasive phenomenon caused by threats to identity. The threats may come from failures to achieve career goals, being forced out by younger men, the empty nest, physical decline, and fear of death or stagnation. The book is filled with dramatic case studies and advice.

Meltzer, H. "Attitudes of Workers Before and After Age 40," *Geriatrics*, May, 1965, pp. 425–432. In a study of male paper mill workers, 120 of them age 40 or less and 93 of them over 40, the author finds that the older workers are much more likely to be satisfied with their superiors, working conditions, salaries, and job. Older workers also scored significantly higher on life adjustment measures. "All in all," he reports, "older workers have more emotional acceptance for traditions, policies, people, supervisors, top management, and pay and are less critical of existing practices and services."

Mortimer, Jeylan T., and Robert G. Simmons. "Adult Socialization," in *Annual Review of Sociology 4*, 1978, pp. 421–454. This article reviews a wide range of empirical findings and theoretical issues relevant to adult development. It places the literature on the experience of midlife in the context of the growing body of literature dealing with socialization during periods of identity change in adulthood. The authors make clear the eclectic quality of the field at this point.

Neugarten, Bernice L. *Personality in Middle and Late Life.* New York: Atherton Press, 1964. Reports on a study of 710 middle class people from Kansas City between the ages of 40 and 90. Making use of both interviews and projective tests, the study finds changes in intrapsychic processes after 40, with the older subjects showing increased interiority and a decrease in personality complexity. Women are seen as becoming more aggressive while men become more passive. Both men and women change their perspective on time, seeing life as time-left-to-live rather than time-since-birth. Changes in conscious, overt behavior are less strongly related to the life cycle.

Neugarten, Bernice L., ed. *Middle Age and Aging.* Chicago: University of Chicago Press, 1968. This edited reader is an excellent overview of theory and research on aging prior to the burst of interest in the area during the 1970s. The emphasis is on social and psychological processes as people move from middle to old age. The book is aimed at a graduate student audience and includes several articles in each of nine areas: age status and roles, the psychology of the life cycle, theories of aging, health, family, work and leisure, social environment, other cultures, and death.

Norman, William H., and Thomas J. Scaramella. *Midlife: Developmental and Clinical Issues.* New York: Brunner/Mazel, 1980. A collection of articles based on papers delivered at a symposium on midlife in 1978 at Butler Hospital. It contains a stimulating range of theory, research, and ideas for clinical practice. The chapters range from analysis of mythology and fairy tales (Datan), overviews of development (Lidz), marital and sex role issues (Gutmann, Notman, Gould, and Mann), to treatment of emotional stress (Cath, Bowers, *et al.* and Turner).

Osherson, Samuel D. *Holding On or Letting Go.* New York: The Free Press, 1980. A thoughtful and careful analysis of the subjective experiences of 20 men between the ages of 35 and 50 who shifted from established positions to careers in creative arts and crafts (actors, visual artists, and potters). The men are unique in many ways, with an average of 2.1 years of graduate education and a total of 13 divorces among them, but the book contributes to our understanding of men who make major changes in middle age. Based on five free-associative interviews with each man, the author conceptualizes the change as stemming from the erosion of the projected self-image of young adulthood. The subjects move from a state of stable organization of self to a stage of crisis. During the crisis stage the subjects experience a sense of grieving for the lost self and re-work separation-individuation conflicts in parental relations. This phase is followed by periods of recovery/reconstruction and restabilization of self. The major focus is on the experience of self in work.

Pineo, Peter. "Disenchantment in the Later Years of Marriage," in Bernice Neugarten, ed., *Middle Age and Aging*. Chicago: University of Chicago Press, 1968. Making use of 20-year follow-up questionnaire responses of 153 of Burgess and Wallen's original 1,000 couples, Pineo finds reduced intimacy and lower marital adjustment in middle age. The decline is explained as a consequence of regression toward the mean level of satisfaction in the population. The couple marries at the highest level of compatibility, leaving them nowhere to go but down.

Rollins, Boyd C., and Harold Feldman. "Marital Satisfaction Over the Family Life Cycle," *Journal of Marriage and the Family* (Feb. 1970), pp. 20–28. Based on a random sample of 852 middle-class couples, this study finds a curvilinear relationship between marital satisfaction and the life cycle, with satisfaction declining until early middle age and reaching its lowest point when children are being launched. Afterwards satisfaction recovers rapidly.

Schaie, K., Warner and Kathy Gribbon. "Adult Development and Aging," *Annual Review of Psychology*, 1975, pp. 65–96. A compact review of five years of research on aging. The treatment of methodological problems in cohort and cross-sectional research is good. The treatment of theories of development is sketchy. The overview of empirical research on psychological and social changes with age makes it a good reference article.

Sheehy, Gail. *Passages: Predictable Crises of Adult Life*. New York: E. P. Dutton & Co., 1976. A popularized version of the age-linked theory of adult development, stimulated by contacts with Levinson and Gould. The methodology is not reported, but the author claims to make use of 115 interviews with members of America's "pacesetter group" between the ages of 18 and 55 .

Shram, Rosalyn Weinman. "Marital Satisfaction Over the Family Life Cycle: A Critique and Proposal," *Journal of Marriage and the Family* 41 (Feb. 1980), pp. 7–14. A good critical review of family life-cycle literature, arguing that the most convincing evidence supports the curvilinear model with the low point in satisfaction occurring in early middle age. However, she argues that we need to know more about "how the transition from one stage to the next is experienced."

Troll, Lillian E. "The Family of Later Life: A Decade Review," *Journal of Marriage and the Family* (May 1971), pp. 263–290. An excellent review of the literature on family relationships in middle and old age. It ranges from extended family relations to family interaction, highlighting variations across class and sex and at different stages of the life cycle.

Vaillant, George. *Adaptations to Life.* (Boston: Little, Brown and Co., 1977). Based on a longitudinal study of 95 men selected from an elite college because they were expected to live successful lives, this study focuses on how men's adaptive and defensive styles influence their development and how these styles change over time. As in our study, Vaillant finds that midlife crises are relatively rare, and no particular year or range of years is associated with a midlife crisis. Crises occur with "roughly equal frequency throughout the adult life cycle." The study is rich with clinical analysis of development under optimal conditions.

INDEX